T0303011

CANDY BARR

CANDY BARR

The Small-Town Texas Runaway Who Became a Darling
of the Mob and the Queen of Las Vegas Burlesque

TED SCHWARZ
AND MARDI RUSTAM

TAYLOR TRADE PUBLISHING
Lanham • New York • Boulder • Toronto • Plymouth, UK

Copyright © 2008 by Ted Schwarz and Mardi Rustam

All rights reserved. No part of this book may be reproduced in any form or by any electronic or mechanical means, including information storage and retrieval systems, without written permission from the publisher, except by a reviewer who may quote passages in a review.

Published by Taylor Trade Publishing
An imprint of The Rowman & Littlefield Publishing Group, Inc.
4501 Forbes Boulevard, Suite 200, Lanham, Maryland 20706
www.rlpgtrade.com

Estover Road, Plymouth PL6 7PY, United Kingdom

Distributed by NATIONAL BOOK NETWORK

Library of Congress Cataloging-in-Publication Data

Schwarz, Ted, 1945–
Candy Barr : the small-town Texas runaway who became a darling of the mob and the queen of Las Vegas burlesque / Ted Schwarz and Mardi Rustam.
p. cm.
Includes bibliographical references and index.
ISBN-13: 978-1-58979-341-5 (cloth : alk. paper)
ISBN-10: 1-58979-341-2 (cloth : alk. paper)
1. Barr, Candy, 1935–2005. 2. Stripteasers—United States—Biography.
I. Rustam, Mardi. II. Title.

PN1949.S7S33 2008
792.702'8092—dc22
[B]
2007046903

∞™ The paper used in this publication meets the minimum requirements of American National Standard for Information Sciences—Permanence of Paper for Printed Library Materials, ANSI/NISO Z39.48-1992.

Manufactured in the United States of America.

CONTENTS

Contents

ACKNOWLEDGMENTS

With thanks to Jean Collins in the Literature Department of the Cleveland Public Library for revealing more about taking off one's clothes to music than I ever knew before.

ONE

Ladies and Gentlemen, Miss Candy Barr!

It was a time of transition in the music industry. The jitterbuggers and the bobby-soxers still moved to the big band sounds of Tommy and Jimmy Dorsey, Harry James, Benny Goodman, Cab Calloway, and so many others, though more often delivered by a disk jockey spinning records than the musicians themselves. Frank Sinatra, the skinny kid with the punk's attitude and a way of delivering a song that brought girls to sexual ecstasy, was still packing the big theaters like the Paramount in New York. But radio had become the entertainment medium of choice, bringing with it shows such as *Your Hit Parade* to which teens could dance in the privacy of their homes. Transporting big bands from city to city had become too costly, especially since the tour dates had fewer and fewer customers. Some band leaders cut the size of their groups. Others retired. Increasingly young people decided that instead of paying to listen to their favorite singer perform live for just an hour or two, they would rather spend the same money on the singer's records, playing them over and over until they wore out.

Las Vegas would change all this, the casino and hotel owners creating a city devoted to the glamour, the excitement, and the live entertainment that had mostly disappeared from cities such as New York, Cleveland, Chicago, Miami, and Detroit. But Las Vegas was just one city, a gradually evolving living museum dedicated to the excesses of the past. Vices that were criminal in forty-seven states were legal, controlled, and so safe to pursue throughout Nevada that the region seemed an amusement park for adults.

Television also altered the entertainment world, though at first no one knew quite how to use it. The producers relied in large measure on old-style vaudeville, cleaning up the acts for family viewing. Ed Sullivan, Jackie Gleason, Milton Berle, and Ted Mack, among others, hosted comics, dancers, singers, ventriloquists, and jugglers.

It was in the 1950s, during this period of transition, that a tiny Texas girl with no knowledge of the world at large began a career that would briefly bring her money, fame, and unwanted notoriety in cities she had previously never seen or never heard of. She was a dancer with a beautiful face, big breasts, and a body as finely tuned as a saxophone player's horn. Her name was Juanita Dale Slusher, but the world knew her as Candy Barr, the last great dancer in burlesque.

Candy Barr never set out to entertain the ever-growing audience of teenage boys overwhelmed with adolescent hormones, old men having a last hurrah with one of their hands hidden under the handkerchiefs discretely covering their laps, and younger men wishing they could trade wives or lovers for the woman on the stage. She knew they came to see her take off her clothes, but she did not care about that. Having to strip was the price she paid to practice her skills as a brilliant improvisational performer. "They weren't there so far as I was concerned. I mean, I just went out there and entertained myself. We [the band and Candy] were doing a show."

And what a show it was! Other dancers used records to help them plan their acts. Three songs, approximately two and a half minutes each, would be played over the loudspeakers. The dancers, including Candy Barr, would come out in costumes. But no matter what they wore, the routine was the same. Dance for one to one and a half minutes, and then remove the skirt. While the second record plays, the blouse is removed, leaving only a mesh bra. The third record plays almost three-quarters of the way through before the dancer removes the mesh bra. The audience gets a glimpse of the dancer with just G-string and pasties before the record ends and she is off the stage.

Burlesque dancers usually moved with whatever style they had developed growing up. Some used jitterbug steps. Others had at least some lessons in tap dancing or ballet. Still others made up their dances as they went along. No one had the innovative brilliance of Candy Barr, who ignored the traditions of the dying art of burlesque.

Candy Barr shunned records, time limitations, and clubs that did not allow her to use a minimum of a half-dozen musicians. She preferred a full orchestra, but if the club owner pleaded economic necessity, she would work with just two players, one on sax and one on drums. However, those two players had to have the improvisational skills of Miles Davis and Charlie Parker, coupled with the musical call-and-response sensitivities of Cab Calloway. When Candy walked on stage, the audience might be unaware of what was coming, but the musicians knew that they were in for a long, innovative ride that might last forty minutes or four hours.

"At the [Sunset Strip] Largo where I was working [in 1955], I was just having a good time dancing and carrying on. So one night I was dancing and I turned. . . . And it was a semicircle bandstand and the saxophone man stood over by the wall. I turned, and I don't know if it was gravity or the perspiration on my back. I have no idea what took, but the wall caught me. And I couldn't get off that thing. I tried and I couldn't. I mean it felt so good just to lay back, you know? The wall caught me.

"And I told Tony [the saxophone player], I said, 'Tony, I can't get off this damned wall.' He's right there next to me.

"I said, 'Do something with that horn.' I said, 'Make me get off this wall.'

"He said, 'Okay, baby.' And he made a peeling sound with the horn. Like just kind of loosing me.

"Okay, I got off the wall, but it just felt so good, I said [to the wall] 'are you going to let him take me away from you?' And you know, the audience would get so quiet, and I didn't know it for years, because I talked to myself. On stage I'd be dancing, I'd go, 'Uuuuhhh, that was good!' when I'd do something unusually well.

"I said, 'George'—he was my drummer that I hired, George Jenkins— he was a black drummer and he was just what I needed—'are you going to let him take me away?'

So he started pounding out one rhythm, and Tony would go with a different rhythm. . . .

"That's the way I danced. I danced the music. I danced the plays and the songs I chose, like 'Autumn Leaves.' I lived it each time, like 'your sun-tanned hands, your summer kisses . . . '

"I felt that most of my dances flowed because I flowed. When it came down to the time of my coming off with them I would be doing pirouettes. What with when the leaves were falling I had my clothes fixed with hooks and snaps, and as I came around I just ripped it right off my body.

"So Tony followed me out and he's standing in front of the semicircle with his horn. I walked, and I was dancing, and I stepped back, and I said, okay, and they began playing off each other. The horn, the piano, the drums . . . " And Candy changed her movements to work with each of the musicians as each played a few bars in turn. "[When] Tony [was] out with the horn, I bent over [backwards] and my head hit the floor. He started [playing music] down my backbone . . . never touching me with his horn. I mean I was so agile I could do it." And he matched her movement with the sound.

"So we did that act, and you know, that act created so much sensation that the law came out and said we couldn't do it anymore because it was 'too provocative.' He can stand back there and play but he can't come out anymore." It was the biggest controversy on the Sunset Strip, and it added to the legend that was building throughout the country.

Candy had to find another dramatic movement, and she liked playing off the wall, though differently than when she would become stuck against it and need the saxophone to peel her from it. "You know I'd hit that wall and I'd say, 'Don't get me again because I can't play with you anymore.' I'd talk with everything—floors, walls, ceiling."

What Candy didn't do was talk to the audience. "I didn't go out there and say, 'Oh, hi, baby. Watch this. Watch this.' " But the wall was there, and she made it part of the show. The only question she had was how to use it.

"I remembered watching all those dancers I loved in my time, you know." They were the athletic dancers who combined strength and agility with grace and ease of movement—Fred Astaire, Gene Kelly, and Donald O'Connor, among others. She remembered dances from movies released in 1951 and 1952 where they did everything from dancing in a room that turned (Astaire) to dancing up the wall and flipping back (O'Connor). "So one night I just said, 'I'm going to see if I can do that. So one night I just went up that damned wall. And I came off that and went into a knee-bend shimmy-shake. They went crazy."

(Later in life Candy figured out that their response was unrelated to what she did as an innovative dancer. "It was because those tits of mine went Zing zing, Zing zing, Zing zing. I realized that years later and it made me almost cry when I found out.")

The management of the theater wasn't thrilled about the wall improvisations. They were impressed with what Candy was doing, but the wall wasn't meant to be a prop. The impact of her body was enough to threaten its stability. "They told me, 'You gotta be careful. You're going to go through that wall one day. Be easy. Be careful. There's no sense in getting hurt,' and I thought, oh pooh!

"One night I'm dancing, and I hit that wall and I felt it give. I didn't go through it because my reflexes were so good. I broke it. And in my step, I gave it a hand. Like everybody said, to the band, to the wall, to the people who bowed. And I went on about my business. But I hit it. I broke it. They were right. I sure was going to go through it.

"I felt it giving. I wasn't totally unaware and I felt it go, and about then you just react. You just move a little quicker.

"Back and forth. Back and forth. And then my little conga player. And I said, 'All right!' We created something brand new, you know?"

But even those who thought they knew, who were aware that the national sensation came from a small Texas town, had no idea the life a woman named Juanita Slusher had barely survived to become the sensation known as Candy Barr.

TWO

The Capture

They called it "the Capture," and it sounded so much like a childhood game that "nice" men could openly discuss their participation. Some were introduced to the experience by fraternity brothers or friends who made it a rite of passage when they turned twenty-one. Some shared the experience with their fathers, who taught their sons the intricacies of this subculture in a rite of male bonding no different, in their minds, than when they taught their sons to hunt, fish, or play golf. Others were out-of-town businessmen who sought an evening's escape from the intensity of deal making in the board rooms where they were meeting with local politicians and executives. And a few, physically, economically, and socially indistinguishable from the others, came to exercise their dark side, to pay for the privilege of being able to do almost anything they desired with a woman. The only taboos were facial disfigurement and murder, and even these might be tolerated in some quarters if the money was right.

The women enduring the Capture knew what it really was—the form of involuntary prostitution often called white slavery. To the men who used these women, they seemed good looking, quick to laugh, and eager to be caressed by strangers. Some of the women worked from small apartments and houses of prostitution, always with one or more men around handling negotiations, providing protection, making certain nothing happened that was not agreed upon before the customer met with the prostitute. They also supplied whatever "reminders" the women needed to not try to go off with anyone, to not try to leave the life.

Other young women worked outcall, going to hotel and motel rooms to provide companionship to a man willing to pay for a "date" with a woman who dressed and spoke well enough so the other guests would not recognize her as a prostitute. In either case, the price was high for the era: $20 for each fifteen minutes in a house of prostitution, $100 minimum for the first hour of outcall, though both fees could rise depending on the man's desires. By contrast, the young men coming home from World War II were given their 52-20— fifty two weeks of $20 a week pay, more than enough to live adequately on one's own or to travel the country, easing back into civilian life.

The prostitutes saw little of the money, however. White slavery was not a career choice. The women did what they had to do to live another day.

It was not by chance that the Capture was centered in South Dallas, Texas, nor was it coincidence that Juanita Slusher, a young teenage runaway, found herself in that city within a city. Many poor, rural Texas girls fantasized that South Dallas was where you could find a job, find a room, have enough to eat, and begin to conquer the world, or at least the small section of which they were aware. California girls pursued their dreams in Los Angeles, and New York girls went to Manhattan. For Texas girls like Juanita—miserable at home, victimized both by people they knew and by strangers, child/women who could pass as adults long before they emotionally reached that stage in life—South Dallas offered the illusion of a new and better life.

The girls who came to South Dallas were partially right about the area. It was an affordable oasis in the midst of a vast building boom comprising office complexes, luxury hotels, and businesses catering to the newly rich. There were plenty of jobs, and though most were menial positions, they paid better than similar work in small towns. A girl could rent a room, buy food, and set some cash aside.

What the runaways and other hopefuls did not know was that South Dallas was the dirty little secret of a larger community in the midst of trying to redefine itself in the years following World War II. What had once been cattle country catering to cowboys and ranch owners was gradually becoming an important center for the oil business, insurance companies, and banking. The expensive hotels in the heart of the downtown area regularly housed sophisticated East Coast business leaders who were being courted by civic leaders to open a Dallas branch or move their headquarters to the Southwest.

The Chamber of Commerce publicly provided the official lures—a temperate climate, a quality education system, reasonable land, skilled construction workers, tax breaks, and the like. Some of the visitors were also interested in theater, music, and the type of sophisticated arts organizations they enjoyed in New York, Boston, Philadelphia, Cleveland, and Chicago. For others, a baser form of entertainment was desired before they made the multimillion-dollar decisions that would affect their home office, two cities, and hundreds of workers. It was for the latter that South Dallas existed with a wink, a nod, and law enforcement officers who wore blinders during their patrols.

The longtime residents of South Dallas were unhappy with the way their community was treated. They were decent, hard-working folk living from paycheck to paycheck. They cared about their families. They cared about their churches. But because they were poor, most "nice" people had written off them and their children. Prosperity theology was becoming a part of the teaching of ever growing Baptist churches in the North Dallas area, and by that emerging thinking, God blessed you with material wealth according to your goodness. Neiman Marcus was not yet offering $250 perfume and his-and-her Christmas Jaguar sports cars in their annual catalog. Tiffany's and Saks Fifth Avenue were not yet present so the country club set could drop in for purchases as frequently as their maids and kitchen help stopped by Woolworth's 5&10-cent store on payday. But the excesses that would soon dominate the lives of the Dallas rich as they pursued ever more ostentatious and inappropriate ways of proving their wealth (e.g., a murder trial in which one of the principals had a necklace of diamonds spelling out the words "rich bitch") were already as irreversibly present as tiny unkempt patches of crabgrass randomly present amidst an otherwise flawlessly manicured lawn.

The prosperity theology that was still in its infancy on a national basis was already a part of Sunday sermons in moneyed white Dallas. Success in life meant God's blessing, prosperity theology taught, so the corollary had to be that the poor had failed the Lord in some manner. Blacks, Hispanics, members of the Choctaw and other Texas Indian tribes, and those with limited incomes were all abominations in the sight of God, for if they weren't, then the wretches would be driving luxury cars instead of hitchhiking or taking a bus. Of course, where the elite white pastors taught prosperity theology to congregations proving their largesse with the envelopes placed in the Sunday collection plates, pastors serving the poor, the displaced, and the downtrodden focused on raising up the meek. It was live for the moment and lesser mortals be damned against live for the future, a room awaits you in our father's mansion in Heaven.

Politicians of the era understood their communities and recognized that South Dallas residents had little clout in the ballot box and too little money to make truly meaningful contributions to any campaign. That was why no city politician would risk his career and accumulated political clout to fight the South Dallas juke joints, cheap motels, disreputable bars, and "entertainment" businesses that revolved, in part, around women who had been through the Capture. While many of the residents were prevented from voting, the profits from these shady enterprises made their way into the pockets of the North Dallas men who had the clout to put a politician in office or shatter his career.

"The white elite of Dallas, Texas, is easy to spot. All the men are Baptists who never have an impure thought, even when having sex with their wives or mistresses. All the women are virgins, no matter how many lovers or children they might have."

—A joke told in the 1940s by the social outcasts in the disreputable South Dallas, Texas

---

Teenage runaways, without jobs or prearranged places to stay, assured the success of the South Dallas illicit entertainment business. They were both the unwilling "play toys" and the eventual currency of the pimps, the hotel porters, and those members of the Chamber of Commerce who understood their entertainment value when properly seasoned. The most beautiful among them were set apart for special clients, provided to visiting business leaders as part of Dallas's efforts to encourage investment in the city. They came without charge—tip optional—so the out-of-towners could pretend they were "dates" who were accompanying them to dinner, dancing, and whatever they desired behind closed hotel room doors because the women found them seductively brilliant, witty, and handsome.

Lesser women were used in the strip joints or as sex bait to keep pimple-faced local ranch boys from waving their manhood in nicer parts of town. In South Dallas, everyone knew their place, understood the industry that fueled the region, and either participated, was a victim of it, or quietly endured.

Juanita Slusher was drawn to South Dallas like so many other girls her age. Texas was home to both large family ranches and massive agribusinesses comprising many thousands of acres under single owners. Small towns evolved to serve the ranching communities, Main Street often nothing more than a courthouse and post office, a bar, a church, a diner, and maybe a general store. A handful of locals were hired to work in the service businesses. The vast majority either worked the land or left the community in search of excitement, opportunity, and a chance to live a different life than the one they had known growing up. And among those who left, South Dallas was often the draw.

South Dallas offered jobs as waitresses and maids, short order cooks, bartenders, handymen, and the like. The work was menial by big-city standards, but it was work at a time when the place they had called home offered little to alleviate boredom other than alcohol and sex.

South Dallas housing was cheap, some motels providing their employees with a free room, meals, and a small amount of cash. The living area might be little more than a converted storage closet, but it had a bed, a place to wash up, and a door that locked. Compared with some of the homes the runaways had previously known, it was a four-star establishment. What none of them expected was the Capture.

THREE

Growing Up in Edna

It was 1948 when Juanita Slusher had a preview of the future she would soon face. She was thirteen years old, her 38-24-35 body making her physically mature beyond her years. Years later she would explain that her job when she returned home from school was to go out to a Chinaberry tree with a rub board and boiling iron kettle. There she would spend up to four hours a day washing the family's bedsheets. "When girls ask me about breast development," she told writer Gary Cartwright of *Texas Monthly* magazine, "I say, 'Honey, get yourself a rub board.'" She had a love/hate relationship with her life at home in Edna, Texas, coming to the conclusion that home was intolerable and she needed to run away to escape the miserable existence.

Juanita felt she could survive on her own because of what she had learned from her father. Elvin "Doc" Slusher taught by example his philosophy that there were battles to be won and problems that were not worth the effort to rouse oneself to anger. He was a heavy-drinking, hard-working handyman and stone mason with a face and build that made him look like a double for actor Henry Fonda.

Doc had few successes in his life. That was why he could be a sometimes violent tyrant at home, trying to keep a firm control over his wife, three daughters, and two sons whenever he was battered by society in ways he could not fight. For example, there was the time he purchased an Atwater-Kent radio so the family could have free entertainment every evening. He was supposed to pay a few cents a week for it, but there were weeks when putting food on the table was more important than the bill for a luxury.

Doc was a proud man. The radio had been a special gift for his family and he saw no reason he should have to lose it just because he and most of his neighbors had fallen on hard times during the Great Depression. Eventually he'd be able to pay what he owed. Just not today. Some businesses understood that reality of poor working folk. Others, including the store owner from whom he had purchased the radio, did not. He sent men to repossess the radio, and they did not listen to Doc's story. They had their own families to feed.

Doc understood this. His battle was with the people who sold him the radio, and that was a battle he could not win. Still, he decided to end the humiliating experience on his own terms. When the repo men arrived, he pulled out his rifle, aimed it at the radio, and fired five rounds into the tubes. "Okay, you can take it now," he said, having maintained his pride. "I don't want it anymore anyway because it don't work."

During the lowest point in the family's finances, two men came to repossess Doc's old Studebaker. The car was battered when Doc bought it, and it had seen a lot of use with the family since then. Still, the car was critical for a skilled laborer who needed to get to job sites. The problem was that, of late, he had been having trouble getting adequate work to pay for it. Without the car there might be no work at all.

"Daddy just got a can of gasoline from the barn and he spilled it in a circle all around the car," Juanita recalled. "Then he lit a kitchen match and stood there, threatening to throw the match at the car. They knew he meant it and they went away."

Perhaps Juanita's life would have been better had Doc been able to be around to protect her while she was growing up. Doc was a man of fairness who loved his youngest child in ways that made her feel wanted and secure. He would take her and his wife, Sadie, to the Pavilion, a big building where there was music for family listening and dancing, and a sealed-off room that was adults only. The latter was where a man or woman could enjoy the naughtiness of a glass of beer and a game or two of dominoes.

Doc liked his beer but he loved his Juanita more. He would stand her on his boots, take her in his arms, and move swiftly about the dance floor. They would fly through the Texas two-step, the waltz, and the other popular dances of the day. He delighted in his daughter's joy, not realizing how much he was influencing her future. She giggled as they moved, but she also paid close attention to the steps her father was taking. She wanted to do those steps on her own. She wanted to become one with the music, as though her body was a sponge and the notes were liquid. She somehow understood that music and dancing would be an important part of her life.

Doc was respected in Edna, Texas, at least respected as poor white trash for whom formal education meant elementary school and for whose family indoor plumbing was only a dream. Part of this respect came from his knowledge of the Indian ways gained, as with many things in his life, as a result of generally unacceptable behavior.

Elvin Slusher's family lived near a settlement of Choctaw and Cherokee Indians who earned some of their income from growing fruit trees. Elvin liked to swim across the river that separated the Slusher home from the Indian land. It was there that he met Sadie, whose father spoke only his native language.

Elvin fell in love with Sadie, and he made amends for his fruit-stealing pranks and showed respect for her culture by studying the Indian ways under his future wife's elders. He became knowledgeable in Native American healing, learning the medicinal plants common in the region as well as how to prepare poultices, teas, infusions, and the like. Juanita's earliest memories of her father's skills were those of neighbors and family members coming by the house when they were ill so Elvin, by then called "Doc," could diagnose the problem. Then he would take a trowel or other digging tool out into the woods to gather bark, roots, or whatever he needed to make one of the Choctaw/Cherokee natural medicines.

There were college-trained doctors who served the region, but they were hard to find in a crisis, and Doc was considered better than the so-called professionals. He certainly was nicer, never charging them for his knowledge, treating them as though they were important instead of nuisance white trash.

Doc's willingness to help others did not make him a saint. Juanita also knew him as a rake, a man who not only healed bodies but also provided "compassionate" assistance to other men's mothers, wives, and daughters when they sought relief from sexual tension. His movie-star good looks made him the target for bored housewives and other stay-at-home women. Many of them would open their doors as he passed, suggesting that they engage in a more intimate exchange than a mere "How'd you do?" before proceeding on his journey. Being a "gentleman," he could find no polite way to refuse. As Juanita explained many years later, "I called him the Pied *Peter* of Edna, Texas."

Doc never wanted a long-term affair with the women he found so amusing. Affairs were commitments in ways Doc knew were wrong. He was a married man with children, and he liked the stability that brought him. An hour or two in the bedroom was one thing. Returning for an encore performance was almost always out of the question.

Not that Doc was fooling Sadie. Truth be told, there were no secrets in the Slusher house. His wife knew other women had tasted the fruit. But this was Texas, and in those Great Depression years, the culture and the law were on the side of men. If Juanita's mama ever caught her daddy in bed with another woman, the law said it was a "minor indiscretion." It was something in the inherent nature of a man who was physiologically incapable of monogamy, and thus it was not a crime. If her daddy ever caught her mama in bed with another man, and if he had acted with the righteousness of a Texan, taking his gun and shooting them dead, no crime was committed under Texas law. The woman got what she deserved, and the man shouldn't have been messing with someone else's wife in the first place.

Doc engaged in "minor indiscretions." Only the women were committing adultery as the law was interpreted. That was why any concerns he had between the sheets were only about the unexpected return of whichever husband he was cuckolding. He did not have to worry about his own spouse.

Juanita knew none of this, of course. Not back then. And whatever her mother knew, she had her reasons for keeping quiet. There would be no dramatic confrontations in the household. There would be no threats of separation or divorce. Instead, Juanita grew up loving her father, learning to respect both her parents, the way children were taught in what only naïve romantics now consider gentler times.

It was just this world of unquestioning respect for one's elders that emboldened an eighteen-year-old neighbor boy to act out his fantasies with the four-year-old Juanita. He seemed a nice youth to the Slushers, someone who cared about their daughter and did not mind taking her out to play for an hour or two so they could get their own chores done. They did not think anything improper might take place. Not in Edna, Texas, in those days before World War II. Child molesters and pedophiles were neither known nor discussed there. Besides, the boy was a neighbor, and in small Texas towns, being a neighbor was the next best thing to being kinfolk.

The youth thought he was being gentle, but his relative size terrified young Juanita. She would go along with anything he wanted because to do otherwise did not seem possible. "He was a big, big man to me," she recalled. "He'd come over to play hide and seek with me. Then he'd pull down my panties and put his mouth on my little bitty thing. I didn't dare tell my parents because I was afraid that *I* would be punished or that my daddy would kill the man and go to jail."

The boy never threatened Juanita. His molestation was made to seem a natural part of their being together.

Equally unsettling was the fact that not all the sensations were unpleasant. The boy was letting his tongue probe places even married couples of the day were not sure their pastors would want them exploring. But he was sophisticated enough to know that the sensations would not be physically hurtful. "Children have feelings, too, and often it was gentle and sweet and felt so very good," said Juanita. Yet it was the pleasure that scared her as much as his acting in ways she could not find words to use to get him to stop.

It was only when the neighbor came over with a friend that Juanita realized she dared not go with the youth again. Her mother was cooking on the wood stove when the two boys came in. As usual he suggested taking little Juanita out to play to give her mama a break.

This time things were going to be different. Juanita knew that. She had no idea how everything had changed or what she might have to experience with these two young men. She just knew that she was having problems coping with the one boy's actions. There was no way she dared leave her mama to go with two of them.

Frightened, Juanita climbed into the wood box behind the stove and begged her mama not to make her go outside to play with the two teenagers. Her mother relented, and though she has no knowledge of what happened after that, it was the last day the girl ever saw the neighbor boy.

Ironically, the one time Doc caught his daughter in seeming sexual activity, neither she nor the little boy she was with knew what they were doing. Her little cousin had seen something fascinating between two adults. He didn't understand it, but he and Juanita thought they should try it, perhaps figure out what it all meant. It was innocent curiosity that resulted from careless, unthinking adults, and it was the one time her daddy saw anything sexual around his little girl.

"My little cousin and I got caught out front of the house. Me with my panties and dress down, and him standing in front of me. . . .

"The only thing that I had done was that oral thing. My daddy came up and caught us and busted our butts. I don't mean busted our butts because we were doing it in front of the house. I really don't know why we got whipped, you know? We weren't doing anything. He had me against the wall, and my dress was up and my panties were down. And his little dinky—we called it that back in those days—his little dinky was hanging out and he was laying up against me. So I don't know who he saw do it that way. It was kind of funny.

"You would think that back in those days everybody did it laying down. I didn't know people did it standing up. Never thought about it. You didn't go around thinking how did Mom and Daddy make out. Well, I never think about how anybody makes out anyway."

The poker parties came next.

Juanita's oldest sister, Kay, was married when World War II brought Doc into the navy to serve as one of the famed Seabees whose construction skills were critical to the war effort. Her other sister, Lee, was a teenager with a life away from home, and her two brothers, Forrest and

Gary, were always off doing something that did not involve Juanita. This left the youngest daughter as the only concern, a problem since her mama had taken a piecework job in a laundry, where she made ten cents for each shirt she cleaned and pressed. She had to work long hours to make enough money to help with the family's finances, and even then the family was frequently hardscrabble poor.

The house was typical of the rural area three hours' drive from the nearest big city. The ramshackle wooden structure relied on an outhouse, a woodstove for cooking and some of the heat, and a bathtub that was painstakingly filled by heating water carried in in buckets. Food that could not be grown or hunted was often in short supply. All the kids knew what it meant to occasionally go to bed hungry. That was why Sadie took the long hours, even though they meant prolonged periods when her then eight-year-old offspring would have to be alone. Again a neighbor entered Juanita's young life.

This time the neighbor, Carter (not his real name), was the brother-in-law of a family friend. He was at home during the hours Sadie Slusher was working, and his offer to help seemed a blessing. The fact that he was in his forties was even better, since he would have the maturity to handle any problem or concern that cropped up.

"The first time Mama was gone, Carter said, 'Your mother told me to check for chiggers,'" Juanita recounted. "And I just didn't have any reason to not go with authority, so that's how it started."

Juanita had no idea how long Carter sat with her, though it seemed to be many weeks. He would come in the morning and stay until her mother returned. For a while he acted as he had the first day. Then he began bringing over a woman friend. Finally, when he was certain Juanita was a properly brought-up Texas child who would not question authority, he asked her mama permission to hold card games in the Slusher home while Sadie was away at work.

Carter had been giving up his spare time to help the Slushers, so Juanita's mother saw no reason not to let him have friends over. She knew baby-sitting could be boring, and this way everyone seemed a winner. Carter had his pals and Juanita had the supervision she needed. Certainly nothing bad could ever come of letting the men have their poker games.

Carter was the perfect card-game host, and little Juanita was to be the key to his special times during those long afternoons. She was small for her age, strong but fine boned. There was as yet no hint of the large breasts, small waist, beautiful baby face, and powerful torso that would excite men from around the country in a few years. At eight she was still a prepubescent little girl just right to delight a group of pedophiles.

Preparations were simple. First he would set the table. There were the playing cards, the poker chips, the cigarettes, and the other necessities for playing the game right. Then Carter would take Juanita and dress her properly for his guests. Her lips would be painted red, and nail polish would be applied to match the lipstick. He put baby-doll slippers on her feet. "And they'd cut a piece of fruit, either a plum or a peach, and let the juices run down ya, and tie it on my breasts with stockings," said Juanita, recalling the sessions so traumatic that, for years, she could neither wear red make-up nor eat a cherry popsicle.

Finally Juanita was placed in the middle of the table, the prize to be won. The gambling was always more intense when the player with the most chips could take the child and do what he wished with her.

Juanita didn't tell her mama. She was too well bred for that. Her mama had said Carter was in charge. Her mama had said Carter was a blessing, looking after her when mama had to work and Juanita wasn't in school. She feared she would be punished if she questioned Carter's actions, even to her mother. She did not know her mama would have been horrified to learn the truth, including the fact that Carter was recently released from prison, something Juanita discovered only as an adult. She didn't appreciate her daddy would have killed Carter and his friends with his bare hands. There was no way she could understand the full import of what was happening. All she knew was that this was the adult her mama had said was in control, the person to be obeyed, and Juanita was a good girl. She would endure without saying anything, too overwhelmed to do anything else.

After all, Juanita Slusher was a Texas girl brought up right and proper. After all, Juanita Slusher was eight years old.

Juanita was nine when her life changed in ways she remembers were more difficult than enduring the sexual molestations. The problem she faced had been coming a long time, since well before Doc went to war.

Doc had hit hard times after Juanita's birth in 1935. Just as Sadie would do when she went to work in the laundry, Doc was doing everything he could to keep the family together and food on the table without having to go on welfare. Each morning Doc would rise early, get his dogs and his rifle, then go after coon, squirrel, and other wild game. He also fished and raised a few hogs, the latter being butchered without waste. There would be the meat for eating, but his wife also made soap, shortening, and cracklings from the flesh.

While Doc was trying to ensure food for the family table, a woman named Etta was hunting for him. Doc saw Etta the same way he saw the fishing and the hunting. She was a rich man's wife, at least by the standards of Edna, Texas, in the throes of the Great Depression. He and Etta made good money, lived in a house with indoor plumbing, and had all the luxuries Edna, Texas, could provide. Etta even had her own spending money, money she could use as she pleased with no accounting to anyone.

The first time Etta wanted Doc, she found him an enthusiastic bedmate. And as was his habit, the second time she sought his favors, he kindly excused himself so he could continue on his way. He had scratched the first itch. Anything more was too much like a commitment for a married man to make.

Etta was not one to be refused. She knew the Slusher family, knew Doc's work depended on the vagaries of the building trades. She rightly figured that a good man trying to care for his family the best he could just might be susceptible to a little bribe, especially if it was for something he willingly gave for free the first time he was asked. That was when she went to her personal stash and began renting herself the most desirable man in Edna, Texas.

There came a time when Juanita's mama learned about Etta, though if she said something, it was out of her daughter's hearing. Instead, she focused on the priorities that mattered for the family, and that meant getting her daughter the best possible education.

21

The Edna, Texas, schoolhouse was tiny—just four rooms. When Juanita's mama converted a closet at home to a small study, the space seemed almost bigger than a classroom. It was the child's delight, a place to read and write and dream. But the quality of Edna's educational system was as great as the building was small. The teachers were dedicated, and they had abilities that would have been in demand in big cities. By fourth grade, with her father in the service, Juanita was doing so well that she acted as a teacher's aide for the English classes. Her teacher had tested her on the information the other students had to learn. Juanita was so far ahead of her classmates that semester, she became a helper, a high honor in the school.

Sadie delighted in her daughter's accomplishments, encouraging her to try ever harder. She did not tell Juanita that life, even with a good education, would always be a struggle for a Slusher. This was an era when small Texas towns were divided by economics. There was little that might be called middle class. Mostly there were the wealthy and the white trash, and in Edna, Texas, Juanita was from the latter. How good you were inside did not matter. Money was the standard for determining a person's value, and money—enough money to live like Etta and her husband—was not something Doc and Sadie would ever experience.

Sadie Slusher may have had bigger dreams for Juanita than she had time to share. Juanita had no future in Edna no matter how well she did. But good grades might enable the girl to leave the town behind, go to college, get a job that would make the family proud in a city where no one knew her history.

Juanita always appreciated the special consideration her mother gave her. "Mama took a closet in this old house we lived in, and she cleaned it out. In this closet she put me a light, my table, chairs, my dog and my dog bed, so that when I came home I could go into this room and study.

"She wouldn't do that for the boys because they weren't concerned about it [book learning and the future an education could ensure], and she made special arrangements so I could [study]. I knew that she knew, and she made it so I could have the best that I could.

"To me that shows something in a person that education didn't teach ya. They just saw that I would be the one to try to achieve, because that's just the way I was." Juanita had a dream, and Sadie Slusher believed that a dream was worth pursuing.

Oddly, Juanita's dreams for her future were further nurtured within the local Pentecostal church, where women were usually considered second to the men they married. Whether the pastor would have approved of Juanita's ambitions for further education is not known. She did not discuss these plans with him, content to find support in the joyful music and the welcoming congregation. The Pentecostal movement was a young one in the United States, its growing appeal originally among the poor and uneducated who felt separated from God because of their difficult lives. The spirit-filled, ecstatic experience was uplifting, and it often involved speaking in tongues—speaking in a special heavenly language one or another member of the congregation would interpret. (Originally it meant that the speaker of one language could be understood by someone who only knew a different language, a situation that occurred for the Apostles of Christ on the first day of Pentecost.) There was a joy to the services, a feeling that each person, no matter how viewed by the society at large, was uniquely important to God.

Actually, Doc and Sadie Slusher wanted nothing to do with organized religion, but they were happy to let Juanita attend with her grandparents and their friends, a pair of sisters with whom they worshipped every Sunday morning and Wednesday evening. "I wanted to be a missionary, imagine that," Juanita related years later. "In a way, maybe I was. I was never religious but I was always spiritual. God and Jesus were the only ones I ever really could talk to. I'd practice talking to them in front of a little mirror, making speeches, declaring myself for God. I'm not born again or anything like that. I *always* had those feelings. I wouldn't be alive today if I hadn't."

It was Juanita's enduring faith in God, even as her life spiraled out of control, that sustained her. She also never felt she was being judged either for what was happening to her or what she chose to do to survive.

It was March of 1944. The war in Europe had changed in the previous few months. Where once Hitler and the Axis forces seemed unstoppable, defeat after defeat was giving the Allies the hope that they would triumph on the Western Front. However, in the Far East, the fight against the Japanese was not moving in a way that could assure either side of victory.

Worse, the kamikaze pilots were destroying ships and ground forces with their many suicide missions. For the kamikaze, to die fighting for one's country was to ensure a glorious afterlife. They were an enemy who would strike anywhere, not concerned about returning from the mission as the Americans always planned to do.

The Seabees were kept busy with construction needs. Doc kept in touch with Sadie and the children, but it was obvious that he would not be home on leave anytime soon. The nine-year-old Juanita had to rely totally on her overworked mother.

Juanita no longer remembers who told her what happened that fateful day. It could have been a police officer. It might have been her grandparents. It might have been a neighbor or even an older sibling. All she knew was that her mama had been in a car accident.

Juanita was never able to know the extent of Sadie Slusher's injuries. She had a concussion, that much is certain, but whether or not the concussion and her other injuries would have been life threatening with treatment is unknown. The doctors did little more than a cursory examination. The nursing staff provided minimal care. Instead of taking X-rays to check Sadie's condition, they checked the state of the family's financial health. When they learned that none of the Slushers could come up with the $50 the hospital demanded to begin treatment, they realized they were dealing with undesirables. Poor white trash was expendable in the county. Sadie was given a bed because the hospital staff was not without compassion. However, they had no intention of doing anything more to help her get better, since she was foolish enough to get herself into a crisis before she had saved enough money to pay for it.

It was only at the time of the Korean War that the family members of servicemen were given special consideration because of the hardships and dangers their husbands were enduring. Neither the hospital nor any of the service organizations such as the Red Cross would make an effort to contact Doc to see if there was a way for the navy to help. He would be granted compassionate leave to visit, but he would not be given the financial help necessary to ensure the care that would save Sadie's life. Instead, after his wife's death, Doc was given the bill for replacing the bed on which she was allowed to die.

Juanita's married sister, Kay, traveled from her home and husband in Oklahoma to try to reach her mother's bedside. She also lacked money yet hoped she could do something, anything to help. Instead, the unconscious, uncared-for Sadie Slusher swallowed her tongue, suffocating herself.

———

"I was smart in school, good at English and Spanish, good in gym and dancing. I wanted to be a cheerleader, but poor white trash like us didn't get to be cheerleaders."

—Juanita Slusher

———

The death of Sadie Slusher instilled in Juanita an understanding of injustice caused by the bigotry of others. Not that she could articulate such feelings at the time. Instead, the concept seemed to have permeated her being, like a seed buried deep in soil where the roots can gain a firm foothold and whose sprouts break through the surface with strength and assuredness. She had not yet become the fighter against injustice that would one day make her an underground folk hero, but she knew her mother had been wronged, murdered by a system of corrupt values. And once again she realized that her life would be about enduring and moving on, getting through the hell that each day might bring, savoring the pleasure, and never looking back.

The now-widowed Doc had broken his cardinal rule about "friendships" with women when he began seeing Etta more than once or twice before joining the navy. Worse for the family, Etta would sacrifice anything to be the permanent resident of Doc Slusher's bedroom. Sadie's death sent her racing to the divorce lawyer even before the dirt had settled on the grave. Doc was granted an immediate hardship discharge from the navy, and with both of them free of their obligations, they married that June of 1944.

Etta had several children of her own, and she saw in Juanita the answer to her own laziness. She assigned the nine-year-old child the chores of a housewife, ignoring the child's passion for school and need to attend. Book learning wasn't important. Etta had done all right in life without it, and a girl had no business dreaming the dreams Sadie had been encouraging. She'd let the child do her studying. She'd let her go to school. But if the hours spent cooking for the family, cleaning the house, doing the laundry, tending the garden, feeding the chickens, and handling all the other chores that befell her meant she would miss the school bus, she could always run the couple of miles to her classes. And if she was so tired she fell asleep over her books or at her desk, well maybe the child should have worked faster.

As the days turned into weeks and the weeks into months, life deteriorated for Juanita. Her father was home by then, but he had to work harder than ever. He frequently left home early in the morning, arriving late at night only to hear Etta's litany about all the bad things Juanita had done that day.

What went unsaid were the sexual games that Juanita increasingly had to endure. Etta may have been bisexual. She may have been a pedophile. All that is certain is that after the men who took advantage of Juanita, there were two women who did the same. One was a cousin and the other was her stepmother. The cousin was the more blatant of the two. She would get Juanita alone, undo her own blouse and bra, and expose her breasts. Then she would pay the child a nickel to lick her nipples. Juanita was trained how to work her mouth and tongue for the cousin's erotic pleasure. The child did nothing else. She never was asked to touch her cousin's genitals, nor was she touched. The five cents was paid for the licking and sucking of the cousin's tits. Nothing more was asked of her.

Etta had a different game. Some of her hatred for and abuse of Juanita came from a probable physical attraction. Again there was no genital touching. Instead, Etta gave Juanita a red Life Saver candy. She told the child to put the candy in her mouth, then bring her lips to her stepmother's and place the candy in the older woman's mouth, using only her tongue. Each time she performed correctly, Juanita would be given a Life Saver of her own to enjoy.

Doc knew nothing of what was taking place with his beloved daughter, though he came to question the wisdom of his hasty marriage almost from the start. There would be no divorce, though. He was still an old-fashioned man when it came to commitment. A husband respected what his wife told him. If she said that his youngest child deserved a whipping, he would take his belt and administer it until the child was in tears. The action tore at his heart, yet he would not question. The social norms of Texas in the 1940s did not allow a man to call his wife a liar no matter what the hurt in his daughter's eyes might tell him.

There were other changes occurring for Juanita, physical changes. Her face was that of a little girl, but her body was developing into that of a woman. She reached puberty early, her breasts large and full, her waist tiny, her legs trim and muscular from all her running. Boys and men looked at her with lust. Jealous girls looked at her with the same expression they might use if they stepped into cow dung. Then, too, Juanita wasn't socially prominent. In many instances, her daddy worked for their daddies. Her mother had cleaned their clothes when she worked in the laundry. White trash girls just didn't get the privileges of their betters no matter how smart they were.

"I was smart in school, good at English and Spanish, good in gym and dancing," recalls Juanita. "I wanted to be a cheerleader, but poor white trash like us didn't get to be cheerleaders. And the men, when I'd walk down the street, would say, 'Hey, get a load of the Slusher kid.' And they would want something from me."

Juanita did not fully understand her appeal when she realized that she could no longer live with Etta. As much as she loved her daddy, she had to get away. The first attempt to flee was when Juanita was twelve years old. Doc had been working steadily and managed to buy Juanita a pair of sandals she treasured above all else. She also had saved $3.74, enough to stake her to a place to live, food to eat, and anything else she might need until she could find a way to earn more. Or so she thought. After all, she had worked hard for the money, doing an adult's job of delivering milk from a horse-drawn cart and shucking corn when the fields were ripe at harvest time.

Juanita put on her sandals, placed her money in her pocket, and then strolled toward the outhouse. When she thought no one was looking, she veered off and started running through the pasture behind the hovel the Slushers called home. Only when she was away from all protection did she see the huge Brahma bull that had been grazing in the pasture.

Bulls are attracted to movement, not color. The bright red cape of a matador is meant solely for the audience. The bull is drawn by the movement, charging it without thought to what it is and what it means. For the Brahma in the field, Juanita was as enticing as a waving cape.

The bull charged. "About a dozen cows stampeded and began to chase the bull," said Juanita. "And there we were—me, the bull, and the cows, all tearing across the pasture."

Juanita was able to outrun the bull, racing to her Grandma Lannie's house. Grandma Lannie was Sadie's mother, and while she always tolerated Doc, she had no more use for Etta than her granddaughter. She agreed to hide the child, but two days later, Doc's sister, Juanita's Aunt Mabel, figured out where the child must be. She angrily came knocking at the door, hauled the girl home, and then stayed while Doc beat her.

The punishment proved worse than expected. After Juanita's flesh was covered with angry welts, she had to watch Doc take her adored sandals and burn them.

Juanita was emotionally overwhelmed. There were nine children thrown together in close quarters creating the havoc of separate families, sibling rivalry within the families, and a need for extra attention neither parent had time or inclination to provide. Etta's bisexuality coupled with her becoming pregnant almost immediately after marrying Doc added to the tension. And then there was the cousin who paid her five cents each time she sucked her cousin's nipple. Years later Juanita saw herself as being a prostitute within the family, a "professional" paid in Life Savers and nickels, and it upset her far more than the Capture where she knew there was no choice.

The relationship with Etta was made worse by the fact that she wasn't kin, she was a rival for her father's attention and a woman Juanita felt he married too soon after her mother died. She realized that she could not continue living with her family in Edna. She needed to go somewhere else, a course of action that her family agreed to allow.

Paris, Texas, proved the answer to the Slusher family problem. Kay, seven years older than Juanita, had already moved there, taking a room with her aunt and uncle. She agreed to look out for her younger sister, and the aunt and uncle saw no problem with housing both girls. Doc was relieved to be responsible for one less child.

The molestation Juanita endured in Edna was the start of a growing awareness that her changing body was causing others to act in ways that made her uncomfortable. Moving to Paris, Texas, did not help as much as she hoped, especially after she became friends with a boy in church.

The immediate post–World War II era was a time when youths with limited education could get good jobs in factories, agriculture, construction, and other labor-intensive fields. The pay was adequate to rent or buy a home and start a family, even if the boy was in his late teens when he went to work, and the girl only fifteen or sixteen. The early marriages also led to earlier sexual relations, a fact Juanita discovered after befriending a boy she met in the church she attended in Paris.

The boy started talking with Juanita from the first day she appeared in the church. They had similar interests, and though he was older than Juanita, she had what passed as worldliness for having come from another town. Most teens were born, raised, and married in the same small town unless they left the area for the military or for college. By the standards of small-town Texas life, Juanita was somewhat of a sophisticate.

The more Juanita and the boy talked each week, the more they found they enjoyed many of the same things, the more the boy wanted to get intimate with her. She was not ready for sex, yet the boy was her friend and she did not want to disappoint him. Finally, after hugging, kissing, and touching the more intimate areas of each other's bodies, the boy wanted more. Not only was Juanita not ready for the experience, the boy was naïve about a girl's body and exactly who should be doing what to whom.

"It got to the point that he would try and have sex, and he would hurt me, and I wouldn't let him try," Juanita recalled. But stopping a boy who liked her and was age appropriate for the experience was different from dealing with a close family member. She became convinced that her uncle had sexual feelings for her and that he would act on them whenever he sensed she was no longer a virgin. "It's just like my old dog knowin' when a bitch was in heat. He knows when it happened or hadn't happened. He can smell ya."

Juanita went to her older sister, Kay, troubled by what was taking place in her relatives' home and with the boy from church. "I told her what's been going on and she said it was about time I was with a man. Now she was probably trying to do [right] for me. If she hadn't taken me out and supervised, I would have been raped somewhere along the line. I wouldn't have been introduced into a sexual relationship with some kind of protection.

"She didn't know how to explain it in the first place. She just said it was time I was with a man, and she probably did save me from some very brutal things."

Kay had Juanita stand by the road while she began waving at men driving alone in passing cars. Finally one stopped and Kay said she would sell her sister's favors for a dollar. Kay, who was trying to help her sister's education, stayed in the front seat of the stranger's car while he climbed in back with Juanita. It was to be Juanita's initiation into sex, a ritual Kay felt obliged to arrange since their mother was dead and their stepmother was not someone to whom Juanita could turn for sex education.

Juanita later assumed that Kay was trying to do for her what fathers did with their sons—giving her a sex education by having her engage in sex while Kay was present to protect her from any possible problems. The difference was that Juanita had no knowledge of what would happen, no desire to experience intercourse, and was never consulted about the plan.

During the "initiation," Juanita neither screamed from the pain nor tried to flee the car. She did not struggle as the man pushed up her white skirt, pulled down her panties, and forced his penis inside her. He was big and strong, but Juanita knew he wasn't trying to rape her. He had no idea that this was Juanita's first sexual experience, assuming that Kay was a pimp and the dollar price for Juanita was what she usually earned for intercourse in the back seat of a car. He was horrified when he comprehended what was happening, especially after he saw the stain form on her white skirt following his breaking of her hymen.

"Why didn't you tell me you were a virgin?" the man asked Juanita.

"I never answered the man because I'd never even heard the expression 'virgin,' and I didn't know whether I was or I wasn't," Juanita later recounted.

"Actually, I suppose I became a prostitute before I knew *that* word, either. When I was small and took the nickel for sucking my cousin's tit, or when my stepmother made me put red Life Savers in her mouth with my tongue and she'd 'pay' me with a candy of my own, *that* was the beginning of my being a prostitute."

Juanita did not understand how her experiences would soon affect her future, but she did know that she was scared, in pain, and convinced that Kay had betrayed her. Worse, she thought her uncle might somehow realize she was no longer a virgin and come after her. She was already earning her room and board by cooking and cleaning her aunt and uncle's house. She felt certain that providing sexual favors might be an additional payment demanded of her.

Juanita went to her aunt's closet when no one else was in the home. There she found one of her aunt's dresses that not only fit her but made her look older than she was. Finally she started walking, going along Highway 59 in the direction of Edna. She did not want to return home. She had no idea what other route to take.

Juanita's aunt discovered the missing dress almost immediately after her niece ran away. One of her relatives was in law enforcement and happy to help the aunt when she explained that her teenage niece was a thief. He contacted her father, who sent her brother Gary to drive Highway 59 and search until he found her. The aunt said she would not prosecute her niece, but Juanita could not return to Paris. She would have to stay with her father and stepmother, a situation Juanita knew would be intolerable.

HIGHWAY 59

Living in Edna again, it did not take long before Juanita realized that Highway 59, if taken in the opposite direction from the way she traveled when leaving Paris, would bring her to larger cities and away from her abusive family members. Highway 59 could take Juanita to big Texas cities like Houston, places so large she could not imagine what the streets might look like. Even better, she knew that there would be crowds of strangers in which she could lose herself. And so Juanita went to the highway, stuck out her thumb in the universal sign of hitchhiking, and waited for someone to pick her up.

Juanita was not afraid to hitchhike because this was a period after World War II when many men and women traveled by thumb. Some were leaving home to try their luck in one of the big cities. Some were taking advantage of money they received after leaving the military, hitchhiking to stretch their dollars further than if they drove or took the bus. Crimes by or against hitchhikers were rare, and many long-distance drivers stopped for anyone whose thumb was pointing on down the road.

The first car to pull alongside Juanita was driven by an older single man who said he was concerned about her safety on the highway. He told her she was too young and pretty to be out by the side of the road like that. He said that though his ultimate destination was quite far, he planned to stop in Houston and would take her that far if that was what she wanted.

Juanita glanced inside the car, not sure what she was checking but not seeing anything unusual. She got in and the two started talking. When the man realized she did not have much money, he told her he would rent her a motel room so she would have a safe place to stay that night. Naïve though she was, Juanita realized the motel room offer could mean trouble. Did he expect to sleep with her? Or was he truly being generous? She decided to wait until they reached Houston before making a decision about staying or fleeing.

The man eventually pulled into the parking lot of one of the new motel chains that had been built to take advantage of the returning servicemen who were using some of the money they were paid at discharge to travel and see the country. The motel was two stories, the rooms were clean and well maintained, and there was a radio set in each room and a coffee shop for hungry guests.

The man rented two rooms quite far apart from each other, giving Juanita the only key to her room. He also explained that he had arranged for her to be able to use room service, the cost of the food, like the cost of her room, being added to his bill. For the first time in many months, Juanita Slusher felt safe, cared for, and able to relax. Compared with the hardscrabble Texas town in which she was raised, Juanita's bedroom was like that of a fairytale princess with its radio, table and chairs for eating, and a young man carrying a tray filled with the food she ordered, carefully laying it out as though she was in a fancy restaurant.

For Juanita, the time between her meal and the knock at her door was the happiest she had known since the death of her mother. She had no idea how thoroughly she had misread her situation, how much danger she was in.

There seemed no reason for caution when Juanita went to the motel room door. She heard two voices, recognizing one as the man who had given her a ride and paid for her room. The other voice was unfamiliar, but when she opened the door and saw the second man was black, she assumed he was a porter who was there to collect her dirty dishes.

Black males had few job opportunities in post–World War II Texas. They could shine shoes, clean toilets, sweep floors, wash dishes, and handle whatever other services were considered too menial for whites. Hard work with little chance for advancement, a constant struggle to feed one's family, and the indignity of being treated as either retarded, a cunning street hustler, or dangerous to white women made survival difficult. Yet despite the bigotry, the majority of blacks married, attended church, and raised their families with love and as much dignity as possible.

Juanita was aware of all this, aware of the bigotry of Texas even with her limited life experience. Her mother was a Choctaw/Cherokee Indian mix, and her father was called "Doc" because he had learned the ways of his mother's people. He knew the various plants and their medicinal values. Anytime a neighbor got sick, he'd go into the woods and find what they needed, fixing a poultice or a tea or whatever would help them. But a poor white man married to a woman with Indian blood made him almost as worthless as a black man in the eyes of the "good" people in the area. That was why seeing the man she thought was a porter raised no more concern than seeing the kindly man who had given her a ride and paid for her room.

Juanita did not realize that the black man and the white man were entry-level employees in the Capture, a service business under the control of some of the most respected corporate executives, politicians, and jurists in Dallas and the surrounding area. They were the urban equivalent of ranch workers, though instead of catching and breaking wild horses, their work entailed the capture and "taming" of young women. Other girls had been kidnapped and repeatedly raped until they complied with the Capture. Juanita was just the latest to be designated to experience that fate.

There was no chance to struggle, and if there had been, Juanita sensed she was helpless to escape. The two men were bigger, stronger, and determined to dominate her. They would be as brutal with her as necessary in order to render her so frightened she would do whatever was demanded of her.

The violence did not break Juanita, not the way the men assumed. She had endured too much physical and emotional pain in her short life. She had lost her mother, been used by her stepmother, and betrayed by her sister, and much of the pain and abuse had been sexual in nature. This was just one more experience to endure, to survive. There would be times to fight back, times when to risk disfigurement or death would be worth the effort. This was not one of them. This time the outcome would be the same whatever she did. The men were going to hurt her and the ordeal would end when they were satisfied she understood her future, not before.

"I was petrified. The whole concept of it . . . the strangeness . . . I don't know how come but I just allowed it all to go on and happen.

"After it happened, I wasn't where I could call the police or any of these things. I just knew I had to run again, so I hid behind the hotel."

Juanita's plight was one the men had anticipated when she was targeted for the Capture. Teen girls did not hitchhike alone on the highway unless they were running away from something—family problems, a boyfriend, the police. Theoretically the girl alone was safe and rapes were rare. But the men of the Capture knew that the culture of the times was such that a girl who would be missed by parents or friends rarely, if ever, traveled alone. Girls who left behind people who would be waiting for a telephone call to alert them they had arrived at their destination almost invariably traveled with a friend. It was less lonely, the anticipation of the future more exciting. That was why, after the rapes, the men were lax in watching Juanita, assuming she would not run because she had no place to go. They certainly did not expect her to sneak out of her room and hide on the property.

"Across the street from the motel was a café. They were open twenty-four hours a day. I knew the best thing I could do was hide behind the motel, watch what was going on, 'cause I could go into the rooms and use the toilet or whatever I had to do 'cause I could sneak. And I knew the café was open right across the street."

Juanita went around back of the café to see what had been recently tossed in the garbage. People often left a good portion of their food on the plates, and when it was dumped, she knew she could grab it and eat. ("I know what it's like to live to eat garbage out of a fuckin' garbage can and hide in the sticks," she later said bitterly.) She was there two weeks, and for most of the time she was lucky. The food she took from the garbage had been dumped recently enough so that it had not spoiled.

Finally Juanita made a mistake. The food she put in her mouth looked and smelled no different from what she had safely consumed for several days, but it had started to turn. Worse, in her weakened state, she was again vulnerable to predators. "I got sick from the food, and I was lying in the grass, and these two boys were messin' around there, and they picked me up and got me in their car." Too weak to fight or run, Juanita was kidnapped and raped.

"They kept me in their car for three or four days," she recalled, but most of the details passed from her memory. "I remember bits and pieces of it, and every once in a while I'd go out of it again. That's God's protection of you when the strain's too severe. But I had that instinct in me that only for a period of time I could stay captive. If I couldn't break away, I could kill."

The awareness of her ability to take a life would become emotionally important to Juanita during the next three years, just as she simultaneously understood that she did not want to murder anyone. She just wanted to survive and would react accordingly to whatever extreme circumstances were forced upon her.

"The fear of my whole life was what I would have to do to [kill] someone." Yet Juanita learned to not feel anger. She taught herself to be in complete control, to use violence as a means to ending an overwhelming conflict from which there was no alternative. But she learned to use violence without anger so that she was never out of control.

Trying to hurt or kill the two boys once they were through using her was never an issue for Juanita. She would gain nothing from seeking revenge, and all three knew the youths were safe from the law. Juanita was obviously a runaway kid, no one to care about her, and no one to miss her. They held her captive, then dumped her back at the motel. Most of the police officers of the era would have reasoned that no harm was done, that all three probably enjoyed the experience.

The return to the hotel was more terrifying than being held captive. But she did not encounter the driver that may have been deliberately looking for single female hitchhikers to bring back to his partner at the motel. She did learn that both men probably went on to the Houston area.

"I got back on the highway. I felt like I was safe, actually. Nobody's going to look for you after two weeks.

"I remember walkin' across Dallas. Then you could walk across Dallas, take you three or four hours, but you could walk across."

Where Juanita eventually ended up is gone from her memory. She thinks she went on to Paris, met her sister Kay, who had personal problems of her own, and returned to Dallas.

Kay had married, had children, divorced, and given up custody of her children to her ex-husband. She was trying to figure how to live her own life as a divorced woman, and taking care of her youngest sister was not something on which she planned. "She was feeling all the torn-up things that a mother goes through when she leaves her children," Juanita said of Kay. "She knew that her kids would be fed and clothed and brought up not to cuss, and not do this and whatever else. But she had me."

Rather than trying to play mother and give Juanita a better foundation in life, Kay treated her as an equal, more mature than her years. It was a continuation of what she had tried to do when she decided that Juanita needed to understand sex through having supervised intercourse with a man. The sex experiment had been a mistake, but Kay seemed to have learned little from the experience. She still felt she could best teach Juanita about life by sharing experiences for which Juanita was not yet ready.

"We went buddying and doing things and going dancin' and whatever else," said Juanita.

The trouble was that what Kay wanted to do for entertainment was not yet appropriate for the younger Juanita. Worse, though Kay felt the need to provide a place for Juanita to live, she also felt jealous of her sister. Juanita Slusher was naturally beautiful in ways few women ever achieve with cosmetics, health spas, and plastic surgery. Men saw her figure and assumed they were pursuing a woman with a baby face instead of a teenager who had matured early. Kay was often shunted aside by men who did not realize that Juanita was underage for their desires, and Kay came to resent her. Juanita eventually understood that she was considered a threat by "evidently every female in the world because of the way I looked and wasn't aware of it."

Despite the strain between them, the sisters knew that somehow Dallas was where they would start their lives anew. It would also be the city where Juanita Slusher, white trash from the wrong side of a dying town, would lose her own identity in just four short years. In her place would emerge a legend, the glamorous, high-paid Candy Barr, the most famous burlesque star who would find her glory while dancing in the night music. But first she had to endure the full emotional and physical bondage of the Capture, and that meant finding a way to survive a world as potentially deadly for women as any war zone.

FOUR

The "Good" People Considered It Tradition

In their youth, the scions of the business leaders, politicians, and clergy of Dallas paid their $20 each so Juanita Slusher would spend fifteen minutes sating their unbridled lusts. Years later, when they matured into inheriting the conservative, respected positions of their fathers, they realized Juanita should have died from her time in the Capture. Life would be more comfortable for them had she been murdered or at least become so hopelessly addicted to drugs and alcohol that all a stranger would see was a wasted body and tormented soul. That would have made her a person to be ignored, a person who would not be believed if she tried to bear witness against them. The women their fathers had enjoyed in their youth had met such appropriate ends.

That was why the Capture could continue year after year, decade after decade, while the "good" men of the community lived their lives with a wink and a nod about their pasts. That an assembly-line prostitute could eventually escape the life and become one of the most famous entertainers of her day was beyond all their imaginations. Had they known, she would have been "rented" to the highest bidders, then quietly murdered, her corpse buried where it would never be found.

Because no one involved with the Capture could predict the future, they used the women like Juanita, fantasizing about having a willing partner. This was especially true for those who used the outcall services, paying a minimum of $100 an hour for the privacy afforded by having the woman come to their upscale hotel rooms. Such women were well dressed, well fed, and seemingly well paid. No man accompanied the out-call prostitute to her rendezvous. No man, including the service providers among the hotel staff, was near to come to the woman's rescue if she got in trouble. (Men handling enforcement at houses of prostitution made their presence known, both in the halls and when they knocked on the doors of the rooms to announce that the fifteen minutes was over.) At a hotel, the woman seemingly could walk away at any time, leaving the life if she so chose.

What went unnoticed was the invisible tether that kept the woman from leaving. Most of the outcall prostitutes had tried to leave at one time or another, sometimes on their own, sometimes with a sympathetic man attempting to help them. Invariably they were caught, most beaten viciously (as was any young man foolish enough to offer assistance), and left in such fear that they did not try to escape again. Those who were too rebellious might be disfigured or killed as a warning to the others. The seemingly free and willing woman coming to the luxury hotels with an appearance that blended in with the paying customers was so terrified both from past violence and the perceived dangers in the future if she did not act as ordered that what seemed her freedom to move about was illusory. As for the money, the pimps made certain each woman received what was needed for shelter, food, clothing, personal hygiene, and the like. The rest was divided among hotel employees, law enforcement officers, and the various levels of businessmen who controlled the Capture.

Adding to the Texas tradition that made the Capture a seemingly acceptable business and an upper-income male rite of passage was the attitude toward women in general in the state. Texas law accounted for what were known as "minor indiscretions." According to the legal system, men and women were mentally and emotionally created differently. A woman became monogamous the moment she married. She wanted one man—her husband—and that man only. She was not aroused by other men. The only reason she might commit adultery was because there was something seriously wrong with her, an inner evil that made her unfit to be a wife, and if her husband so chose, unfit to live.

A man was different, however. He was physically and psychologically incapable of sexual monogamy. He would love his wife with all his heart.

He would want to be in a meaningful relationship only with her. But from time to time it was his nature to have to commit "minor indiscretions" with other women. There was nothing personal about it. The sex had nothing to do with love. Good men and scoundrels were all wired alike. It was their nature to engage in "minor indiscretions," the adultery to be tolerated if discovered.

The outrageous double standard was part of the Texas legal system when the men were attempting to break Juanita for the Capture and for several years afterward. A man who shot his wife or her lover when he found them having sex in bed was considered to have committed a misdemeanor. By contrast, a woman was guilty of a felony if she killed her husband or his lover on finding them in bed together. Her deed was vile and went against what everyone knew was the true nature of a good woman. He, on the other hand, had simply committed a minor indiscretion.

There was more to the hypocrisy of Dallas, Texas, than its attitudes toward women and sex during the era in which Juanita was trying to start a new life. There was also the Citizens Council that had been founded by banker R. L. Thornton in 1937, two years after Juanita was born.

Thornton, who died in 1964, looked at Dallas and realized that it had everything and nothing to offer. The city comprised 280 square miles but had a relatively small downtown area with clusters of high-rise buildings. There were few natural resources, a fact that led Thornton and others to focus on finance. The money in such businesses could be used to control everything from the municipal government to the types and location of major construction projects to the ultimate desegregation of a city where water fountains were marked for "white" and "colored" and the jail had different visitation days for whites and blacks.

The Citizens Council members looked at every issue in Dallas as it related to economics. The clamoring for civil rights had led to embarrassing demonstrations in other parts of the country, but Dallas had no such problems. Thornton and the other members decided that desegregation would help the financial and tourism industries, and to not seem to be leading the way could cause economic setbacks. However, they also knew that they had to proceed cautiously.

First came the state fair where everyone was made welcome. Black, white, Hispanic, and Indian families came together peacefully, each recognizing that they were enjoying the same experiences for the same reasons. Then came the integration of downtown restaurants and hotels. Community opposition, if any, was tempered by the fact that neighborhood businesses serving the residents, not visitors, were not affected. However, the fact that business increased downtown led to many of the suburban areas also becoming more open.

Schools came last because of fears of the students' emerging sexuality and the idea that integration could extend to dating. However, by the time the school integration effort was made, the city had changed enough so that there was acceptance with limited hostility.

The Citizens Council, through political connections, the buying of advertising space (or withholding of advertising dollars), and similar methods also controlled the media. Nothing appeared in newspapers, on radio, or on television that went against the image the Citizens Council was trying to portray. This would eventually become so extreme that Judge Joe B. Brown, a man who would soon have tremendous influence over Juanita, was provided a public relations man by the Citizens Council when they felt press control and judicial censorship were necessary.

It was also from the ranks of the Citizens Council that the How Dare You squad was created. It is uncertain whether the How Dare You squad was the name the members gave themselves or the way others started referring to them. In the 1950s, these men decided what was moral and proper, what was not, and how best to stifle that which might prove an embarrassment. These were also the men who, in their youth, had been participants in the Capture, many of them having paid for their own time with Juanita.

It was in this world of sexism and misogyny, of controlled press and law enforcement, that the pursuit of "expendable" young women for the Capture was played out in a variety of ways. The gentlest was the least used because it required more time than the rape Juanita endured. It also created possible witnesses who could challenge the men involved. The targeted young woman would be spotted working in a coffee shop, cleaning hotel rooms, or handling some other job that required little training. If she was new to South Dallas and lived alone, it was probable she was a runaway.

The pimp would begin dating the girl, taking advantage of her loneliness, her fears, and her low self-esteem. They would go from friends to lovers to planning for a future together. Then, when the man thought the young woman was committed to him, he would suggest that they could make more money faster if she would have sex with other men. Sometimes he talked her into it, convincing her that sex could be separated from love. Sometimes he beat her when she refused, her fear of the violence coupled with a fear of losing him so that she went along with his request. And sometimes he arranged for friends or sex business co-workers to rape her, often for a fee. The brutality would continue until she was emotionally broken and willing to endure sex with anyone.

Other pimps—the majority in South Dallas—were more direct. Kidnapping would lead to rape. Rape would lead to prostitution. Simple. Effective. And if things got too rough, you could kill a runaway with little chance that anyone would come seeking her. Missing teens were presumed to have gone on to some other jurisdiction, to be some other sheriff's problem. Their parents did not care or did not know where their daughters had gone. There was no husband or lover pursuing his beloved. The girls had no attachments in a nightmare world where your lack of local history meant complying with the pimps or dying.

An occasional employer might suspect the worst when a young employee did not turn up for her shift, but business owners also knew that they were hiring drifters who might settle down or might disappear from the area as suddenly as they came. They also knew that some of the pimps were long-term customers whose loyalty was more important than what happened to some runaway.

Ultimately a girl who was properly broken would be placed in some type of residential facility to ply her trade—a motel, rooming house, and the like—or she would be trusted with outcall. The latter usually was handled through the porters working in the downtown luxury hotels.

The fees for women in the Capture were consistent. Oral sex was $20, a week's mustering out pay under the GI Bill for the first year that servicemen returned from active duty in World War II. The man was told he could have an hour with the girl or he could stay until he achieved orgasm, whichever happened first. The girls were told they had better hone their skills with lips and tongue so the man could be serviced and the room tidied in under fifteen minutes. The pimps expected the girls to handle four clients an hour and to service at least twelve men a day, seven days a week, so that the average low-end prostitute would generate $80 per hour or $80,000 a year in gross income (4,000 clients).

It is hard to know which was worse, the turning of a woman into an assembly-line sex worker or that the quotas were met, the latter indicating that many men in Dallas were repeat customers. Given the high cost, the most regular were obviously men of wealth and privilege.

The girls also offered more traditional sex involving full intercourse. The same rules applied, but most men took the full hour for a fee of $100, the same as the minimum charge for outcall. And some men were willing to pay a much higher fee in order to name the experience they wished to have, including the right to be the first person to have sex with a newly kidnapped girl. After delighting in the screams and tears of the girl they had "rented," the men returned to their homes, perhaps to their wives and children, often in upscale neighborhoods where they were active in civic affairs, church life, and always willing to help with community good works.

Juanita Slusher arrived in South Dallas when she was fourteen years old, the perfect age for the Capture. She had the baby face of the pre-adolescent but the taut figure and big busts of a young woman at the peak of her beauty. Her sister Kay, who knew nothing about the rapes, the kidnapping, and the violence Juanita had endured, was willing to share her home with Juanita, who lied about her age to obtain work at the Trolley Court Motel and Restaurant.

Juanita was too young and inexperienced to realize that in an area where white slavery was common, a girl with her looks and naïveté was going to be targeted by anyone in the business, not just her two assailants. She fantasized that the past had been a set of singular experiences, never to be repeated now that she had escaped from her assailants, obtained her first job in a big city, and could start a new, better, happier life.

FIVE

Carhops, Truckers, and Jack Ruby

The injustices and twisted law enforcement in South Dallas of the era did not mean that the people of greater Dallas were without a sense of morals and values. The successful white men who were old enough to have increased their wealth either sitting out World War II or working in non-combatant roles had become philanthropists concerned about business growth, education, health care, and the economy. Some, such as Earl Cabell and Eric Johnson, even sought political office. Cabell was a successful dairy farmer who also owned a chain of profitable convenience stores called Cabell's. His wealth was great, and when he became mayor of Dallas, he was viewed as incorruptible, a man who could not be bribed by special interests and thus an individual to be trusted. Likewise Eric Johnson became mayor after being co-founder of the highly successful Texas Instruments Company. His firm brought greatly desired manufacturing jobs to Dallas, further expanding the city's economic base while offering work that brought more and more people to the growing city.

Some of the visionary community leaders fought for the creation of reservoirs that remain key to Dallas's success to this day. Rain is erratic in Dallas. In any given year, there can be an excess of water that overflows rivers, damages crops, and is more nuisance than blessing. In other years, drought and intense heat scorch the land, potentially crippling the agriculture industry and forcing water rationing. The reservoir system was designed to hold enough water to meet the city's current and projected needs for fifteen years. Such holdings far exceeded the cumulative time of worst drought, the volume assuring business leaders considering relocation to Dallas that neither their employees nor their production would be hindered in any way.

Other wealthy individuals gave of their time and expertise when they formed the Citizens Charter Association, which came to dominate the local government. As former banker and judge Joe Ashmore recalled, "If I had an inclination to become a city councilman, man, I'd have to pass all kinds of saliva tests, be conservative as hell, and I'd have to have their philosophy, and so forth and so forth for me to get the support to even run for office."

Conservative was the key word, though the term seemed to have meant then a self-righteous attitude quite obvious to the disenfranchised in the community. Among the poor minority groups living in the city there was the joking suggestion that Dallas's wealthy white elite had divided themselves into two categories. All the men were rigid Baptists who never had an impure thought, even while having sex with prostitutes. Their wives and daughters were all virgins, no matter how many lovers or children they may have had along the way.

Juanita Slusher never paid much attention to the evidence of the growing economy. She never saw the Dallas of the late 1940s and early 1950s that the Chamber of Commerce was justifiably proud of, the area with buildings under construction, luxury cars plying the streets, and children who were well dressed and well fed. Instead, she found herself in the dire part of town that the "nice" people never admitted existed, in the one place that asked no questions of a teenage runaway. Juanita continued living in Number 22 of the Trolley Court Motel after her sister moved out, working there to earn her keep. "I cleaned up the rooms and she had a different job. And then I'd carhop the hours that I could carhop at the drive-in, 'cause they had the Trolley Drive-in. They had old trolley cars, and I would carhop the hours I could carhop, the hours they didn't sell beer."

Drive-in restaurants were a popular form of dining out in the postwar years. In 1949, new roads, new cars, outdoor movie theaters, and inexpensive motels meant that American youth delighted in living in their cars. Unlike the fast food designs of a few years later, many restaurants offered their regular sit-down meals inside the facility or outside in cars. A car would drive into the section of the parking lot where the carhops worked. These were almost invariably attractive young women in uniforms that included short skirts and fairly tight, relatively low-cut blouses. There was nothing offensive about their uniforms, especially since many worked in conservative communities. But they were as sensual as the standards of the day allowed, and the fact that the carhops frequently had to bend forward slightly to talk with the driver added to the appeal.

The carhop would bring the food on a tray designed to set on the open window. Usually the teens and young adults eating at such places ordered burgers, fries, and milkshakes, though if something was on the menu, it was available. The carhop would check back from time to time, much like restaurants that today offer outdoor tables in warm weather. The restaurants used the same dishes, glasses, and silverware for food served in cars as for food served at the tables inside. Nothing was disposable in those bygone years.

The novelty was so popular that competing drive-ins looked for gimmicks. The Trolley Court Motel was a quirky location, fitting the South Dallas area. All the rooms, the office, and the restaurant were converted trolley cars placed on permanent bases, plumbing for the bathroom and kitchen sections added to the interiors.

Truckers were the most frequent customers, the owner luring them with cheap prices for food and lodging, and a massive lot for parking their big rigs. Pimps also took rooms in the Trolley Court. Some lived there and others used the place as an "office" for matching truckers with their girls. Rooms were not rented by the hour and prostitution was not permitted in the rooms. Instead, arrangements could be made for a girl to come to a trucker's cab. Anything more that might be desired had to be arranged with an area brothel.

The women who serviced the truckers were usually older, physically and emotionally worn prostitutes at the end of their productive value. Many were alcoholics and drug addicts, their faces showing the ravages of the harsh life they had led. But Trolley Court truck parking-lot sex was invariably at night, the rigs angled so the cabs' interiors would be in shadow. It was not noticeable to most passersby, including those like Juanita who lived and worked there.

47

Juanita worked as a maid for part of each day, a waitress for the rest, talking with the customers, getting her tips, able to pay her rent, eat, and go dancing at the nearby Singapore Club, owned by a woman named Eva Ruby, who had moved to South Dallas from Chicago.

Eva Ruby and her two years' younger brother, Jack, had also had difficult childhoods. Their father was an alcoholic carpenter, a Russian immigrant who frequently abused his wife when he had been drinking. Their mother endured the verbal and physical abuse, sometimes seeming to accept what was happening and sometimes separating from her husband. During the separations the children were placed in foster homes, and in her later years, their mother spent months in a mental hospital.

Jack was a hustler from the time he was nine and bought and sold fireworks for a profit. He worked the streets as he got older, selling pennants, scalping tickets to sporting events in Chicago, selling shopping bags at Christmas time. Then he moved to California in 1935, the year Juanita was born, so he could sell racetrack tip sheets and subscriptions to the William Randolph Hearst newspaper in San Francisco.

None of the hustles, legitimate or otherwise, panned out. World War II came, and Jack continued his activities, ranging from being a union organizer to seller of punchboards, a gambling device placed in bars and restaurants near the checkout counters. He was not patriotic enough to enlist, but he was drafted in 1943, and when he was finished with his service, he decided to join Eva in her nightclub business. He would be involved with clubs in one form or another ever after, learning from his sister how to handle underage girls like Juanita.

Eva Ruby's nightspot was an oasis of safety for a girl like Juanita. The older woman had strict policies about behavior that customers followed or were thrown out. The first rule was that everyone who entered the club had to be treated with respect, except the cops whose presence had a way of making some of her less reputable customers uneasy. There was music and dancing, liquor and food, a place where pimps and truckers could relax side by side without doing other business. There were also the North Dallas swells who liked to go "slumming," enjoying a nightspot that seemed to have a hint of danger while being perfectly safe for everyone who entered. No one was allowed to get drunk. No one would be drugged and rolled. The place was a joint but a straight one, and it had the approval of the Citizens Council, which periodically arranged for visits by people from out of state and guests of Chamber of Commerce officials.

Juanita, a lonely kid who worked hard, found an end to loneliness through sneaking a stray puppy into her room and going dancing at Eva's place, where Jack Ruby had come to work a year after his sister opened the place. Juanita was a good-looking kid who didn't drink, didn't hustle anyone, just loved to dance after her long workday at the Trolley Court. They ignored her age, welcoming her and knowing that many of the male customers stayed longer and spent more just to be near Juanita or watch her dance.

Sometimes Juanita came to the club alone. Sometimes she came with other girls who carefully followed the rules. None of them tried to drink if they were under age. None of them were interested in the advances of the men if it meant the men wanted to do something other than dance.

Jack Ruby was so taken with Juanita and her friends that he began acting like her big brother. Let one of the men get out of line and Jack would have a quiet word with the overexuberant male or, if need be, he would take him to an isolated place and beat him senseless. That was the way a good club owner maintained a respectable clientele when the joint was on the streets of Chicago. He saw no reason to run his sister's place any differently in Dallas.

SIX

Turning Professional with Shorty

Shorty Anderson was the next man to radically change the teenage Juanita's life. He saw her at the Trolley Court during the first few weeks she was on her own, had no idea she was just fourteen, and may not have cared had he known. He knew she was a runaway from either family troubles or a bad marriage, because no girl was on her own in that part of town for any other reason. And he lusted for her with an intensity that had no room for any feelings Juanita might have had. He wished to possess her and was amoral enough to not care how he did it.

Shorty, a man of average height whose nickname Juanita never questioned, was accustomed to getting his way. He also fancied himself a professional's professional in the business of stealing other people's valuables. When he wasn't taking what did not belong to him, he ran a school for burglars in his home, a trailer under a bridge. Shorty taught his students how to case a building, how to enter, how to crack a safe, and other necessities of the trade. His vocational school accepted any applicant who was enough of a lowlife to see Shorty as someone worthy of emulating, a judgment call so bad that many of his graduates were prematurely retired by the police.

Shorty's "straight" job was connected with the chain of Glow Coast service stations in Dallas. Juanita was never certain what he did, though she thought he might have handled general maintenance. She became involved with him when she was looking for higher-paying, regular work so she could pay her rent in the Trolley Court.

There was a gas war going on, and Shorty and a friend had Juanita drive them from station to station. She never knew how old a man Shorty was at the time, though she thought he was at least in his forties. She also did not realize that instead of checking on the stations and maybe looking at the books, they were actually involved with petty theft. One would distract the clerk while the other grabbed the paper money from the register. Then they would quietly leave, having Juanita drive them to the next station.

Eventually Juanita realized that she was working with thieves, a fact that meant nothing to her. The girls who came to South Dallas were usually runaways seeking ways to get by. The boys who arrived there, the ones without families who were not in the Capture, found a close-knit community where stealing was considered a profession deserving various levels of respect. Basic burglary, such as Shorty taught with more enthusiasm than skill, was at the low end. The burglars never knew what they would find. They also made very little money on the endeavors and were likely to get caught when they tried to spend too much too fast in all the wrong places.

Given time, both practicing their profession and going to jail, the best and brightest of the South Dallas youths learned the skills needed to make a good living. They knew which police officers to avoid, which to bribe, and which would change the charge against you for a percentage of the take. They learned such advanced skills as safecracking. And within the South Dallas community, being a safecracker who entered a building with purpose and knowledge was as honorable a profession as medicine or law might be in an upscale community. The difference in the hierarchy of thieves was the same as the difference between a hospital orderly and a member of the surgical staff.

Juanita came to feel honored to have Shorty, a burglar who cracked safes, interested in her. She began going with him as he committed crimes, not realizing that he was seeing her as someone to possess sexually, not just someone who was his part-time assistant.

"I didn't know it was going to turn into a masochistic situation where he would become obsessed with me," said Juanita. "It never crossed my mind. I mean, we were workin' buddies. I hit the gas stations. I went in and did what I was told to do. I got a little money here and a little money there. Listen, that was another way of life at that time."

But Shorty was not Juanita's friend, though she didn't know that at the time. Although he was never without a knife or a gun, she was not afraid. Weapons, especially low-caliber rifles, were common among teens in small-town gun country such as Edna, Texas, where weapons were carried to school so the boys could shoot squirrels, rabbits, and similar wild game on their way home. Hunting and trapping were how they helped their family have meat when money was tight. She did not realize that being armed in South Dallas was not normal, that the weapons meant Shorty was at least as dangerous as the men who had raped her in their attempt to put her in the Capture.

Juanita also did not know that Shorty was aroused by a woman's helplessness. His sexual feelings were heightened when the woman became terrified after realizing that he didn't care if she lived or died when she resisted his sexual advances. That was why, when he knew he wanted to have her sexually, he announced his intentions by holding a knife to her throat. Then, when he had stripped her, he held a revolver to her head, his finger on the trigger as he entered her. She dared not move, knowing she would be dead if she resisted in the slightest.

"I don't know how he saw the necessity to rape me. I knew that evidently that's the only way he knew to do it, to make me do it, 'cause I had never voluntarily done or never made advances to him.

"It was unpleasant because I didn't want it to be happening, and he left me off at Zangs Boulevard, left me there afterwards just to teach me a lesson, and the police found me sittin' out there."

The police involvement mattered little. Shorty had made clear that Juanita was nothing more than a piece of meat that could be snatched up, used, and discarded at the slightest whim. Yet the psychopathic Shorty simultaneously made her the subject of his sexual fantasies. He was excited by possessing and perhaps destroying her beautiful face, her flawless figure, her intelligence that was obvious even though she lacked much schooling. So long as Shorty was free, Juanita would always be one moment's madness from death or disfigurement. That was why she did not hide from him when he came back to see her again and again.

Soon Juanita was like a caged bird willing to endure whatever might be done to her, yet always watching the door, always looking for that momentary mistake that would enable her escape. "It was like I could have been locked up forever. Nobody was going to come and see about me. If I hadn't had . . . the energy to know that this is what my heart wants to be or do, I would have accepted it and just let it go. I got to thinking so little of myself that I wouldn't have cared anymore. I mean you can just be punched so much and misused so much."

The only thing Shorty avoided with Juanita was trying to drug her. Perhaps it was her size, "no bigger than a minute," that enabled a large man to physically restrain her when necessary. Perhaps it was because she came to fight back. Drugs were as likely to agitate her as make her docile, and that was a risk predators like Shorty would not take. As she said about drugging, "I don't know why they never did that to me anyway, unless they figured I was such a Looney Tunes anyway that if they put drugs in me I'd really go berserk."

Billy Dabbs became Juanita's open cage door. He was a youth of similarly hardscrabble background, though one with a dream. He wanted to be a professional man, someone who would rise above poverty to take a respected place in society. That was why he went to Shorty's trade school. That was why he became a safecracker.

As Juanita recalls, Billy came up to the drive-in and "Shorty introduced me to him. Billy had been in jail, which I didn't know. But he just came two or three times. I didn't know what he did for a livin'. I didn't ask him."

Billy's profession was not an issue for the fourteen-year-old Juanita when he made an offer that seemed the ideal escape. "He said, 'You want to get married?' And I said, 'Why not?'

"See, marriage to me means you got someone that's going to see about you." It was the way she saw her dad, Doc. No matter what he may have been like, he took care of his wives. He kept them safe. He provided for them. He was a man who would never have allowed men to hurt her the way she had been hurt since arriving in South Dallas. "Nothin' about love ever entered into it.

"Every time someone said 'Love' to me, I knew the 'lastic in my panties was tryin' to get stretched. So we ran off and got married."

Word of the marriage reached Shorty, who was livid. He considered Billy Dabbs to have stolen his property and he would do anything to get it back pronto.

Juanita and Billy were not concerned with Shorty. They drove about an hour to Rockwell, Texas, where a justice of the peace didn't give a damn how old she was so long as the couple had the few dollars necessary for his fee. The girl could be wearing a training bra stuffed with tissue and the boy's voice could still be changing. If the customers had the money and said they were legal, the wedding would take place.

The newlyweds wasted no time going into business for themselves in Dallas. They saw safecracking as a noble profession. There was no violence or threat of violence. Entry was always into an empty building. Breaking into the safe was a skilled job, and the rewards were disproportionate for the time involved.

Billy's education had been thorough, even if he was not the most apt pupil. He at least knew the proper procedure for breaking and entering, and he taught his young bride to be his assistant. First came the casing of the business to be burglarized. Juanita would go into the building to look around. She would check for the best escape routes, including the doors and windows. She would try to determine whether there was a night watchman, and the location of the safe.

Billy had his new wife buy the specialized equipment for the break-ins. Perhaps he wanted her to be a full partner in the family "business." Perhaps he felt that if they were caught away from the job, the judge would go easier on him if she was the one in possession of the burglar tools. And perhaps he was selfishly protecting himself from the volatility of some of what she obtained. She bought fuses, caps, and the highly unstable nitroglycerin. No one ever asked her name or age, not that she would have told them the truth. There were businesses that would sell such items to anyone who came in their establishments. Some catered to criminals in need of particular tools, such as dynamite. Others made extra money by selling legitimate stock to people with less than legitimate reasons for buying it.

"I didn't know nitroglycerin could kill you if you don't walk right."

Juanita also drove the getaway car. "We had an old souped-up Plymouth with a signal whistle that I was supposed to use if the cops came while Billy was inside a building. They would send me into stores to see what kind of safes they had. I just felt it was part of my job. I thought business was business, you know?"

Juanita had an unerring sense of spatial distance and could move the car between two others with only an inch or two to spare. She learned to drive fast, drive well, and always to be aware of every possible escape route.

The routine was always the same. Juanita would park outside the building in a place that would not arouse suspicion. The car windows would be rolled down so she could listen for anyone approaching by car or foot. She would constantly watch through the windshield as well as checking the side and rearview mirrors. And if there was trouble, she was knowledgeable about the surrounding streets, the back alleys, the driveways, and the private homes.

Billy would enter the building with his tools. Sometimes he could go through a door or window. Sometimes he had to find a way onto the roof, from which he would lower himself to where the safe was located. There were alarms in those days, but they were almost always perimeter alarms. If you could get in and out without setting it off, you would be free to search around inside undetected. You just had to worry about being seen through a window or having someone notice while you were breaking in.

Once inside, Billy would follow the directions his wife had sketched out for him. Sometimes he had to blow the safe, a procedure requiring a drill, the careful placement of explosives, and the necessary time to accomplish this. Do it wrong and you could be left with a lot of noise but the safe intact. Or you might drill too deeply, use too much explosive, and destroy the money, jewelry, or other valuables kept inside. There was also a chance that Billy could get hurt, misjudging both the blast and where he crouched to avoid being struck by flying debris.

Once the safe's door was opened, Billy had to work quickly. The explosion often caught the attention of neighbors or passersby. This would lead to the police being summoned, their arrival time always unpredictable.

One of Juanita's tasks was to wait in the car and listen for the cops. The moment she heard the faint sound of the sirens, she would sound the whistle and Billy would grab what he could and race out of the building.

Juanita would have the car rolling the moment Billy opened the auto's door. He'd fall onto the seat as she sped away, rapidly turning corners, always traveling in the direction opposite to the sound of the police. She would turn a corner, then another one, checking her mirrors, keeping her speed to a level that hopefully would not attract the notice of a traffic cop. There were times she had to slip between cars or trucks, using a space so small there was no margin for error. Her task was to ensure they would not be stuck in traffic, no matter how heavy it might be. Then she pulled into a residential driveway as though she belonged there. She and Billy would not run. They would do nothing to call attention to themselves. They were just a young couple sitting in their car, unaware of the excitement that was bringing the police to the nearby building.

Billy developed other scams. He had Juanita pick up men, slip them knockout drops, and then steal their identity cards for use when cashing stolen checks. She was never happy with the crimes she was committing, but most of the people she knew in South Dallas were engaged in similar activities. At least she and Billy never did physical harm to anyone. She could take pride in that and in the fact that the marriage seemed to be working. Billy may even have loved her, but what mattered was that he was keeping her safe.

Despite the "success" of her marriage, Juanita was still a troubled teenager, not a woman. She and Billy began fighting, and she realized his insistence on their committing crimes together was inappropriate. She returned to Edna for a visit, Billy following to try to persuade her to go back to Dallas. But Juanita wanted nothing more to do with Billy Dabbs.

Doc Slusher was never told that his daughter operated a getaway car for her new husband. He just knew that Juanita was not happy with her husband, so Doc made clear to the youth that he was to leave his daughter alone. Billy, inwardly outraged, had the good sense not to challenge his father-in-law. That did not prevent him from having a temper tantrum before he withdrew from his wife's hometown. He spent one night breaking into as many of Edna's stores and businesses as he could, stealing whatever he could find. He took jewelry, money, and other valuables. It was a crime spree the likes of which no one had seen, and whatever he did afterward was not enough to avoid getting caught.

"I don't know when Billy was arrested. I don't know where he was arrested. I just know that one day Lou, the sheriff, came to get me. He had Billy in jail and he wanted me to spend the day with him. I told him no. I told him I wanted nothing more to do with Billy Dabbs, but he said, 'Come on, Nita. He's your husband.'"

Juanita didn't know what to do. She felt she had no choice but to accompany the sheriff to the Edna jail. The sheriff's building was an odd one. The first floor was the sheriff's living quarters. Then you went up a long stairway to the second floor, where there was a series of cells. Three sides of each cell unit were solid. The fourth side was a door of bars through which anything going on in the cell could be seen by the jailer.

Juanita had been brought to the jail for a conjugal visit with her husband despite the fact that several of the cells were filled with men arrested on one charge or another. The situation was embarrassing, yet she had no idea what to do about it. The sheriff insisted, this being Texas, where a woman had certain obligations to her husband. So far as she knew, she had no choice. She was Mrs. Billy Dabbs, after all, and the sheriff represented the law in Edna.

Juanita's aunt had the solution. She brought a bedsheet, and Billy and Juanita used it to cover the bars. Anything said could be heard by the other prisoners, and everyone knew exactly what they were doing. That did not matter. Billy wanted her. He was going off to the state penitentiary, and Juanita was only a woman. She had no rights compared with Billy Dabbs. She just had to go along with it, and then take the sheet down at the end of the day, walking past the cells as the other inmates commented on what had taken place down the way.

If anything killed a chance for reconciliation, the visit to the jail did. The coldness of the experience was yet another violation in Juanita's young life. She hated the sheriff for what he did, but she despised Billy more for demanding that she do it. She knew it was time to leave town and return to Dallas, increasingly the place she considered home.

Billy would eventually die after being released from the state prison, a fate that brought her neither pleasure nor pain. She had dismissed him from her mind by the time she returned to Dallas, looking for work that would keep her eating.

SEVEN

Corky, Juanita, and Jack

It was around 1950 or 1951, the exact date no longer remembered. Once again Juanita had a job waitressing in a café on South Ervay Street, just a hoot and a holler from Jack and Eva Ruby's Silver Spur (Jack's new name for what had been the Singapore Club). The brother and sister operators boasted the best rhythm and blues entertainment within walking distance of the café and the nearby rented furnished room Juanita called home after leaving both Billy and the Trolley Court.

Not that the Silver Spur was her first choice of nearby nightspots where Juanita danced after working the late shift as a waitress. She would usually first go jitterbugging at the Round-up Club. That nightspot had a country-western group whose music reminded Juanita a bit of her daddy, his boots, and the Pavilion. But the Round-up Club closed at 2:00 a.m., far too early for a late-shift restaurant worker to be heading home to a sleeping puppy she had sneaked past the landlady, and a cold bed. Her feet were still dancing to the music that lingered in her head as she moved on to the Silver Spur. "They stayed open until 4:00 in the morning, and they had rhythm and blues. I lived right around the corner and walked everywhere."

The life was a quiet one, a happy one, an existence that she wanted to enjoy forever. There were a few friends, including Mary Lou, Ginny, and Maria (not their real names), and her frequent dancing partner, Corky Copland. "One night out at Jack Ruby's place, there was Corky. And

Corky, he was excellent. He was smooth and on time, so we began to dance together."

All of the friends lived for the moment, working hard, playing hard, and letting tomorrow take care of itself. But the best times were with Corky because there was no sexual tension, no risk of a Shorty getting jealous and trying to hurt him, no risk of a Billy feeling cheated on while in jail. "Corky was just a friend. We used to dance country-western dance," said Juanita, noting that the two of them would try all the clubs that would let them inside.

Corky and Juanita became regular dance partners, not lovers. She was still too young to know what love was all about, too young to care. What she did know was sex, and most of that had been so brutal, there was no sensuality and rarely any pleasure.

Dancing had stolen her heart, and Corky was the only partner who could keep up with her moves, working with her to stretch their abilities. Dancing was her lover, something Corky understood. Besides, Juanita was still married to Billy Dabbs, though the relationship was over. She felt she owed Billy, just because she had been his wife in what passed as the good times together. She made an effort to see if she could get him out of jail, but a fifteen-year-old wife had no influence over and little understanding of what Billy faced.

Juanita knew she would be getting a divorce sometime in the future, and she liked having a male friend for companionship and security. She just made certain he didn't get the wrong idea about their relationship. Shorty was still gunning for her, and she was certain Shorty was the type who would destroy any male caught seriously dating the teenager over whom he still obsessed. She did not think about her tendency to return to the same places again and again. Either Shorty was less of a daily threat than she feared, or he wasn't concerned enough about Corky to make a move.

Dancing was a relief from the daily fight for financial survival, but the hard work she had to do to support herself never bothered Juanita. She knew she had the best job she could get at the time. She was making $22 a week, almost half of that going for rent. She had a puppy and was constantly delighted by the way its tail would wag, its ears pick up, and its face get what you'd swear was a grin every time she came home. The puppy was family enough for her in Dallas. That an occasional club owner like

Jack Ruby would take a genuine interest in her added the comfort of what was almost a surrogate uncle. Or so it seemed to a kid for whom nothing else in life had ever really worked out.

Juanita did not understand the impression she was making on Jack Ruby when she went dancing in the Silver Spur. He watched her at first to make certain she wasn't one of the South Dallas characters his sister Eva had somehow misjudged. But Ruby found he liked the teenager's style. She didn't drink, and she wasn't there looking to seduce a customer out of his last few dollars before she went home. She was a dancer, a kid who lived for the music and the movement. The times she was there with Corky, they looked like South Dallas's answer to Fred Astaire and Ginger Rogers. And when she couldn't go with Corky, she was often there with the slightly older girls who were also respectful of Jack's club rules. The kid wasn't particularly close to anyone, and that also drew Ruby's notice. He called himself a "black Jew," a term he never explained and which other Jewish club owners, such as the Weinstein brothers, neither used nor claimed to understand. Jack seemed to be saying that he was an outcast in a religion of outcasts, at least in the Dallas area, and in Juanita he noticed a kindred spirit.

Not that Juanita realized why Jack and the other club owners kept her from being hassled when she came to dance in liquor joints where her very presence was not quite legal. "I was under age, but they looked after me the best they could, probably 'cause they knew if they didn't look after me, somebody [making inappropriate sexual advances] would be going through a plate glass window." Juanita was tough as nails. Her willingness to fight was similar to Jack Ruby's pugnacious attitude when confronted by what he perceived were societal injustices.

Only later did she come to see that she and Jack Ruby had both been on the streets, both knew how hard you could fall if you didn't watch your back, and both knew to avoid a fight unless you could come back quicker, meaner, and harder than your assailant.

EIGHT

Under Age and Making It

Juanita moved from serving food to seeking a series of higher-paying jobs as a cocktail waitress in just about every club within walking distance. She lied when she told the club owners she was eighteen, and they lied when they said they believed her. "Course, maybe they did think that," Juanita mused later. She had a baby face, but the men who ran the clubs might not have gotten up that high when their eyes gave her body a look over. No way were her breasts those of a little girl, and as for the rest of her figure, all that running to school when Etta's list of daily chores made her miss the bus had given her shapely legs, a small waist, and a flat stomach. Juanita had all that and those big breasts. Maybe the club owners didn't notice how her face gave away her true age.

There was also the work ethic. Juanita was the most reliable waitress the clubs employed. There was no daddy to support her, no boyfriend exchanging a little bedtime for a roof over her head. She needed the money to eat, and she was willing to tackle any job with enthusiasm. She followed directions and she pleased the customers. She would smile, joke with the men, and move enticingly in time to the music that might be playing. They thought she was a sight worth enjoying enough to continue drinking instead of going club hopping. She enhanced the customer base, and the managers knew it.

For a city where the clubs were not allowed to stock hard liquor, alcohol was a big part of the nightspots that Juanita tried to work. Beer was on tap, but the customer brought everything else in. The clubs were BYOB (bring your own bottle), with the waitress supplying the glasses, the ice, and the fixings.

The customers trooped in looking a little like redneck winos, their bottles "hidden" in brown paper bags, and they were looking for more excitement than they could get drinking in the cabs of their trucks. Sometimes this meant attempting to share with the waitresses in the hope that they'd be loose enough at the end of their shift to agree to spend time in a cheap motel. Drinking on the job was always against the rules, though some waitresses sneaked drinks when they were offered. That made Juanita's inability to consume so much as a beer a highly desirable trait. Her bosses knew she would never steal drinks as some of the girls did, and there was no chance she would call in sick from a hangover.

The first Texas Liquor Control Board (LCB) bust was by chance. The agents were in the club where Juanita was working, and at least one of them managed to look at more than her figure. He saw the round-cheeked, little-girl face with the laughing eyes and dazzling smile. She wasn't coming on to anyone. She was only sexual in some man's fantasies. But her personality and that chest, well, nobody seeing her forgot the appearance of Juanita Slusher Dabbs, teenager or not, and that meant she was regularly targeted by the liquor agents who inspected the bars. Juanita moved from club to club each time the liquor agents forced the owners to let her go. Always she would do her best, helping the manager improve his bottom line with all the attention she got.

Juanita was seen as a little girl with an attitude when she needed one—big breasts, big smile, and not afraid of the cowboys who came into the joint looking for a stiff drink and a willing woman. She didn't take the smartass talk, the butt pinching, the money they flashed trying to impress her. She did her job and encouraged some casual customers to become regulars who bragged to their friends that they'd be the one to tame the filly and teach her what a real man was like in bed.

No one knew about the kidnappings and the rapes. No one saw the defiant anger that kept her alive. Few knew about her criminal past, and fewer still would have cared even if she had done jail time. This was South Dallas, where actions that would have been the dirty little secrets of upscale families brought you bragging rights in the bars.

The agents from the Texas LCB became part of a hide-and-seek game like that played by high school kids running from the truant officers. The agents couldn't miss the kid from Edna—sweet baby face and a figure as potent as the A-bomb that the newspapers said the Russians had just exploded, heating up the Cold War a notch or two and making the soldiers on leave nervous. The club managers who knew her wanted her working for them. When she moved to new clubs, having been evicted from the previous one by the agents, the managers tried to hide her in their offices, going along with her pretense that she was eighteen. But they all knew. They just didn't want to lose the best worker they had, regardless of her age.

Unfortunately there were times the agent got inside the club and spotted Juanita before the manager spotted him. And there were times when the agent was on rotation from somewhere else, his face unknown as he sat at the bar, acting just like a regular customer, watching, listening, and then pulling out his badge.

It got so Juanita thought there was some magic to her being caught. She never saw herself as a unique person. She never saw her looks as being something that would make men drool till they tripped over their tongues and made fools of themselves on the floor. She never realized she was unforgettable in South Dallas.

For their part, the LCB agents were frustrated with the underage teenager who wouldn't get their message that she didn't belong in BYOB joints. They thought she should be home with her mama, going to school, growing up right.

One time Juanita was "deported" by being placed on a bus to Edna with the instruction "Stay home, little girl." But Edna wasn't home anymore. It hadn't been home since Etta became her stepmother, and especially when Billy Dabbs embarrassed her by getting himself busted. The only thing to do was get off the bus, buy another ticket, and head right back to Dallas, where she finally accepted reality. She went back to slinging hash in the café. The money was less, but so were the hassles.

What Juanita didn't realize was that she was the type of easy arrest the law enforcement officers liked. Dallas had a vagrancy charge that covered a lot of territory. You could be taken into custody if you didn't have a roof over your head and a means of supporting yourself. You could be arrested if you were working illegally in one of the clubs. You could be arrested for being a prostitute. And you could be arrested just because a cop wanted you off the streets of "his" city. And all those arrests were lumped together under the heading of "vagrancy."

The cheap misdemeanor busts under the vagrancy statute helped the lawmen look good. Their numbers of arrests passed inspection, so no one ever questioned why they ignored more serious violations in the joints owned by Pappy Dolson, Abe Weinstein, and Jack Ruby, among others. Pappy, Abe, Jack, and to a lesser degree Abe's brother Barney, were among the most prominent men in the Dallas entertainment industry. They owned the bars up and down Commerce Street. They had the slot machines. They had their own version of the numbers racket. They had underground horse betting and other types of gambling. It all made big money, and it was all illegal as hell.

"What happened was that the Abes and Pappys, and the Jack Rubys, they were all politically connected with city hall, and with the mayor's office," explained former Dallas judge Joe Ashmore. "You know, they kind of took care of that segment, and when the city needed some help so far as the sheriff's department or the police department—they were looking for a criminal or needed some help in nailing somebody—well, they'd go to the Abe Weinsteins and Pappy Dolsons and Jack Ruby. They'd put the word out and they'd get what they needed—information. They had a network and a system of stool pigeons so to speak, but the point being, even though there was that kind of seedy side, it was controlled, it was in the hands of a very select few, and they had their fingers on the pulse of it. They were able to keep it under wraps, to grow it, to make money out of it."

And though she had no idea just how that world existed or what it would mean, there would come a day when Juanita was as old as she claimed to be, a day when Abe Weinstein would give her a job she was ready for, and the legend of Candy Barr would be born. For the moment, though, she only wanted to work and enter that world as a customer, dancing through the night.

======

"Like a butterfly, I'd go around transforming. I created myself. I called myself a self-made schizophrenic."

—Juanita Slusher

======

Without the hassle of the LCB agents, Juanita briefly found complete happiness. She'd work, then walk to this club or that one so she could dance the night away. She frequently had her partner, Corky. She often had the slightly older girls she could hang with. She had everything she wanted, everything she needed. It was the greatest freedom she had experienced in her life, and it lasted until the day she went to jail just a few years later.

NINE

Shorty Had to Back Off or Shorty Had to Die

If there was anything good in the time Juanita spent in the BYOB clubs, it was the Dallas Police Department cop on the rise that she met there. His name was Fisher, and he eventually made captain. He understood girls like Juanita. He had seen a lot of them, mourned more than a few when they escaped the streets only by being murdered.

Captain Fisher couldn't change Juanita, change the streets, or find a new life for her. The times were wrong for that sort of thing. A teenager was an independent woman so far as the law was concerned. Maybe that wasn't right. Maybe it wasn't realistic. But this was Dallas, Texas, after World War II, and that was the way girls like Juanita were perceived. Still, with Fisher she had a friend in the right place when she needed one. She just had to have the courage to reach out, and that courage seemed to come only when it involved Shorty.

Shorty had become Juanita's bogeyman, the person she feared might turn up at any time, hurting anyone with whom she was friendly. She ignored the fact that Corky never saw Shorty, never was threatened by him in any way. Instead, the danger occurred when she went to live with her mother-in-law, an action she thought would provide protection. What she did not realize was that she was a product of her times and culture. It was expected that, in the late 1940s and early 1950s, a Texas teenage wife without a husband, regardless of the reason for his absence, would move in with her in-laws. Wives were still their husbands' property, and even if she did not have trouble getting along with Etta, a bride's first duty would be to her husband's family.

Shorty was also a product of the Texas culture. He knew that a teenager like Juanita would almost certainly spend some time with her in-laws. Finding her now that she was with Billy's mother was easy.

"Shorty grabbed me from behind and put a gun in my back in the front yard about midnight or one o'clock and took me off, and I think that's what began the next day keeping me in a motel, and I don't know where he took me back unless it was to my in-laws."

Shorty tried to force Juanita to live with him two or three times. "It was very difficult to be away from Shorty. I eventually had to run and hide in the attic [of her in-law's home] for three days, and I finally called Officer Fisher. He knew I had been under quite a bit of abuse from these people, and also the police department. Rookies on the beat and in the patrol cars, when there was a hot piece of ass movin' around there all of them will use you."

It was the unspoken agreement among many of the younger patrol officers in the South Dallas area and the attractive prostitutes that a trip to jail could be prevented if the men were provided a free romp in the back seat of the police cruiser. Each prostitute an officer desired would be stopped for vagrancy and then given her choice of being booked or servicing the officer in his car. A booking, though a misdemeanor, would require calling her pimp to pay the money needed to arrange for her release. She would lose the night's work and he would be angry about being bothered. The women, and at times this meant Juanita, endured the back seat to avoid the problems that came with facing a trial.

Captain Fisher did not use the women on the streets, and Juanita had come to trust him. She explained that he "was extremely aware of the problems I was having." He arranged for surveillance on Shorty, yet some of the younger officers still were hassling Juanita for sex. "He knew I was a victim of all this and I wasn't a participant with all this crime with Shorty. I called him and told him what was happening, and he said he'd be over to get me, and he came and got me so I could get a bus and go somewhere else. Otherwise I would have been in the attic and Shorty would have found me.

"I had to get away because I was up against the wall, and I really feel the pressure of Capture. Then I decided to kill."

Juanita's decision to kill Shorty came when she realized that she would never escape him. He would hurt her, rent her body to other men, and delight in her pain. Running away was not effective, and if he became too angry, she knew she would simply disappear like too many other girls. Murder was the only way to free herself. But Shorty was stronger than Juanita, and trying to kill him while he slept was too risky. She decided to use the one weakness she knew against him. She would murder him with chocolate-covered cherries.

"Shorty would make me lay and feed him candy-covered cherries with a knife on me, 'cause he liked to eat the cherries, and then he'd make me indulge in sexual relationships or whatever he chose to do. So I knew that's one way I could get him. I could put cyanide in the chocolate-covered cherries. That's a hell of a thing for a kid to know, but I became desperate."

Juanita knew where she could buy the cyanide, no questions asked. It was the same store where she had bought the explosives for safecracking. There were stores "back then for the gangsters. They black-market everything. Just because they're gangsters, they had black-market things for them, too. So this is what I planned to do, and I knew if he captured me again, I would carry my plan through.

"I knew no one else would free me from him. I didn't think of anything else. Shorty was everywhere. You'd drive down the road and stop at a stop sign, and he'd jump in the car and stick a knife in my belly just to do it. He really persecuted me. I wasn't paranoid. Once you reach the point of what reality is and deal with it, then there's no place for paranoia. No matter how extreme anybody thinks it is." Fortunately for Juanita, Captain Fisher eventually put a halt to Shorty's pressure.

Juanita remembered little about the day that marked the beginning of the end of her terror of Shorty other than she was between fifteen and sixteen years old. She had stopped worrying about his appearances, accepting the idea that he would come and go in her life without warning. She would not spend her days looking over her shoulder, and when he found her, she would not resist. It was a decision that saved her life when, unexpectedly, he appeared, grabbed her, and held a knife to her throat.

There was no fighting the bastard. He didn't care if she lived or died. He was going to rape her whether she could feel every thrust or his orgasm matched the last beats of a heart drained of blood. She did as she had in the past, enduring the violence and believing his threat to see her anytime he damned well pleased and to do with her whatever he wanted.

This time Juanita retaliated. She called Fisher and asked to charge Shorty with rape. The captain agreed and then asked her where the assault had taken place. They both thought he had probably stayed in the area, and when Fisher checked, he found that there were a series of criminal charges, both federal and state, pending against Shorty unrelated to Juanita. Several officers converged on the area; Shorty was located, arrested, and tried in both courts. The sentences he was given should have put him behind bars the rest of his life, and in a sense they did. But this was Texas, the last victim was "just" a young woman, and Juanita would soon learn that all celebrations were premature.

Juanita did not know the future, of course. She thought she had won and did what she usually did under such circumstances. She went dancing.

Troy Phillips was an occasional visitor to both the Trolley Court and the Singapore Club (later known as the Silver Spur). He was married, in his mid-twenties, and had an eye for new girls in the area. He owned a rooming house where he officially made his money, but his real income was from the Capture.

Troy had no interest in seduction. It was slow and could only get a married man into trouble. Even if the girl was ripe for breaking, there was still a courtship period, and no man's wife was going to tolerate his being away from home for so long a time. That was why he chose the direct approach—grabbing a girl on the street, terrifying her with a knife or a gun, and then taking her to a windowless room where her screams would not be heard, where she could be bound and gagged if she resisted too much.

Maria, one of Juanita's dancing buddies, had a clunker of an old car that brought her freedom when she and her friends were done serving chicken fried steak, burgers, fries, and whatever else a customer wanted. Juanita usually walked to any place she worked or danced, but if something was happening too far away, she knew she could usually count on Maria to find a place for her in the car. That was the case when Maria gave Juanita a ride to Jack Ruby's club early one morning.

Among those in Ruby's club was Troy Phillips, who was making a play for Ginny, the other blonde among the waitress friends. Troy was overbearing, dressed to be noticed, and had no skill on the dance floor. And Juanita "had this thing" about men who could not dance. "I don't like somebody who couldn't dance. I don't like somebody who gets out there and slobbers all over me, 'cause I was just a kid."

Troy suggested that he take everyone over to a café called Cowboys when the dancing was over at the Silver Spur. The nearby restaurant was open twenty-four hours and served as a quiet place to go if you were a cop, an entertainer, a pimp, or a hooker. Anybody who had to be up all night knew they could eat in Cowboys when everything else around South Ervay Street had closed.

Maria had Troy and the girls pile in her car and they drove the short distance to Cowboys. "I didn't want to go, but all the girls did. It was a free meal and I guess they figured in numbers they were safe. 'Course, he was making a play for this other little blonde-headed girl." The slow-to-trust Juanita assumed she would be left alone because of Troy's attentions to the other young woman. She had long ago learned that a few girls together were no protection from a violent, aggressive male.

To Juanita's dismay, Troy "sits down right between me and this other girl, and he starts making his play. Then he eats out of my plate. I couldn't stand that anyway. I just didn't like him." The group ended up at the house that Troy and his brother shared, "and me and the other girl were the only two that couldn't leave." The girl with the car had left them at the house, which was too far from Juanita's room for her to walk home. Troy could drive them, though he had no intention of doing so that night.

Juanita went home the next morning, but later, "he was waiting there in the café, waiting for me to get off work. He was just overbearing." What she didn't know was that she was about to become a madam for his sex business.

TEN

Ten Tricks a Night and Outcall Looks Easy

Juanita discovered how the game was played when Troy Phillips stopped her on her way home from working the last shift at the café. It was dark, the streets mostly empty. He knew no one was expecting her in her furnished room except the puppy she had been hiding there from the landlady. He knew she went dancing, but the clubs were chosen at random and she didn't show up every night. Her marriage was long over. No one would miss her if she just disappeared.

Juanita was annoyed rather than on her guard when Troy came into her life. She was a decade younger than the married man, who was separated from his wife at the time. Maybe he wasn't old enough to be her father, but he was so many years ahead of the teenager that he might as well have been for all she cared. She was just a kid, after all, and she had hoped she had made clear that she wanted nothing to do with the likes of him.

What happened next was remembered as a blur. One minute she was free, the next manhandled and forced to go with Troy to the rooming house he owned. She was taken to an upstairs room with no way out except the door. Then she was stripped naked and locked inside.

It was only when Troy came back with a friend, saying, "Wait till you see what I captured!" that she understood her life would never be the same again. What she did not expect was to have to endure Troy's playing with her body for the next three or four days before she was taken to a hotel in Waco and turned over to what Troy called the "nigger porter." The porter promised Troy that he would get her in shape to be one of the best prostitutes Troy worked. To Juanita's horror, he kept his word. Unlike when she was attacked after hitchhiking, this time there would be no escape until she was psychologically under their control.

Juanita was naïve despite all she had experienced. She had an intense instinct for escape, but she had no sense of how to survive once she fled the building where she was held prisoner. In her mind, freedom meant reaching the streets. She did not realize that she had become a commodity, something that could be bought and sold for large sums of money. She did not realize that she had a value worth pursuing. That was why she went to the nearest dance club, a place catering to the enlisted men serving at the air force base just outside Waco. She thought she could celebrate her freedom by dancing, a method that always brought her peace.

Juanita began dancing with a young test pilot who had come to the club with a few friends, hoping to find a pretty girl with whom to dance, drink, and enjoy a conversation. His name was Joe Benaventura and he spotted her almost at once. She was dancing with the abandon of a caged animal suddenly set free. There was something sensual about her, but more compelling was her complete abandon. He knew he had to meet her, talk with her, and dance with her. To his delight, the girl agreed.

Juanita didn't know why she decided to talk with Joe as openly as she did. There was nothing special about his appearance that she can recall today. He was a Texas boy with the short military haircut and polished shoes typical of all the young soldiers on leave. He was out for a good time, no different from hundreds of youths whom prostitutes in the area knew as potential one-time tricks. But this one wasn't interested in a night of cheap sex. This one had come to the dance hall to enjoy the music, and if he got lucky enough to meet a girl, he wanted a friendship before anything else happened between them. That was why she told him about the Capture, about the porter in the Waco hotel, about Troy and the violence she had endured.

Joe wanted to help Juanita get away, but they never had a chance to run. Troy knew the teenager was a creature of habit. She was happiest going out dancing, so he told the porter to look for her in the nearest dance hall. The man was a professional in a world of politically connected criminals. Whatever he said to Joe made clear that Juanita was a prostitute who was wanted badly enough, if Joe made a move to stop her going back to the hotel, he and any friends who helped him would be beaten or worse. Juanita did not want to see Joe hurt. She had endured enough pain herself, so she didn't scream or resist, and Joe seemed to assume that this was a choice she had personally made.

There would be a second escape, this time after she was returned to Dallas to work in Troy's rooming house. She had been "broken" and trained in Waco, or so the men thought. In reality, she was still determined to flee, still naïve enough to go to the nearest dance club. Once again this was a hangout for airmen, in this case those stationed in nearby Fort Worth. Once again a pilot tried to come to her rescue. The youth's name was unpronounceable, he told Juanita when they began talking. "Just call me Johnny Harper. That's what all my friends do."

Juanita trusted Johnny with the story of what had happened to her, and he seemed to have more sense than she did. He realized she would not be safe unless she fled the area. He told her he would help her, and together they started to leave, just as Troy and his friends caught up with them. Johnny started fighting in order to distract the men and give Juanita a chance to flee. She found a way to climb to the roof of a nearby building, where she could lie flat and not be seen from the ground. There she had to listen in horror to the sound of Johnny being severely beaten.

Hour after hour Juanita hid on the roof, knowing she would never get away. Finally she came down, accepting the inevitable, returning to Troy. He beat her, though far less severely than Johnny. He wanted no marks on his merchandise so she would immediately return to work. Johnny, by contrast, had been taught a lesson about the ways of the Capture that Troy felt would keep the airman from interfering with another man's business.

"They finally had to tie me up," Juanita recalled. "They do it a lot nowadays 'cause the girls won't stay. I finally knew this was serious. I wasn't going to get back to the Round-up Club and dance.

"You can see how simpleminded I was. I didn't know that this was a serious world. I figured this was some of the games people played all along my life. So I would end up right back where I felt best, at the Round-up Club, and go dancing.

"The problem was that I kept breaking out and going back to the Round-up Cub, and they knew where to find me, and they'd come and get me. And every once in a while I'd have to have a little fight. It was too early to go home. Then they'd take me back down there.

"After a while it got to be a humiliation for the trophy Troy had captured. She wouldn't break." It became a joke among the men Troy associated with. "So they told him to turn me over to them so I'd come back right."

Juanita was broken, at least to the point where she realized she could no longer fight the system. It wasn't what was happening to her: there was no greater violence they could do to her unless they wanted her disfigured or killed. Instead, she reached the point where she felt resistance was futile and escape impossible. Instead of recognizing that her own behavior was like a beacon calling the men to retrieve her, she decided that she would have to do whatever was requested of her. And when the men who paid to have themselves sucked or fucked praised her, Troy decided that it was time to try her in outcall.

Juanita was obviously perfect for the outcall services. She was young, beautiful, and seemingly a willing participant. She had come to accept whatever a man wanted to do with her, never letting him be aware that she hated his lust, hated his actions, hated the fact that he was undoubtedly cheating on his wife while visiting Dallas for business. At the same time, "I was embarrassed. Everyone knew what a woman alone going into a hotel was there to do. I was embarrassed when I went up to the bellman who would take me to the room where the man was waiting.

"I wasn't ashamed of that. How could I be ashamed of something that I had no control over? I would only be ashamed of something I willfully, voluntarily did as a way of life.

"I had a choice. Which was the better to do—running in and out of those hotels or be given to some porter 'cause I misbehaved? But I was embarrassed."

Part of the lie for the men who used the prostitutes was the price paid for their services. A man could easily raise a family of four in luxury on $100 a week in 1950. The Teamsters Union membership thought life was wonderful when they earned $35 a week. A prostitute going to a hotel to service one of the guests received a minimum fee of $100, the maximum charged in the whorehouse Troy ran with his drug-addicted brother.

Troy's whorehouse workers earned between $5 and $50 a trick, depending on the services desired. All the women were expected to do whatever the men wanted, unlike some establishments where the prostitutes could choose their specialties. The $100 fee covered an overnight stay, again the fee covering anything the man desired.

This could include the girl's being prepared by Troy, his brother, or some of their friends, who would tie the girl to the bed so she could not resist. She would be gagged if the man wanted the illusion of cooperation with a particularly undesirable act. Her mouth would be free for screaming if he enjoyed hearing her suffer.

The financial split for prostitutes was meant to give the illusion that the women were independent operators. The pimp got a portion of the money. The owners, managers, porters, and bellmen of the hotels and motels received a cut. The police obtained their share, though usually they got it directly from the pimps and madams. And the women were presumed to go home with their percentage. Sometimes they did. More often all the money went to the pimp who paid for her clothes, her room, her food, and other necessities, never letting her accumulate the funds to escape.

What went unsaid, what went unseen, was the violence and the horror.

"No one looked for me," said Juanita about her time in the Capture. "I wasn't the type to just disappear like that. I was reliable at the café. I paid my room rent every week. I regularly talked with my sister. And my puppy . . . "

It was the puppy that still caused great pain more than fifty years after the Capture by Troy. No one seriously questioned Juanita's disappearance. No one really cared. When the rent went unpaid and Juanita could not be found, the landlady emptied the room of everything, including the puppy. Someone who found it wandering the streets might have taken it in. It might have been killed. There was no way of knowing, though Juanita knew that its chance for survival was almost non-existent. The loss and presumed death were so overwhelming that, to this day, Juanita still weeps from the memory.

The one person who knew she was missing, knew she would never have just run off without saying something to both her and the owner of the café, was Kay, the sister with whom she once shared a room at the Trolley Court. Men like Jack Ruby undoubtedly noticed her absence, but that was not unusual. Young women lost their jobs, fell in love, and otherwise found reasons to stay away despite once having been regulars. The idea of some sort of foul play would not come to their minds. Kay, by contrast, should have noticed. Instead, she was so busy enjoying her freedom from family and responsibilities that she lied to herself, later explaining that she assumed Juanita had just chosen to go off somewhere. The fact that such an action was completely opposite to the teenager's character was not a concern. Juanita might as well have been dead.

ELEVEN

South Dallas's Dirty Little Secret

When she was spotted for the Capture, Juanita was young and had a wild streak—much like the city of Dallas itself. The city's population doubled in the years between Juanita's birth in 1935 in Edna, Texas, and her arrival in Dallas in the late 1940s. Within a few more years, the population would be approximately 650,000 and growing, and the skyline would make it seem closer to New York or Chicago than to a former cow town.

The young college graduates in Dallas had their own wild streaks, but where Juanita was like a wild caged bird fighting to get free, they were users of the dark side of the city. Many had been raised in privilege, their fathers being the men who had orchestrated the changes in the city. Their destiny was to be the next generation of local leadership. Their family wealth meant they could indulge their unspoken vices. They would rarely get arrested, almost never face adverse publicity from a run-in with the law. Their fathers arranged for a promotion here, an envelope of cash there, perhaps a job for the son of a police officer who would always remember why his son was a business executive and not a dead-end street cop.

The youths knew the clubs and bawdy houses in and around South Dallas. They were familiar with the club owners who would arrange private entertainment for a price. And they were acquainted with the "nigger porters" who would act as go-betweens, making certain a desired woman was available in whatever way requested.

The porters, actually no more than a handful of African American men who were held in contempt in their own neighborhoods, worked for the pimps and for tips from the college men. They were a part of the white slave trade that flourished in South Dallas, and because they were black, they were dismissed as being as unimportant and interchangeable as the women who were the victims of the business.

Dallas law enforcement had the same attitude as much of the rural, white Deep South. A white person could commit a major felony against an African American, including murder, with impunity. The porters who acted as go-betweens for the pimps were considered typical of their race, rarely facing jail even though the majority of blacks wanted them taken off the streets. Ignoring neighborhood demands, the law enforcement officers saw the porters as part of a service business that was white dominated and utilized by the politically influential. As for the women kidnapped and brutalized so they would work for the men—white and black—most of the police officers went along with the fantasy that they were willing participants, and as such the lowest scum on the streets. These women were thought to "enjoy" their work even if the customer arrived at the designated motel unit to find his woman for the hour tied to the bed, gagged, and bearing bruises that indicated she had been beaten. This was merely a turn-on for the customer who managed to convince himself that she was found the way she liked to have sex.

To the residents of Dallas, there was no corruption (bribes, theft in office, and the like) in the city as most people would define that term. "We didn't have a corrupt police department. We didn't have a corrupt sheriff's department. We didn't have a corrupt court system. And the reason being is that the people elected to office were people who were philanthropists and wealthy in their own right, so they didn't have to go stealing anything. And they were giving something back," explained former judge Joe Ashmore when reminiscing years later.

But corruption can take many forms, and the world of South Dallas remained a world many men did not want to discuss. It was where they could go to engage in acts they might joke about with men their fathers' ages but which would never be discussed in polite society. They did not tell their wives. They did not tell their lovers. They did not tell their pastors. And they did not expect to ever get exposed for their deeds, because none of the women they abused would ever be in a position of power to do so.

What they did not count on was a female who would one day achieve international acclaim at the same time they were making their move into the upper levels of business and politics. They did not expect that a woman they had used and abused would come to have the ear of journalists and gossip columnists, not just in Dallas but throughout the nation. And while Juanita had no intention of destroying anyone's life, the men did not recognize this fact. They knew they had revealed their dirty little sexual secrets while standing naked before her, and so they would one day fear her knowledge of the dark corners of their hearts.

Women of the Capture like Juanita had few, if any, connections with people who would question their disappearance. That was why the approaches were so effective. Once the woman realized the world into which she had been brought, she understood that any effort to run away would lead to her being hunted down and retaken. If she was able to place a telephone call to the police, she usually found that the men who might be assigned to investigate such a complaint were sympathetic to the businesses, not the victims.

The most shocking example Juanita encountered was during a period when she was living with Troy. They were in a South Dallas apartment building when a police detective came knocking on the door, asking Juanita to come downstairs. To her amazement, the detective had brought Shorty to be with her.

Shorty had become a "snitch," turning in people who worked for him or setting up someone innocent if a corrupt detective wanted the person taken off the streets. One of Shorty's scams, run from jail, was to arrange for a friend to commit a robbery. Then another man would deliberately be arrested for the crime, the officers involved making certain enough evidence was planted to ensure a conviction.

The benefits for Shorty were great, including being allowed to live in the local jail instead of the penitentiary while going through his various trials. He faced a lengthy sentence in the state penitentiary but had managed to convince Dallas-area law enforcement officers to delay his trip there by keeping him in the local jail. Shorty would not have impressed the warden at the state pen. He would not have had special treatment and might have been killed by the men he had helped to imprison. The local jail was quite different. He was the king there, and the police were his servants. That was why the detective was surprised when Juanita refused his request to allow Shorty to have sex with her.

Shorty had been so helpful, the detective explained, and now he had needs that required servicing. He specifically asked for Juanita, and since the police knew she was working as a prostitute, they were certain she would do them a favor. "I'm married to Troy Phillips," she told the detective. "I'll go ask him if he'd like me to have sex with Shorty."

The detective panicked. He knew Phillips was a hothead who was always armed. Troy wouldn't hesitate to shoot both Shorty and the detective if he became angry, and he most certainly would have been livid over such a request. Shorty and the detective fled.

As Juanita slowly moved from assembly-line prostitution, servicing between 400 and 500 men a month, to the outcall work where she was trusted to be on her own, she came to understand what the other women forced into the trade had endured. Each victim was taken any way that was necessary. She might be threatened with a gun or knife. She might be rendered unconscious by drugs. She might be grabbed unexpectedly, beaten immediately, and then literally carried off. All that mattered was that the girl was quickly removed from the streets without calling attention to the Capture.

The girl would be taken to a house, apartment, or motel room. It would always be located where either she could not be heard or the people who heard her would ignore her screams. She would be stripped of her clothes to reinforce the sense of helplessness and reduce the chance that she would run.

Men would be brought in to rape the girl, the first rapists chosen for their brutality and lack of caring. Some of the girls would mentally break, going insane or trying to take their lives by hanging, cutting, or even drowning themselves in the toilet. Others would come to an understanding with the pimp. They could have clothing, food, and the freedom to move around South Dallas provided they serviced every man the pimp ordered them to do. They would work three weeks a month (unless some

84

customers liked to have sex with a menstruating woman, in which case there would be no breaks), and as many hours a day as there were men willing to pay to have them.

Sometimes the external violence was minimal. The girl would be drugged and used, preventing resistance that might result in a man's over-reacting with his fists and feet. She would be left exhausted, emotionally battered, physically violated, and with no place to turn, though without bruises, dislocated joints, or broken bones.

Still other times the victim would be tied, gagged, and "rented" to men who liked the idea of a helpless woman. Sometimes the men would have the fantasy that this was the way their sex partner enjoyed it, that "no" meant "yes," that her struggles were foreplay and her arousal depended on her being overwhelmed. By keeping her helpless, they fantasized they were giving her the best sex she had ever enjoyed.

Sometimes the men would know she was new to the life, their interest heightened because of her helplessness, fear, and anger. In such circumstances the pimps would be able to get more money for the unique thrill of being one of her first violators.

Some procurers began making note of the tastes of their customers, selecting girls who could be made to go along with whatever was desired. Others didn't care. In Troy's case, for example, he insisted that Juanita do whatever the customer wished. He would physically make certain that happened, preparing her through bondage, beatings, or whatever else was felt necessary. He also made clear that if she did not cooperate, she would again be turned over to one of the porters for brutalizing.

It was the latter abuse that held the greatest fear for her. Still, she never stopped trying to escape. She also never stopped paying the price each time she got away from Troy's control for a few hours or a few days. But when she was under his power, she never disobeyed in a way that would return her to one of the hotel porters involved in that world of violence.

Juanita was also forced to manage other girls who worked out of a house Troy owned in South Dallas. "There were tricks who came to the house," she said. "We had bedrooms upstairs."

Most of the work was fast, oral sex, a task that could be performed many times a night. This was not a fantasy date where the girl had such a wonderful time that the man was guaranteed to "score." This was nothing more than a woman helping a man with masturbation—cold, impersonal, and so against society's norms that "decent" men never engaged in such activities. Or such was the illusion.

"I didn't know how to handle Troy. All my life I'd been owned by somebody, force-fucked by somebody.

"At first Troy was so good to me. But then I became scared of him. He'd get drunk five nights out of seven, and every time he got drunk and could find me, he'd hit me so much I thought he'd eventually kill me. He was filth, the 'bacteria' of my early dreams. And after I became Candy Barr, he saw me as if I were a little racehorse and he was determined to break me. His friends were all junkies or dope pushers or gangsters. Finally, to appease him so he wouldn't hurt me anymore, I became a madam for his eight girls. I'm ashamed of that but I had to do it to survive. Do it and get through it."

Pimps, including Troy, were often not satisfied with their agreed-upon portion and tried to find ways to cheat the prostitutes who worked for them. Juanita would not let Troy do that, seeing herself as the protector of the others who shared her hell. "That was the only good thing that came out of me working the girls. I wouldn't let him rob them. The girls got their money. He got his money. They got their money."

Troy believed that the prostitutes expected him to have sex with him, that they would somehow show more enthusiasm if he was regularly having intercourse with his "employees." "You know he felt like he was supposed to service everybody. I didn't know if it was because he was a good fuck or a bad fuck, but a lot tried to run off from him. But I tried to be fair. I know what it's like to walk into a hotel and up to one of those rooms."

There was never any way to know if a customer was going to take advantage of a girl. Sometimes the man was a psychopath who felt he could do whatever he desired because he had bought the prostitute. Sometimes the John would change the rules once the girl agreed to a particular sex act. The prostitutes could not dictate what they would and would not do with an outcall. So long as the trick paid what the pimp or madam demanded, the girl had to go along. The danger came when the trick paid to restrain the girl before sex and then took advantage of her helplessness. "Back in those times they were throwin' girls out the window. People were taking things off them and carvin' on them and killin' them. It was dangerous on the streets."

Again this was the dark side of Dallas. There was no way of knowing which trick was going to prove to be a psychopath. When the police learned of such a deranged soul, they knew it was in the interest of the city's image to have the man be a disreputable drifter. They wanted him to be the disheveled loner who slipped into town with $5 and a horror-movie agenda, then slipped away after carving up his anonymous sex partner. He was no longer the Dallas Police Department's concern and no longer a threat. It was just a relief to know he had only cut a whore. The truth was more likely to involve the offspring from a rich and prominent family.

The prostitute's best protection was to be working in a house like Troy ran. There were at least enough controls so surprises were unlikely. A trick would pay for specific desires he wanted to act out with the prostitute. The screams of a woman who was being hurt would be heard in the house, and if her reaction did not match the agreed-upon sex act, usually someone would rush into the room to stop him. This also prevented the prostitute from making a separate deal with the John, pocketing the difference in cash between the act for which he paid and the more extreme act the two agreed he could perform.

The "proper" men of Dallas who wanted to hurt girls learned to rely on outcall service. This meant being able to afford a hotel room as well as the $100 minimum, though the evening could cost several times that, depending on the man's idea of perverted "fun." The cops might want to claim that a prostitute's killer was from out of town when a trick went too far. They would claim the man registered with a phony name, and family connections would ensure an alibi for the real trick that night. And always the hotel clerks went along with the ruse, maintaining that no matter what name was used, the person who rented the room was no one they had ever seen before.

The few caring pimps would give their girls a schedule to keep, based on what the customer paid for. They knew the time necessary for different sex acts, and the trick was made aware that there was a schedule. If the girl did not return within a few minutes of when she was expected, the pimp would break in the door to get her.

Troy had no interest in protecting the girls, considering them readily replaceable, but when Juanita was forced to act as madam, she decided to personally ensure the girls' safety as much as possible. She did not worry about herself, though.

"I had already learned early in life to do it and get through it, whatever it was. See, the least resistance is sometimes the easiest pattern, 'cause that's what they want you to do—resist. Then they can show their power over you, and they feel justified in beating you up or brutally attacking you, 'cause you were a woman who fought them. Being brought up in a male/female world, don't raise your hand against a man. But you got to get on top of it and be concerned for the girls when you send them off. They can sure get hurt."

Juanita always went armed when confronting the men who were abusing the girls she sent to service them. Usually these disgruntled characters would threaten to call the law, something Juanita instinctively knew would not happen. Most of the customers were family men. They had wives. They had children. They had reputations to maintain. If they called the police, they were risking exposure for what they were doing. What she did not understand was that her threats made them worry that she knew who they were, where they worked, and where they lived.

The users of the prostitutes pretended the higher-priced women had complete freedom of choice in the lifestyle in which they were engaged. No one thought about the fact that their pimps had found whatever inner terrors would keep them compliant. Instead they looked upon the well-dressed, often extremely attractive young women as individuals enjoying their dates when they came to the city's luxury hotels to service them.

There was no special outfit the prostitutes wore as they might on the street. Women standing on street corners, waiting to be hired for whatever the man desired, often wore clothing that was easily removed. Dresses were usually shorter than the contemporary styles, and some had zippers along the sides so a woman could take off a dress in seconds without worrying about a man tearing at the fabric.

In the hotels, the women on outcall would wear whatever was appropriate for women staying in such locations. Juanita was usually in a dress or a skirt and blouse. Older prostitutes would wear heels, a hat and gloves, and whatever other clothing matched the styles of the guests. They might even shop in the same upscale stores, such as Neiman Marcus. It was ironic that women like Juanita, forced into the lowest point of their lives, victimized by every male with whom they had contact, appeared to be just another of the upscale ladies, another upscale wife.

TWELVE

The Reluctant Movie Star

Troy did not want Juanita working from the house they shared. He gave her the choice of doing outcalls in the hotels and occasionally in someone's home, or becoming a street-corner hooker. "I couldn't stand to be on the street. I'd been on the street a couple of times and I couldn't stand it. Believe it or not, I was really embarrassed.

"I would watch the girls work. It was easier to sneak into the hotels. In a room, it was private. But to stand on a corner—it was embarrassing for me. And I knew I had to try, 'cause if I didn't, I had some severe punishment to my way of thinking."

Outcall work had benefits lacking in street and brothel work, despite the element of danger. Among these was the fact that the majority of customers seemed to see the experience a little like a date, albeit without the preliminaries of wining and dining. The woman was a guest in the man's personal space, especially if he was from out of town and spending more than the time it took to have sex. Thus the experience could be physically gentler than what took place when a woman had to please a man who came with enough money to do anything he desired.

Still, Juanita recalled, "I didn't go to a trick unarmed. I either had a switchblade or some small weapon because I was aware." Yet she said of most of her experiences at the hotels, "There was nothing unusual about my tricks, believe it or not."

Sometimes, however, she had to accompany another prostitute who would turn a trick while all Juanita had to do was sit naked in a chair and watch. "I don't know what they did, to tell you the truth. But they wanted me to be naked in a chair, and for that they gave me $50, gave Troy $50."

A pseudo-lesbian issue arose on some of the outcalls. There were times when Juanita was sent with a second girl and they were expected to have sex with the trick or in front of him. They would always fake the sex they were supposed to be having with each other, knowing the trick wasn't going to get up from his chair to check exactly what they were doing.

On outcalls, "the porter usually knows what the trick wants. He calls the girl. If the trick's a butt fucker, the porter will call the girl that allows that. He knows whose pimps have their whores trained to do anything they want to, even to the point of throwing them out the window. And most of those girls are havin' to depend on drugs, or their men are really mean and they're really scared, or they really like it. I don't see how anybody could enjoy that kind of life of being a pressured whore, hitting the streets every day with no choice in the matter."

The clothing was surprisingly demure, often pedal pushers or shorts and a halter top. "But we didn't go around braless. Those things didn't happen even with the prostitute in those days. Not in my bracket. I had no idea what the pros did. I'm a novice and stayed a novice until I finished. And I kinda feel I should have gone ahead and become a pro. Boy, I would have been one hell of a woman to go along with my reputation.

"I'm a pro in the arts," Juanita said, referring to her dancing and singing, "not a pro in the prostitution." She explained that she never spent time "learning all the things they learn to do to make people feel good."

Juanita gained a sex education in the perverted wishes of some men during this time. One man wanted the girls to urinate on him, and "when we knew he was comin', we'd give them beer," she said, so they could accommodate him. "And I know these things happen because I'd peek every once in a while, because I couldn't believe these things happen. Thank God I didn't have to become a part of it.

"Now squattin' over the old man's face and peeing on him would be no chore. Drinking the beer to me would have been traumatic. That's the truth. The act of what was to happen I was accustomed to because of the programming, but the drinking of the beer . . . " Four or five girls would drink the beer, "and they'd go in there and pee on him and he'd leave. That's all he wanted."

It was 1951, a time when pornographic filmmaking was in its infancy. The cameras were usually silent and used amateur 8mm film for the most part, although some 16mm films were made, the quality similar to what older Americans may remember from watching educational films in public school classrooms. The smaller 8mm was cheaper to use and easier to sell because it could be packaged with inexpensive hand viewers or battery-operated projectors. Floodlights could be obtained inexpensively. A "professional" 8mm pornographic film could be made for no more than $100 worth of equipment. A few producers tried for what passed as a quality product, but actors in porno flicks were never paid as well as they would be a decade later. Instead they were either forced into their roles or chosen because of a drug addiction that kept them working for anyone who would feed their habits.

The man who grabbed Juanita was a talent scout of a sort for a new type of film company, at least for Dallas. He was planning to make a pornographic movie, and she was going to be the star. Unbeknownst to her, the man had Shorty's permission, and in the world of South Dallas, that was what mattered. No one was interested in the woman speaking for herself.

One of the men who was involved with the film production had "auditioned" Juanita in a Dallas motel room, though he led her to believe he was just another trick. The man was another regular at the Round-up Club, a place whose customers often included pimps, drug dealers, and whores. Not that Juanita realized any of that. She came to the club to jitterbug, and if she wasn't on the dance floor, she was about to return to it to dance. The man who was part of the film project had been her partner for a dance number or two, but all she remembers is that he must have been good enough to hold his own. The very best and the very worst dancers remained in her memory. Those she considered adequate were just pleasant ways to pass a song or two.

―――――――

"They may have drugged me, or maybe I blocked it out of my mind. I suppose they took me to a motel, I don't know where. In Dallas, I guess. I had been forced into screwing so many times, I wasn't really aware that his was different."

—Juanita Slusher, talking about the pornographic movie *Smart Aleck*

―――――――

Exactly what happened next is gone from her memory—she was only fifteen years old at the time. The suspicion is that she was drugged at the club and then taken to the motel room. All she knows is that she found herself with Shorty and his friends, acting out a story of sorts. She no longer remembers how Shorty came to be free. It is possible that some of the men were connected with the jail, letting him out long enough to make the movie so they could all benefit.

The basic plot of the movie was simple, as was typical for what passed as pornography in those days. Almost three decades would pass before production equipment, make-up, and the complexity of a porno film would be similar to Hollywood standards. And four decades would be needed for camcorders to become popular production tools. However, at the time, the movie was considered a groundbreaking classic, perhaps because it was so widely distributed that it could be seen on college campuses and even at the Wolters Air Force Base NCO Club in Mineral Wells, Texas.

Smart Aleck starts out by a swimming pool where a traveling salesman and a young brunette (Juanita, who would eventually became an "unnatural" blonde) are enjoying the day. Then the traveling salesman invites Juanita into his motel room and gives her liquor, to ensure that he can have his way with her. Juanita and the salesman begin kissing and hugging. The action gets more intense, starting with French kissing and erotic touching while both remain dressed, then proceeding to more passionate kissing while partially undressed. Soon the couple has stripped each other of their clothing and moved to the bed. He takes one of her breasts in his mouth, sucking on her nipples. He works his hands down her body. Finally, he is insistent that she take his penis in her mouth, at which time she rebels.

The rebellion was not part of the scenario. Almost fifty years later, Juanita remained haunted by this particular type of sex act she was forced to perform as a prostitute. "I'll never get the odor out of my nose, out of my mind." There was no way she was going to cooperate for the stag movie, even when she was physically attacked in an effort to make her compliant. Drugged or not, she refused to go along with the stage directions.

"It came time to make me suck his dick and this was alien to me. I hadn't done those things except when I was a young girl with that older man. I wasn't going to do it and he was going to make me do it, and you can see in this movie it became a fight scene. He clipped me on the chin. He said, 'he will,' and I said, 'I will not,' and I didn't care what they did. I didn't care if they did shoot me. He was not going to put his dick in my mouth."

The challenge was serious. "They told me they'd kill me if I caused a ruckus and caused them to get arrested. So I didn't cause a ruckus until they tried to make me suck that man's dick, and they said, 'Well, just forget it.' " As Juanita explained years later, "Shorty knew they'd have to stomp my face in order for me to do it. Then it wouldn't be a good movie."

Instead, the filmmakers had Juanita use the telephone in the room to act out making a phone call to another girl. The telephone call was not part of the original story. The phone was present because all the motel units had them. Having Juanita pretend to make a call was an ad-libbed action. She did not know that a second girl was there or why she was there. Perhaps the film was going to be shot differently if both cooperated. Perhaps she was there for something else. She did what she was ordered to do, and Juanita is shown sitting and watching.

The movie was a radical change from the types of films previously available, despite its simple story line and limited sexual action. Juanita was perceived by the early audience of sexually aroused but relationship-challenged young men as enjoying what was taking place. They could pretend to be the salesman and fantasize that she was enjoying kissing and touching them. The truth of her situation did not matter. It was only the results of the audience imagination that made the film enduring.

95

Smart Aleck had no real plot. It was made for people who wanted to see a couple having sex. However, it was made at a time when hypocritical moralists were publicly "outraged" and privately titillated by all manner of what they considered naughtiness. The National Organization for Decent Literature was working to coerce booksellers to remove the works of novelists they felt were corrupting America with "filth." The suspect writers included Ernest Hemingway, George Orwell, John Dos Passos, Emile Zola, and William Faulkner, all of whose classic writings are studied in high schools and colleges today. Television of the day had nothing more controversial than quiz shows such as *The $64,000 Question*, not yet revealed to be rigged so popular guests would have the correct answers ahead of time, allowing them to return to play week after week.

In the 1950s, most people believed that evil centered on communism, a menace noted by blowhards such as Senator Joe McCarthy, who became famous for finding communists where none existed. Organized crime was also being discovered. Senator Estes Kefauver headed a committee that traveled the country, holding hearings that revealed illicit activities. Many of those activities would eventually be made legal in Nevada.

Sexual concerns centered primarily around new media such as *Playboy* magazine, which debuted with one of the calendar photos of Marilyn Monroe. Feature films with the French actress Brigitte Bardot were eventually banned from being shown in Philadelphia. Sex scenes available today via the Internet and cable or satellite television were purchased as still photos in magazines sold from under the counter of various stores or by mail in the form of 8mm movies running perhaps five minutes.

Smart Aleck was a shockingly long film for the day, a fifteen-minute one-reeler, and there was an instant demand to see it. It was one of the first "blue movies" to get widespread distribution in the United States. Part of the legend surrounding the movie was that the girl who is first brought into the room by the traveling salesman is having a wonderful time during the sex. The idea that she could enjoy something she was forced to do intrigued Juanita enough so that she finally saw it for the first time approximately twenty years later. "Everybody told me what a good time I was havin', which made them question the fact that it was done under duress."

Some of what viewers saw in the film could be explained by drugs. Back then, Juanita recalled, "I became aware of hallucinogenic, LSD stuff, and how people could put stuff in your drink and alter your whole personality." About seeing the film years later, Juanita explained, "I went mainly to see how I reacted, and true enough, after I got the beverage I became someone else.

"The point I'm trying to make is I suppose that was the time I had my first real drugs. But I watched it 'cause I wanted to see if I was showing having pleasure in it.

"I remember it shows where I'm having the beverage and then I watched myself very closely 'cause I know what that's like, the trip. I give myself the possibility that there may have been something to make me cooperate."

There was also the possibility that she acted no differently than she had in the past. "At that time I didn't know what was going on. I had been forced into screwing so many times, I didn't think this was any different. It was just an order from the pimp."

What Juanita could not anticipate was the reaction to *Smart Aleck* within law enforcement in Dallas. The movie came to the attention of the higher-ups as well as those concerned with vice. They were outraged, not at the men who had made the movie. Instead, they were shocked by this whore, this teenager who willingly participated in so nasty an act. Just as "nice men" didn't use prostitutes, even though they were the primary customers in the city, so decent women never had sex on the screen. The issues of white slavery, of rape, and of abusing a minor were not considered. Juanita was being branded a sinner for what was done to her. It was a situation that would come back to haunt her in the years ahead.

Smart Aleck began making money almost immediately. There was an instant demand to see it. Copies were screened in college fraternity houses and men's smokers. Business leaders and blue-collar workers viewed it. And it excited women as well. It was not unusual to see couples attending the various showings or buying the film when it became available for purchase.

Troy Phillips used the film as a marketing tool for Juanita's services. She was "rented" to gatherings of the wealthy young Dallas business and professional men's associations, as well as to fraternities having a major gathering of members. The base price for her presence was as much as $500. Other fees were charged if any of the men touched her.

Juanita never talked about these events in later life. It was all part of prostitution, all part of the Capture, even if she didn't have to have oral sex or go to bed with the men. They were there to see and touch a body, not a woman, and she felt used and debased.

The film remained a major money earner in the Dallas area until Juanita gained fame as Candy Barr a few years later. Sales easily grossed a million dollars, and historians of the pornographic film industry compare it to the popularity and success that *Deep Throat* would have more than a decade later.

———

"My brother came over and said to me, 'Guess who I saw in a movie?' And I said, 'In a movie? Was it Candy Barr?' And he said, 'Yup.' I said, 'God, I'm glad it wasn't me!'"

—Juanita Phillips, aka Candy Barr

———

Juanita's time as a prostitute was a difficult one for her to remember in detail. Her recollections of events a half-century ago are sometimes slightly contradictory. One example is oral sex, which she mostly indicated was always a taboo for her. She hated the idea, and it was not a sexual act in which her husbands wanted to engage.

When Juanita talked about her months in forced prostitution, however, she talked about having to perform literally every sex act imaginable. She often did not describe them in detail. She did not want to remember such experiences. Yet she made clear that anything one human being can do to another in the name of sex was probably done to her and done many times. The few specifics she chose to share were often hauntingly unpleasant, because the acts were never done for erotic enjoyment. They were meant for dominance and pain against the woman.

Juanita did have experience with oral sex during her time as a prostitute. Yet it was so upsetting for her that she would often remember herself as not having experienced it since childhood, as when talking about the movie *Smart Aleck*. Most likely this memory glitch was another of the "black holes" to which she often referred when she had forced something from her mind because it was too painful to continue enduring.

THIRTEEN

Candy Barr Takes the Stage

Juanita never considered what saved her from being mentally destroyed by the Capture. Perhaps it was the fact that she was a rebel, determined to best those who would hurt her by escaping to a better life, whatever that might mean. Perhaps it was because she refused to let her destiny be narrowed by the four walls of rooms where men were trying to contain her in emotional and at times physical bondage. Whatever drove her to survive, her method of choice was music and dancing.

Forced prostitution was an entertainment medium, a part of an evening's entertainment for men who chose to get liquored up and turned on by a night of drinking and dancing in a less than reputable club. With inhibitions down and libido elevated, they would be approached by a man offering a room, a "willing" woman, and a chance to party privately for a price that, by then, seemed worth paying. This meant that the rooms where Juanita had to work were always a short distance from where the music played. So long as she worked when and where Troy insisted, she could use her down time to dance, a pleasure no man could steal from her.

It was Barney Weinstein who first recognized the potential in Juanita as a legitimate employee of his South Dallas Theater Club. He probably did not know that she was caught up in the Capture. His club catered to businesspeople and tourists, often husbands and wives who might enjoy a little naughtiness but were not there to cause trouble or pick up women. That was why, when Barney and his wife, Mae, saw Juanita's flawless body, her friendly manner when the music was playing, and her jitterbugging in a way that kept the single men lingering—and ordering—just to watch, they knew they wanted to hire her. The club needed a cigarette girl, so Barney asked her age to make certain she was legal, then accepted her lie so she could go to work for him.

Troy was too short-sighted to understand what was taking place with Juanita. She told him of the job offer and he was ecstatic. Barney Weinstein's new cigarette girl would draw more men to his club than ever before, and Troy would be in the area to convince the customers to try his prostitutes. He might not be able to use Juanita to service as many men, but she would do just fine as bait for willing fish.

Cigarette girls were hired for their looks. Their job was to walk around the club, going from table to table with a wooden tray that held various packs of cigarettes. A strap around the cigarette girl's neck supported the tray so that it rested below her breasts, so the customer could see both types of merchandise.

Cigarette girls were not prostitutes or entertainers. They were there to bring visual pleasure and sell a high-profit item to the customers. In more upscale clubs, especially in the East and Midwest, there were also camera girls who walked around with a 4x5 Speed Graphic, the press camera of the 1940s and early 1950s. They took photos of the customers, then went to a back room to process and print them to sell to customers as a souvenir of the evening. Like the cigarette sales, this was a high-profit service, though fewer customers took advantage of the photos. The more expensive the nightclub, the more likely it was that a man might have a different "wife" each time he came for dinner, drinks, dancing, or a floor show. A photo recording his adultery was not something he wished to purchase.

Barney's place was not upscale enough for a camera girl, but Juanita was making more money as a cigarette girl than she had ever seen in a straight job. She made $15 a night, far more than was possible as a waitress in a café. The only part of the job Juanita did not like was acting as a "B-girl" when she wasn't working the floor.

The B-girl was an employee, invariably attractive, who would sit at the bar to talk with the customers and let them buy her expensive drinks. She was not a prostitute, and though some turned tricks on their own time, a B-girl who used the club to arrange for prostitution was usually fired. The club owners made too much money with the innocent flirtations and had too many hassles when the cops and liquor control agents learned they employed a whore. The B-girl was a simple scam, the man paying for the most expensive drinks in the house while the girl got something that matched only in color.

Barney Weinstein's B-girl scam involved Champale, an inexpensive drink that was made to look like champagne. It had the same color. It had the same bubbles. It even had a little alcohol, but it was closer to beer than to champagne, especially in cost to the club owner. The customer ordered the most expensive champagne for two, and the B-girl was served Champale in an identical glass. The girl appeared delighted by the man's largesse, delighted to spend whatever time she could spare from selling cigarettes to enjoy the drinks, and he ran up a bill far greater than he expected.

Many of the cigarette girls accepted the time sitting at the bar as a part of the job they did not mind. Juanita was different. The Champale made her sick, and she had to pretend she enjoyed being pinched and touched by sweaty, foul-breathed men.

According to Juanita, because she "really wasn't hustlin' business" as a B-girl, Barney Weinstein asked her to dance as a stripper. She would not dance full time, nor was she considered a draw by herself. The club had times when amateur strippers could perform. It is unclear if they were paid when they danced, if they simply became a free part of the show on off nights, or if they were gaining experience before moving on to becoming featured performers. Juanita's pay was primarily for working the cigarettes, but she was intrigued with the idea of getting on stage.

"So I asked Troy and he said that would be great. Course in his mind he was still thinkin' in that line of movin' some tricks into that house. High-class tricks he would call them, those hundred dollars a trick guys to the girls, and then do it through me. And if they didn't want the [other] girls, then if they do it through me they're going to want to fuck me, not the girls. I couldn't handle it."

At this time, Juanita was still living at Troy's house. But one night, after picking up a trick to take to Troy's for sex, Juanita recalled, "I had a bad feeling about it. He said he needed to make a phone call [before getting to Troy's], so I stopped at the corner market and I said 'Bye,' and I drove off. . . . That's the last time I had to be concerned with that stuff 'cause I moved out."

Juanita had difficulty putting time sequences into perspective when she began discussing this period more than four decades later. She had been horribly traumatized by everyone from family members to the men she thought were going to help her. Kay Slusher taught her about sex by selling her virginity for a dollar to a man who assumed she was experienced. Troy Phillips taught her the business of sex and the brutality of power when he kidnapped her and had her raped repeatedly while tied naked to the bed whenever she balked. She stayed safe by doing what she was ordered, hating the men, hating South Dallas, and living only to dance. It was better to not think too far ahead. It was better to view "tomorrow" as having no meaning, to just get through today by going along with whatever was requested. She gave up all control to others, except for the dancing.

Troy wanted Juanita to marry him even though she had walked out on him. He seemed to think it was better to make Juanita his wife than to have problems with her as a girlfriend/prostitute for his customers. There were also possible concerns with *Smart Aleck*, since she was a minor when it was filmed. Texas law and attitudes within the courts made wives secondary to the men they married. Troy would have more control over a wife than he would a girlfriend and employee.

"We had our conflicts, so Troy decided he better marry me. So anyway, somewhere along in there we got married. It wasn't a question of choice. He arranged it. He dressed me up in black—a black Tam [O'Shanter] and a little black strapless dress and black ankle straps, and he took me to the J.P. [justice of the peace]. I'll bet I looked like fire." Juanita, originally a brunette, was now a blonde—another of Troy's ideas. "Can you see me with that blonde hair and that strapless black? 'Cause I always picture myself in those black baby dolls. Nobody wore those things except Marilyn Monroe.

"I don't even know when we married. And we moved into the Ambassador in Dallas and I was dancin' at Barney's."

There was the minor problem of whether Juanita was still married to Billy Dabbs in those early days after the ceremony with Troy. He told her not to worry, that he had a smart lawyer handling the proceedings.

The lawyer, who later became a well-known, well-connected criminal defense attorney, first cut off her relationship with Billy. The lawyer made certain there could be no further jail visitations between Billy and Juanita. There was a time when Billy was briefly free from jail, on bail between trials and staying with his parents in Dallas. Juanita managed to go see him, an emotionally difficult time for both. However, he explained to Juanita that what was happening was not her fault. It was an arrangement the lawyer and Troy had worked up that prevented her from seeing Billy.

Billy also never knew that his wife had been forced into the Capture. "He really didn't know until he got out of prison and they told him what they had done. It really upset him, but it was past the point to do anything. It was just one of those things. I was married to Troy."

Juanita's new life was not much better than her old, except the sexual pressures were reduced. Dancing at Barney's club meant little more than taking off her clothes to music without a unique style or a real act. However, she received a $10 per week raise over what she had earned for just hustling cigarettes.

This was the era of burlesque, but the Theater Club was not a burlesque house. There were no comics, no singers, no athletic dancers popular on the vaudeville circuit, and no satirical plays. A girl got on stage, and if she had a great figure, she could turn on the men watching her. If she could parade around without falling as she dropped her clothes, she would be called a dancer.

This was a rather odd hiatus for the teenage Juanita. The opportunity to dance on stage meant little to her as yet. She lived a portion of each day in fear and in danger of being the victim of brutality. The stage was an escape, but it was not yet a world she could fully embrace. Instead, Juanita kept weighing her options.

"I really had a sense of ethics," Juanita said about those years. Money was never the concern. She knew that the most cash she could earn came from selling her body. She had been happier working all night, five days a week, for $22 at the café than she was making almost the same money having five minutes of oral sex with a man. Prostitution "wasn't what I wanted my life to be. I fought it. I still fight it. Here I was at the Theater (as a guest), asked to dance every night. Seemed like a chance of a life-time," to be paid to dance even though the pay for the week would be far less than she received "when I could go with one guy, once a week, one night, and make a hundred." According to Juanita, "The whole rationaliza-tion of it is absurd" if your only concern is making the most money you can in the shortest amount of time.

Perhaps Juanita's career would have begun and ended on Barney Wein-stein's stage had it not been for his brother, Abe, who owned the upscale Colony Club, also in Dallas but catering to the city's elite. The brothers had two different personalities as well as two different clubs. Abe was the natural leader and promoter. Barney was the follower. When Abe decided to open a school for strippers, the brothers asked Barney's wife, Mae Wein-stein, to operate it.

The school for strippers was never meant to be a long-term business. Abe figured they would need one real class, enrolling the broadest range of young women they could find, milking the sessions for all the public-ity they could get, then putting the best of the women to work if they needed jobs.

Abe thought that a kid like Juanita was a natural. She was already working, had danced a little, and had the face and figure that would bring in the men. She was also a contrast to the less well endowed students who had the range of body types and enthusiasm more typically found in a YWCA exercise class. There were secretaries and cleaning women, clerks, women who worked in the media, and a handful of dancers just starting their careers. The classes were genuine, and the women were periodically brought together for publicity photos.

Juanita was the most beautiful woman in the class. She was also the least competent by the standards of the curriculum. Even such basics as the stripper's walk were beyond her abilities to learn. As she later explained, you "just go out there with the rhinestones and lipstick and stuff, and hunch yourself and do that stripper walk. 'Cause being a young person like I was, and with all my attributes that I wasn't aware I had, you get a lot of incorrect information from the older girls 'cause they already know. They're threatened and you think they're helpin' you and all they're doing is hurting you." When she reverted to dancing her own way, "in a period of sixty days I was headline, which made everybody hate me."

Juanita's comments were not brags. There were five girls in the show, with Red Ford as master of ceremonies, and Juanita was different from the start, her only interest being in the dance. Other women collected their paychecks for undressing without regard to their performance, certain that was all the audience cared about and not willing to develop an act. One or two also delighted in sexually taunting the men in the seats, trying to get them aroused in whatever way they could, short of leaving the stage and touching them.

By contrast, Juanita was oblivious to the audience and had no interest in sexually arousing the men watching her. The music made her come alive. The awkwardness that marked her early days of being on the stage ended as she began using the shows as time to teach herself new moves. She focused on the dancing, removing her clothes as the price for mastering her art form. The difference was obvious to the audience, and within two months she was starring at the club.

The Weinstein school lasted longer than the initial publicity because it proved to be both good business and good for business. The Theatre Lounge was a nightclub that also became known as Strip-Tease University. Each new class ran six weeks and was divided into subject areas such as make-up, music, and singing, as well as the all important "undressing with finesse." There was no charge because, after the first class, Barney and Abe Weinstein realized the students could provide new talent in a business that had a shortage of good dancers. The women who graduated were expected to sign with Barney Weinstein as their manager, should they wish to continue as professionals, something not all of them did. He felt that the ones who loved it would have the skills needed to provide him with a steady income from his commissions for booking them.

Weinstein also added a short course lasting three days. It was meant for professional entertainers who needed to add some of the skills of strippers for a part in a show or a movie, or for a stage act they were developing. Among the more famous graduates of the three-day intensive training was Broadway star Carol Channing.

But no matter which course a woman took, graduation involved going on stage with new stripper names in the Theatre Lounge during business hours, demonstrating the skills they had mastered. The several hundred graduates ranged from Candy Barr to Honey Bare and Black Velvet.

It was during this period that Juanita had her name changed for the show, though exactly how that happened is unclear. Many individuals have taken credit for it, including both Weinstein brothers. One version says that she was sitting in a coffee shop, eating a Snickers candy bar, when Barney asked her to dance. Another story has Abe Weinstein doing the naming because she was always eating candy. While some of the girls at the Theatre Lounge apparently called her Candy Barr, it was only one of her names. Another was "the Sugar and Spice Girl." But Juanita thinks the name change did not occur until she left the Theatre for the sophisticated Colony Club.

"All I ever asked for at the Colony, if I came off the stage and *wanted* to sit with someone, was a candy bar. I used to say I liked eating Snickers and Millionaires [candy bars]. It wasn't any big thing, becoming Candy Barr. It just evolved."

The switch to the Colony happened quickly in Juanita's new career, but not before she had problems with the other strippers in Barney's club. She thinks the tension among the strippers came because they felt that Juanita had an appeal to women as well as men. Juanita did not understand what they meant or how they could think that way. "I was very muscular." She was a taut 119 pounds on an approximately five-foot, two-inch body, with breasts that naturally filled a D-cup. "My backbone sunk in half an inch when I was dancin'. The other strippers used to tease me in the dressing room. When I brushed my hair, my muscles would flex, but see, they knew that and I didn't. They knew about lesbians and fuss and stuff because they'd been in the business and they just knew. And I just walked into the world of burlesque, and you know everybody has been always tryin' to get to your body, but you can't believe that women are. Until you realize that they either want you for themselves or to take you home to daddy."

Another possibility is that some of the other girls may have been sexually interested in her and that was the cause of the banter. "I took it just [as] razzin' me because I was new and they didn't like me anyway. I really didn't understand it, but it was because I was voluptuous.

"I didn't care. I didn't want their place in line." The burlesque dancers were paid more money as they became popular. The new girl was the first to dance, the rest waiting backstage in what was called the line, though they actually stayed in what was usually a communal dressing room. The last girl to dance was the star and heavily promoted. Only the most brilliant and popular performers were allowed to jump several places in order to star before they had worked their way to the top.

"I didn't want anything from them. I just wanted a paycheck, have a job. I was that clean in my head about it. I didn't know they fight for stardom, and this place [in the lineup of when they appear on stage] means this, and this place means this.

"They always used to tease me about my muscles, and they'd run their finger down my back. 'God damn, that's a half-inch deep in there, and that's like a young boy's back.'

"So that's how I looked. But I was sinewy, being long waisted and short legged. I looked like a filly tryin' to be broke. That's why Troy said, 'I got me a racehorse.'

"But I turned out to be what is really a disgrace in the world of prostitution. I turned out to be an outlaw. When they tried to buy me, I really got upset. Just like when that girl called me a whore after I knew I didn't have to be one anymore."

The incident to which Juanita was referring occurred when she was working as a dancer at Barney Weinstein's Theatre. She was about to go on stage with another stripper named Tammy Lee. A third performer, Eva Du Broc, went out in front and said to the emcee, "Red Ford, you work with a couple of prostitutes back there, Candy Barr and Tammy Lee."

Stage performers have always had a reputation as being morally suspect. Women traveled unchaperoned from city to city, and in burlesque, they exposed themselves in ways "nice" women did not. The dancers were part of a gypsy-like counterculture, but they were rarely immoral. Many of them married comics and other men in the shows. Despite this, the public often suspected many of the women were prostitutes. One performer calling another a prostitute was the worst insult that could be given. Worse, while Eva was right about Juanita in the past, the prostitution had not been voluntary, and the Candy Barr character she created on the stage would never have her body sold to others.

Outraged, Juanita decided that the best revenge was to not perform. She alerted the trio of musicians she was going to put on the minimum performance as a way of getting back at the verbal abuse. "So I waited my turn and I told this little trio, I said, 'Now you just play what you want to but if you don't just play while I drop my clothes, then you're going to be up here playin', 'cause that's all I'm going to do." It was the only way Candy could think to rebel. The men in the audience were paying to see a show. They wanted the girls they watched to dance enthusiastically as they removed their clothing. Candy Barr refusing to come on stage would not have mattered. Candy Barr coming out, dropping her clothes, and walking off was a shock. Cold indifference to the audience was the height of rebellion, the ultimate shock for the customers and club owner alike.

"I walked out, dropped my clothes, I said goodnight, just put my clothes on, and she [Eva] was bent over talkin' to Mae Weinstein. I turned her around like this and I said 'whap' honey," hitting her.

"This is the truth. She slid across the plate into the pit where the customers were. Troy jumped up and started cussin' me. 'God damn, crazy son of a bitch, all you do is fight,' 'cause that's all I ever did is fight. Anybody, anywhere, anytime they pushed me against the wall.

"She shouldn't have said that. More special, not 'whore.'

"The next night that girl was a mess. I remember her arm was black where I grabbed her. Her face was blue. So Barney gave me to Abe."

The fight had actually not been Juanita's first one. Before Barney promoted her from cigarette girl to stripper Candy Barr, she had become fed up with sitting with the patrons. "I have hit his customers," she admitted. "Now I didn't know drinking Champale, eating potato chips, I was supposed to let people pinch my pussy and pinch my tits. That wasn't part of the job. That to me was prostitution. I should get extra pay. And so I had slapped a few customers and created a scene, but that was it when I whipped Eva in front of a whole group of people, so he gave me away to his brother."

Abe Weinstein understood the potential of Candy Barr when Barney did not. He immediately offered her $85 per night to go to his Colony Club, delighted that Candy Barr "just simply drove everyone crazy, men and women alike. She wasn't lascivious like some of the other strippers," said Abe Weinstein in a 1983 interview with Muriel Davidson. "She was just so happy, so lovely, so beautiful to watch. Hell, I didn't make her a star. She did that all by herself. But I knew how to exploit her talent, and she *was* talented. She really knew how to dance. Not, you know, just taking off her clothes."

Candy later recalled, "People have different impressions of me. I was quite earthy. I had long blonde hair, a peaches-and-cream complexion, big green eyes and dimples. I had a baby face that didn't match my woman's body. My muscles have always reacted to rhythm. People told me I looked like a wild filly up there saying, 'Break me if you can.' Others said I reminded them of a cat. Some of the girls even put me down as a bull dyke. Everybody had a different image of me."

Candy was also able to relax at the Colony. "I loved it at Abe's. I didn't have to sit with the lousy customers anymore while they touched me and hurt me when they pinched too hard. I didn't have to drink any more of that awful Champale while I tried to get guys to buy what they thought was champagne for me."

Corky and Juanita worked together on her dancing every Saturday night. "When I got off at Abe's, everybody knew I'd hit that club. We'd go dancing between shows. That's what I wanted to do. Corky would be there and we'd dance for half an hour, and then I'd get back in time for my show. So we would do dance exhibitions. Above the Comedy Club [which also had stripping] they had a dance studio. I would go up and dance. I learned the mambo, the samba, the rumba. But I would watch the people do this whip, and I would watch and I knew I had to know how to do it before I got out on the floor.

"Corky wore things that looked like zoot suits. You ever see 'em? One time when my daddy was sick, I had Corky come down and we danced for him, 'cause he never saw us work out. We were really good. We were sensational.

"There wasn't any other kind of dance partner but Corky, and anybody that's ever seen Corky and Candy, they remembered it. I get excited about it, 'cause we were sensational, but we didn't even know it. We just knew we could do that dance better than anyone in town, and then the kids from the studio would come up."

Juanita and Corky enjoyed participating in the competitions at the dance studio. They would all compete with the tango and the mambo. "Nobody ever entered the swing. Just Corky and me." And everything

Juanita mastered with Corky, she worked to include in her stage act, never realizing how it would influence her future.

For once, life was going well for Juanita, now that she had become Candy Barr. "I was satisfied with a good job, a good paycheck, a little prop money, not havin' to live with Troy, clothes to wear. . . . It was dancin' and whatever else, but I didn't have to do all this other stuff and be other things. To me, $400 a week, 375, or 350, that was a nice paycheck.

"I didn't know about stardom. I didn't know about entertainment. I just knew that this was a job.

"I didn't know about all these other things. Nobody ever told me. If they had've, they would have lost their cookie. They would have to pay me for what my potential was.

"If you don't know about show business, you don't know about show business. You think stars are in the movies. I mean, it was a shock to me to find out that they had burlesque stars. How gross, really. How gross. Anybody can be a stripper. Yeah, they could. I'm saying anybody could be a stripper if they had an attractive enough body.

"Anybody can take off their clothes. Look at the Go-Go girls. Anybody can do it. It's all classified as stripping. All you have to do is take off your clothes." But that she was becoming such a star, "no, I didn't know. I really didn't know."

There never was a Candy Barr burlesque routine. She never followed the traditional stripper route that the vast majority of the women, including Linda Brooks, would follow throughout their careers. She never desired or needed a gimmick to get attention. And she never tried to be sexual, to turn on the audience. Truth be told, she cared little how the men and women responded to her presence on stage. What mattered was a duet she performed between her body and the music.

"I never thought about it being different," said Juanita. "I was doing just what I knew how to do. The way I liked to do and it made me feel good.

"I had to have a routine 'cause that was one of the rules. I did the routine, and then I did what I wanted to do. I had it worked out with the band that I would work as long as I want to, and then I'd let them know when I was tired."

Candy did not realize that though she was the star, she was still supposed to do the three songs and then get off the stage. The club managers
assumed she understood the routine to follow. She didn't, but she also did
not care. She created a performance that was unique. "That's why I became such a hit. They loved me on stage at the end.

"It's like when I go dancing. I dance four hours solid. When I get
wound up I could dance forty-five minutes sometime and stay out there,
but I knew I had to get off sometime."

Abe Weinstein quickly realized that Candy should dance alone. The
Colony Club would also have a singer and a comedian on the performance bill most nights, but Candy was often the only dancer. Later there
would be other girls, usually acting as a chorus, and eventually she would
star in lavishly staged production numbers. But at first she would be left
alone with what, for the audience, was an erotically charged evening. Ironically, Candy never thought about the impact she was having until many
years after she had stopped dancing.

"I didn't even know they were getting turned on. This is the truth. I
figured they were flirting [with their shouted comments and gestures].
That's what people do in show business," she thought, the audience and
the performers playing off each other. "I watched it a thousand times. But
as far as getting sexually turned on, no, and I'm serious."

Today, as much as fifty years after the time when Juanita was in the Capture, there are old men who reminisce about their encounters with the
teenager who would soon become famous. They did not think of themselves as rapists. Most of the men knew her from stag events that were
perks of their youth and privilege. Some had sex with either Juanita or
with Candy Barr. Others say they did not. Given their positions in the
Dallas business and political world, all asked for anonymity. What they will
admit is that Juanita/Candy was hired for stag parties sponsored by such
organizations as the Junior Chamber of Commerce. The groups rented the
location, then enjoyed a night of dancing and sex. The cost for using
Candy went as high as $500, and it was not unusual for the men to drop
more than a thousand dollars during an evening.

While Juanita and the other girls were considered local hookers or the property of one of the club owners, no one minded their participation in the stag parties. It was only when Candy Barr became famous that they feared she not only knew who they were but also kept a diary of some sort with their names and, perhaps, their sexual preferences. This was a common practice of madams with a high-priced clientele, and it was a practice used by some of the hookers.

Juanita was different. She kept a black book of sorts. The book listed men by first names. It listed their telephone numbers. It had no other details.

The brutality of what amounted to assembly-line prostitution was experienced during a troubled adolescence, a fact that added to the daily roller-coaster of emotions Juanita experienced. The first names and telephone numbers she recorded were of the men who were nice to her, who took the time to talk, to be gentle. These were almost all men she met at stag parties for which Troy supplied the entertainment. The youths present were usually wealthy, educated, and the future leaders in the community. Some had never had sex with a girl who did not charge. Some were as lonely as Juanita. Some liked to fantasize that Juanita was just another date at the party, one who found them fascinating and succumbed to their seductive wiles. It was these youths, in their own way as emotionally lost as Juanita, whom she liked to consider friends.

The youths, when married and moving up in society, thought about Juanita. Some feared that she would come back into their lives to blackmail them. They did not understand that blackmail was something she would never consider. Even if she loathed the men, their sexual preferences, and the way they handled her, she was always aware of their families. They had wives and children who would be even more humiliated by the knowledge of what the men were doing than she was embarrassed by her participation. She had known too much pain herself to ever deliberately inflict such pain on others.

But the fact was that she knew too much. It was one thing for an unknown hooker in Troy Phillips's stable to call you Sam or Fred, Dan or Joe. It would become quite another when the woman achieved fame as Candy Barr and could discuss her personal relationship with your past. Each day she was in the life, each day she was heading toward the time of stardom, Juanita was ensuring she would have to be destroyed.

FOURTEEN

The Lights, the Music,
the Clothes That Came Off

"Juanita Slusher was a prostitute. Juanita Dabbs was a prostitute. Juanita Phillips was a prostitute. All those Juanitas probably turned four thousand tricks a year. But Candy Barr was a dancer, an entertainer, a star. Candy Barr was the very essence of myself."

—Juanita, reminiscing in 1983 on when
she became the dancer Candy Barr

Perhaps it was always about survival. Perhaps it was the enduring faith in God to which Juanita would cling throughout her adult life. Perhaps it was the love of dancing that kept her focused on getting through to another day. Whatever kept Juanita's spirit alive, it did not allow her to consider Candy Barr a prostitute. She considered her life to have been divided into two distinct periods—when she was forced into white slavery through the Capture, through marriage to a violent pimp, through community law enforcement that saw teenage girls as secondary citizens, and when she became the dancer Candy Barr.

Ultimately Juanita saw the Candy Barr persona as a virgin and a feminist. Juanita was a victim, and even when she fought back, she was still overwhelmed and out of control. Sometimes the bondage was physical—ropes, gags, and locked rooms. Sometimes the bondage was psychological. Either restraint was effective.

Candy Barr was a woman in charge of her body, her relationships, and her work. She was a professional dancer, not a whore. She had sex because she wished to do so, not because some man was paying her. Even in the early years of stripping, even when there would be stag parties where the youths thought they were hiring Candy Barr, Juanita knew better. Candy Barr never attended such gatherings. That was Juanita's job, her forte, her tragedy. The fact that the two women were the same did not matter. They had been split to allow for emotional survival.

Juanita was a prostitute. Candy Barr was a dancer whose stage was a part of the world of striptease. Their histories were different in ways she would not know until many years after she became a star.

It was an irony of history that the striptease and the Mafia's desire to take control of the liquor industry occurred in the same year in the same city. It was 1928—seven years before Juanita Slusher's birth and almost thirty years before she became one of the biggest names in the entertainment industry that came about, in part, as a melding of these two concepts.

According to pop culture history, Carrie Finnell, the burlesque queen who is believed to have invented the striptease, arrived in Cleveland, Ohio, early in 1928, although the exact date is unknown. She was booked into the Columbia Theater at East Ninth Street and Prospect Avenue, one of only two burlesque houses in the city. The limited number of such venues—in a few years there would be five on East Ninth Street alone—was due to fashions. Short hemlines were in style. When long dresses came back into style in the 1930s, the number of burlesque houses immediately increased. Or such was the talk of the press in those days. More likely the Great Depression resulted in the closing of many more traditional nightclubs, as the legalization of alcohol caused speakeasies to shutter their doors. The public seemed ready to enjoy stage shows of all types with what little cash they still had, perhaps because of the variety of entertainment which would not be matched in any other form until television developed vaudeville-style programs such as *The Ed Sullivan Show*.

Changing moral standards that evolved with the acceptance of illegal drinking and gambling establishments also may have boosted the interest and attendance in burlesque houses.

The Columbia was successful because it was located a short chauffeur-driven ride from the mansions that remained along the parallel Euclid Avenue stretch once known as Millionaires' Row. The Great Depression did not end wealth in America; it just shifted it into many different hands than in the past. In Cleveland, Euclid Avenue was the main street in a city that had more corporate headquarters than any other metropolitan area outside New York. The avenue also had upscale retailers, high-priced law firms and doctors' offices, accounting businesses, and architects, engineers, and similar professionals. More important for the Columbia, it had a ready audience: randy young men of means, riding the crest of the stock market rise; couples seeking entertainment that would shock their Victorian-era parents; and liberal old men who delighted in bawdy entertainment. They comprised the regular audience of the Columbia, where a new show with new, uh, faces was guaranteed each week. Or such was the case until Carrie Finnell came along.

By the time Candy Barr entered the world of burlesque in 1954, there were two classes of strippers. One group was the circuit dancers, women who would be part of a show that would travel from city to city every two weeks. They would tour by Greyhound and Trailways Bus or drive in their cars. They would be heavily promoted. The female performer with star billing within the group would conduct interviews in newspaper offices and on radio stations. And they would stay in whatever hotels the management arranged for their stopovers.

The other group was the stars, the women whose work stood alone so that their names became familiar even to those who never saw them dance. They toured, but not as part of any single touring company. They would be booked individually and play at the biggest theaters on the circuit as well as clubs that normally did not have such acts. Gypsy Rose Lee was in this category, as were women such as Ann Corio, Lili St. Cyr, and Tempest Storm.

The star may have traveled the circuit at one time, paying her dues, developing her skills, and gaining ever more attention for her work, though not necessarily. Her name alone would draw an audience, and there were clubs around the United States where she would be asked to head a periodically changing revue, performing week after week at the same locale for as long as the audience came to see her. She would be as famous as a film star, and once she made it, she could name her own working terms.

Carrie Finnell, who loved taking off her clothes to music, was a circuit dancer who tired of the gypsy life and realized she would never become a star. Her contracts, like all the other burlesque queens of 1928, ran just one week per theater, a schedule so grueling that they would soon be doubled to cut down on the traveling. At the time, though, she could look forward to living in a different, unfamiliar furnished room for just seven days before heading for the next town and the next boarding house or inexpensive hotel.

Carrie decided to change her act in Cleveland, announcing that her dance would have an extra-added attraction. Instead of stripping to music, she took off just one item of her clothing, promising that there would be more removed the following week. No one had ever taunted the patrons like that. The audience, amazed, demanded that she be held over to satisfy their curiosity.

The timing was right for Carrie's gimmick. Burlesque had long been considered risqué even in its early days when the stars did production numbers such as the Can-Can and had the audacity to reveal their ankles. Burlesque queens always were on the cutting edge of erotic entertainment. Baring ankles were daring in one era. How a woman took off most of her clothing was daring in a different era. The tease was a new element, and repeat trips to the Columbia Theater became a ritual during Carrie's stay.

True to her word, Carrie took off two items of clothing each performance during her second week's run, encouraging the audience to return the third week for an even greater erotic experience. That she only cut a portion of a third garment that third week did not matter. Carrie's teasing of her audience was increasing the take at the box office. By the time Carrie had gone as far as the law would allow, she had spent an entire year in Cleveland, and the striptease was about to become a part of burlesque.

Carrie had other abilities besides a sense of how she could extend her stay in Cleveland. She also was what might be called the Olympic champion of tassel tossers. Using a combination of pectoral muscle control and remarkable skills with her mammary glands, Carrie could spin one or two tassels from her breasts. She could spin them in different directions. She could spin them at different rates of speed. She could even have one pop out of her blouse and rotate like an airplane's propeller while the other remained demurely quiet inside the fabric. However, while Carrie's tease was the forerunner of the business in which Candy would find fame, the tassel tossing was always too crude for a dancer of Candy's skill.

Tassel tossing aside, the history of burlesque has always been far more honorable than the contemporary memory corrupted by crude present-day clubs offering in-your-face tits and ass, table dancing, and private blow jobs. In fact, it was not burlesque that brought staged nudity to the theater. It was the far more respectable revues such as Broadway's Ziegfeld Follies, George White's Scandals, and Earl Carroll's Vanities that delighted in using naked or near naked women to decorate parts of their shows. Burlesque had historically been a serious art with deeper purpose than titillation.

Burlesque actually began as a form of social satire, and burlesque shows often featured plays along with singers, dancers, and comics. Anna Held was probably the first woman to take off her clothing, but only the stagehands might have seen her naked. She was the first wife of prolific Broadway producer Florenz Ziegfeld, and she did her strip number in 1908 while singing "I'd Like to See a Little More of You." Her silhouetted figure was showcased behind a screen on the stage of Los Angeles's Mason Opera House. It is not even certain that she was fully naked. No matter what, the audience experienced eroticism more in their imaginations than with what was actually taking place on stage.

Seven years later, an entertainer called Mlle. De Leon shocked the audience at the Pittsburgh Academy of Music. She was in a show called *The Girl in Blue* during which she came on stage wearing a full-length opera coat and carrying a parasol. She eventually removed the coat revealing that she had on only tights and a leotard.

Today the actions of Mlle. De Leon would be meaningless. However, in 1915, a woman wearing tights was subject to arrest. Back then, even female circus performers who desired the tights to make their acrobatics easier and safer were forced to wear long skirts.

The actress Theda Bara, actually a sweet Jewish girl from Cincinnati named Theodosia Goodman, agreed to a Hollywood makeover and performed the Dance of the Seven Veils in one of her silent feature films in 1916 at the Fox Studio. The sensuous movements by a woman publicists had nicknamed "the Vampire" because she allegedly could suck the soul from any man, at least according to her press releases, was as close to stripping as the censors allowed. But twelve years later, in a Cleveland burlesque house, Carrie Finnell forever changed the entertainment world.

New York racketeer Lucky Luciano probably never saw Carrie Finnell perform when he came to the Statler Hotel on December 5, 1928, even though the hotel was only three blocks away. He was not there for entertainment, and even if he had been, Cleveland's most notorious criminals—the Cleveland Combination, the Mayfield Road Gang, and the like—had no connection with burlesque in those days. They were primarily the eastern European Jews, Greeks, and Italians who ran restaurants and smoke shops that fronted for high-stakes gambling joints or handled racetrack betting, loan sharking, and prostitution. Their involvement with the nightclub entertainment business had yet to occur.

Luciano had no interest in Cleveland's nightlife when he scheduled his meeting. He only wanted to meet with the leaders of organized crime such as Giuseppe "Joe" Profaci, the boss of the Brooklyn Mafia. There were twenty-three men in all, thirteen of them armed, and they might never have been noticed had Luciano been more adept at common sense than he was at skullduggery. In his mind, the group would not be discovered if they met at 4:30 a.m. He reasoned that the hotel would be quiet and almost no one would be moving about. Instead, the sight of men slinking through the halls at that hour was so unusual that it caught the eye of police patrolman Frank Oscowski, who was on duty in the hotel. His curiosity, which would not have been aroused if the men had gotten together at a more normal time, led him to discover that they were meeting to take control of the bootleg liquor trade.

That the two seemingly disparate events—Luciano's meeting and Carrie Finnell's tease—would eventually meld in some way would have seemed impossible to both of them. However, Luciano's plan was to take control of the drivers of bootleg alcohol, since distribution was the key to the success of all other aspects of the illicit business. He was unsuccessful during Prohibition, but he formed alliances with such men as Bill Presser, the first Jewish Teamsters official (of Cleveland Local 51) and the man who broke the Irish control of that union, which led to the election of James Hoffa as the Teamsters Union president. Hoffa was the leader who made the Teamsters the strongest and allegedly most corrupt union in America. He, along with his friend Bill Presser, also helped control the Teamsters' Central, Southeast, and Southwest Areas Pension Fund whose $200 million (in 1950) helped underwrite the construction and operation of Las Vegas casinos where dancers such as Candy Barr, an artistic heir to Carrie Finnell, would be showcased.

FIFTEEN

This Became Burlesque

"I make $500 a week. I own my own house in Gardena, California, and I have a car—all paid for. My parents have a house around the corner from mine. I've got all that and I'm just twenty-one. I think I'm doing all right."

—Crystal Starr, a burlesque dancer in 1955

Juanita, and perhaps the men of Dallas who would soon conspire to destroy her, had no idea that, when she became a dancer in the world of burlesque, she had entered a business with a rich cultural tradition of mocking the social, political, and financial elite. Candy Barr, the dancer, had no interest in making political statements or attacking hypocrisy. She went on stage, bathed in the spotlights, her soul uplifted by the music. Juanita later described her onstage persona by saying, "Candy Barr was a dancer, an entertainer, a star. Candy Barr was the very essence of myself. Dancing in my special way was all I ever really cared about. I was where I wanted to be. I didn't need those bigshots anymore, and I laughed in their faces when they came after me."

Juanita did not realize that her hostility toward the hypocritical members of the business and political establishment was typical of the origins of burlesque. The major difference was that the original burlesque shows deliberately mocked people of power and influence as part of their performances. (The word *burlesque* comes from the Italian *burlare*—"to laugh at or make fun of.")

From the early days of American burlesque well into the 1950s when Juanita began dancing, many burlesque theater performances included satirical plays. These were often quite bawdy, but the men who were in positions of power in the 1920s were no different from the men in power in the last half of the twentieth century. Mistresses and one-night stands were commonplace, and it was in burlesque plays that the audience could experience satire openly mocking what everyone normally only whispered about.

The tradition of dancers in often erotic dress (at least for the day) seems to have come from the British. During the American Civil War, a dancer named Lydia Thompson was electrifying the London stage despite the popular belief that only the Spanish truly could dance with passion. And among the Spanish stars in the 1860s was one Perea Nina, whose footwork was considered the greatest of the day—that is until Lydia Thompson dared to challenge her to a dance-off using the Spanish dances that were Perea Nina's specialty.

The contest should have been a foregone conclusion. Thompson was a little-known dancer, someone whose career on the stage was both recent and going nowhere. Perea Nina commanded top dollar wherever she went. However, when they began dancing, challenging each other to ever greater feats of physical dexterity, the audience was amazed by the results. First Nina would dance, establishing the challenge. Then Thompson would dance, amazing the audience by matching her rival step for step. When Nina danced faster and in more complex patterns, Thompson matched, then topped her, eventually being declared the winner. She was acknowledged to be the greatest dancer in all of London.

Lydia Thompson's husband, Alexander Henderson, felt that such brilliance should be exploited. He arranged for his wife and several other beautiful, highly skilled dancers to form an act that he brought to the United States in 1869. They were known as Lydia Thompson and her British Blondes. Henderson, assisted by American manager Samuel Colville, promoted Thompson with a marketing blitz that included circulating cigarette cards, a gimmick similar to the baseball cards added to packs of chewing gum several decades later. The dancer was shown in various poses and costumes, including tights, a white dress, short pants, a hat, and umbrella. They were all slightly naughty for their day, yet mild enough that a man could bring them home and share them with his spouse.

The cigarette cards dramatically helped the sale of cigarettes, then a new commercial product. Most men smoked pipes or cigars, or they rolled their own smokes. Commercially produced cigarettes were still a relative rarity, and Lydia Thompson's pictures greatly boosted sales. The cards were also hung in bars, the "art" serving as a strong advertising medium.

Thompson's stage routine was typical of the early days of American burlesque. The blonde beauties in her troupe all were quite heavy by today's standards. When Henderson and Colville advertised for talented young women who might want to join the British Blondes tour, the ads stated that the women had to weigh a *minimum* of 150 pounds. Had Candy Barr been trying to enter the profession in those days, her 119 pounds would have disqualified her.

Lydia Thompson and her British Blondes did not just dance. A burlesque show always included a play; in this case, it was the story of Ixion, the ex-king of Thessaly. The play was written by F. C. Burand, and its high point was the chance to show off the girls' bodies. Ixion, a male played by Thompson in the drama, meets French and English sailors, as well as various goddesses, when "he" journeys to Mount Olympus.

Burand's play was confusing to watch. The musical sections included both the dancing of the Can-Can and the singing of a psalm. When the burlesque production opened at the newly renovated Wood's Theater in New York City, the critics panned the show. There was also moral outrage against the offering because women were performing. Lydia Thompson was married, which was a fact in her favor. However, while it was common knowledge that the British Blondes were strictly chaperoned, it was believed that any female on stage was a potential target for sexual exploitation and debauchery. Women were the weaker sex, easily led astray, and no father who had any decency would place his daughter in jeopardy by tolerating her having a theatrical career.

Despite the criticism, the promotion of Lydia Thompson's American tour led to the popularization of burlesque queens. Chewing-tobacco packages had pictures of sensual women performers, all of them dressed.

Some of the poses showed them with bared ankles, the maximum flesh the law allowed and thus quite daring in its day. Years later, male art school graduates who attended live figure study classes in the era laughed about what they found erotic. They explained that the figure model, often nude or draped to show an uncovered breast and thigh, was of no interest to them other than for learning to re-create the line of the human body. However, after class they used to check the hemlines of the more counter-culture among the women who studied with them, to see which ones left a hint of ankle, a sight they considered almost overwhelmingly erotic.

Burlesque in the manner of the shows that would still be popular when Juanita obtained her job at the Colony was invented by Michael Levitt in the late 1800s. He opened with an all-woman minstrel type of performance, followed by vaudeville acts. Finally there was a burlesque farce making fun of whatever seemed appropriate: politics, local issues, sexual relationships, or other concerns.

Burlesque houses always had at least two male comics. One was the obvious comic while the other acted as the straight man, his clothing flawless, his pointed shoes highly polished, his pants perfectly creased. There would be a boutonnière in the lapel buttonhole of his jacket. His hair was slicked back in the style of the day, and any girls on the stage were immediately interested in him.

The straight man was a stereotype, an individual who seemed to have it all. He was obviously successful at work and in romance, and he held the comic in disdain. He made a point of constantly putting down his companion, an individual who represented "Everyman." The vast majority of the audience could see themselves in the comic's position, and the more offensive the straight man became, the more they were rooting for the comic to take his revenge, to give the straight man his comeuppance. Abbott and Costello got their start in burlesque, Bud Abbott being the straight man and Lou Costello the comic.

Depending on the city, the comic and the straight man would do ethnic acts that matched the ethnic make-up and attitudes of the city where they were performing. The men might use accents that were Irish one night, Dutch another, and French a third. It was an opportunity to hone their skills, and with the birth of television, many of them became nationally known for the professionalism they learned on the stage. Typical were men such as W. C. Fields, Buster Keaton, Ed Wynn, Jimmy Durante, and Bert Lahr, all of whom mastered their craft on the Columbia Circuit of Burlesque theaters that Sam Scribner formed in 1900. Comics such as Danny Thomas, best known for television and nightclub work, also got their start in burlesque, albeit a generation later.

W. C. Fields's sense of humor was perfect for burlesque. In one town, he went into the hotel nearest the theater and asked for the bridal suite. The clerk told him he had to have a bride to rent that suite. Fields said, "That's okay. I'll pick one up in town."

Rubber-faced Joe E. Brown began his show business career as an acrobat and athlete turned circus performer. A friend of his, Frank Prevost, thought Brown would be great at visual comedy and convinced him to try an act with Prevost as the straight man. For their efforts they would be paid $60 a week.

In the act, Prevost and Brown came on stage wearing top hat, tails, and gloves. Prevost was the dapper one, fitting his formal wear as though he had been born in it and experienced it like a second skin. Brown was disheveled. The act began with Prevost taking off his gloves and putting them in his pocket. This was followed by Brown taking off his gloves, and taking off his gloves, and taking off his gloves. Brown had paid his landlady to sew several stockings to each glove, so the glove seemed to go on endlessly. The men got their first laugh of the evening.

"They laughed," Brown wrote in his autobiography. "Kept saying that over and over to myself. It was one of the highlights of my life. To hear people laugh, to think that they were laughing at something I did!"

A number of comic routines that could be seen in theaters around the country involved a straight man and one of the chorus girls. Typical were jokes like the following, so commonly used that it has not been possible to determine the originators:

COMIC: Do you believe in the hereafter?

CHORUS GIRL: Yes.

COMIC: Then you know what I'm here after.

In one typical pantomime routine, a chorus girl is with a drunken man. She keeps trying to pick his pocket in order to steal his wallet, though she is constantly foiled. Finally she manages to fool him, obtaining the wallet and proudly holding it up for the audience to see. The drunk realizes what has happened, looks at her, looks at the audience, and shrugs his shoulders in acceptance. Then he signals to the audience to look at what he has managed to steal without the chorus girl catching on. As the audience applauds, he delightedly holds up a pair of what are supposedly her panties.

Both vaudeville and burlesque had a tradition that one's salary was determined by one's placement in the show. When you worked in vaudeville, you were hired at a certain level and were unlikely to move up your billing with the particular circuit. However, if a performer was fired on the road, the nearest entertainer known to the manager would be contacted to act as a replacement at the same level, even if his or her fame to date should not have warranted that. Bob Hope experienced this chance when a brother and sister act near the top of the billing had to be replaced while in Akron, Ohio. Hope, in nearby Cleveland, just thirty miles away, was the only act available. He took their position and went on to develop the skills that led him to the top. But when he was summoned, he was not yet ready for prime time.

Burlesque dancers earned their position with their skills. The last dancer was the most important person in the show, a coveted spot that could bring great wealth. The featured dancer on the one-week (and later two-week) circuit of theaters would often make as much money as a successful corporate executive. It was a life where she could afford furs, jewels, expensive cars, and other luxuries.

Some of the burlesque dancers tried to gain prominence on the circuit by creating a gimmick that would get them noticed by both the public and the men booking for the different circuits. For example, the dancer known as Little Egypt became famous a few years before World War I when Middle Eastern dance was little known in the United States.

Called "belly dancing" by most Americans, traditional Middle Eastern dance involves specific forms of movement. There is the "cifitelli," the slow, sensual movements often seen in early movies where a harem or slave girl dances erotically for some usually evil potentate. The second part of the dance is the "karsilama," the joyous, rapid movement that is the more exciting part of traditional Middle Eastern dancing. A "belly dancer" would begin with the cifitelli. The audience would clap for her, urging her on. But where clapping normally follows the beat, this clapping would lead her. The audience would clap faster and faster, urging the dancer into a blurring series of karsilama movements.

Little Egypt knew none of this. What she understood was that the traditional Mideast dancing costume was the most erotically charged clothing any woman could wear in public. She developed her own dance, using the traditional music, some of the movements, and of course the clothing. She called herself Little Egypt in case anyone missed the point. The high point of her career came when she danced at the 1904 Columbian Exposition. According to the publicity, Little Egypt had managed to flee a harem and was now keeping body and soul together by being paid to dance in a way that revealed the sensual secrets of the sheiks. One unusually smart publicist occasionally paid police to stop traffic near where she danced because her movements were said to be so fast, forceful, and erotic that they could trigger an earthquake. Only when she was finished was it safe to continue traveling near where she performed.

Yvette Dare moved to top billing in the immediate post–World War II years by using the circus concept of the trained animal act. Dare used a trained parrot for her "Dance of the Sacred Parrot." The bird would fly about her, plucking off her clothing one piece at a time. She would dance and the bird would strip her.

Lili St. Cyr, who also was famous in the 1950s, used a chain and lock between her legs. Then she tried a costume that included a pair of six guns worn so that her guns covered the front and back of her G-string. A G-string was a jewel-like ornament strategically hanging between a woman's legs and held in place by a string that went around her waist. Some strippers wore panties or flesh-colored gauze as well as or in place of the G-string. The G-string was a deliberately naughty device, since it would fly up and down during a bump and grind, one of the traditional moves of the burlesque dancers.

Rose La Rose, a demure businesswoman off stage, had an act in the late 1940s and early 1950s in which she would remove her clothing while reciting lyrics about her dates with movie stars. To add to the excitement, her bra and panties were often made from masks.

Rose La Rose created stories about her sex life that may or may not have been true. For example, she explained to the audience that her ex-husband had her strip for him prior to sex. Their foreplay required her to perform for six choruses of whatever music he chose while he played the tune on the harmonica. Her stories made newspaper columns in the towns where she played, and no one ever questioned if they were true. What mattered was that they were good gossip, and gossip sold additional papers.

There were other traditions in burlesque. Tenors were regularly hired to entertain the audience and be involved with various acts. Sometimes the singers were highly skilled. At other times they might best be described as "enthusiastic." A few went on to major careers. Others had their careers solely in burlesque, often doubling as the straight man for the comics and for the girls in chorus numbers where there would be stripping taking place behind the oblivious singer.

Souvenir offerings were also common. Coca-Cola in six-ounce bottles was sold between the acts, along with "provocative pictures from Paris" and pamphlets with risqué stories and a "special page." The pamphlets, called "books" by the men who hawked them, supposedly had a secret that would be revealed when you took it home and put a certain page under water. Those who were foolish enough to buy into the ruse discovered the secret of the page. When you put it under water, it got wet.

SIXTEEN

Abe's Joints, Pappy's Joints, and Other Histories Seldom Told

Candy Barr entered the well-established world of burlesque entertainment with no knowledge of its history nor any sense that she was so revolutionizing the typical dancer's stage performance that she was getting attention well beyond the Dallas city limits. This widespread attention was especially surprising since she did not go on the circuit. Her commitments were for the long term, not the gypsy lifestyle of two weeks in each town.

Most new dancers performed in the various circuit clubs around the country. A circuit club booked talent for two weeks at a time, just long enough to draw the bulk of the patrons who could be counted on to fill the seats. By contrast, an independent nightspot might hire some of the girls who routinely went on the circuit, but usually the talent was hired on a one-on-one basis for so long as the person was a customer draw. The performer might appear for one or two nights, then move on to another booking, or she might headline in the club for several weeks. It all depended on her popularity.

In Dallas, Abe Weinstein's Colony Club was one of the most popular of the independent clubs not connected with the burlesque circuit. And it was Abe who took control of Candy Barr's professional life, recognizing her unique skills and manipulating her career so she gained fame and fortune in just four years.

Abe Weinstein was never a member of organized crime. Neither was Pappy Dolson, the other famous Dallas nightspot owner during the period just before, during, and after World War II. They were entertainment entrepreneurs, and that meant they were an important part of the Dallas experience in which tourists delighted and the locals pretended did not exist. The club owners could make or break a new performer, and had Juanita not been hired by Abe, it is doubtful she would have become known by people outside those who utilized women forced into the Capture.

Abe was always a promoter of entertainment that focused on the availability of women. His first club was the Triangle Club, which was a taxi dance hall. There a man spent ten cents to buy a ticket and then handed the ticket to the female employee of his choice. She would take the ticket, dance with him for one song, and then turn in the ticket for her pay. She split 50–50 with Abe, each taking five cents a dance.

Taxi dance halls were considered immoral in Dallas, especially since the girls could use their contacts with the men to turn tricks on the side. Not that Abe encouraged such things. He never tolerated hustling in his clubs. Some of the women accused him of making inappropriate passes at them, but he did not tolerate the customers harassing or trying to use the girls in any way.

The 25 Club was Abe's next spot. The cover charge was a quarter. The beer was a quarter. Everything he sold was twenty-five cents in the club. In 1940 Abe began Abe & Pappy's in partnership with Pappy Dolson. Seven years later he bought out Dolson and changed the name to the Colony. And always he made girls available for private work, taking the attitude that what the girls did away from the club was their own business.

"Being in the business I was in and being who I was, I never did anything crooked," Abe Weinstein explained. "I never been to jail in my life. I was like Frank Sinatra; I went my way. I was propositioned by everything—Mafia, by the prostitution, by the gambling. No. I treated my business like it was a shoe business. Consequently I made good friends in the district attorney's office, and the sheriff, and the police. They all knew that Abe was okay."

Juanita was fortunate to have gravitated to Dallas at a time when all the major Texas cities were on the move after World War II. Dallas was fighting to get what it considered its share of the growth. Many companies were looking to relocate, but to them the Texas cities were superficially all the same. You could open a business in Houston, Fort Worth, or San Antonio just as readily as in Dallas, and those cities were aggressively marketing themselves. But the Dallas business leaders had a philosophy the others did not, according to Joe Ashmore, a former judge. "You wined them. You dined them. Gave them all the drinks they wanted and let them screw their brains out, so that's why Dallas was selected over anybody else." And Candy Barr was certainly the best looking lure the city had seen in many years.

Not that the corporate executives in decision-making positions would ever admit to being swayed by too much liquor and one or more willing women. They could site statistics about roads being constructed, the quality of the schools, the availability of land and skilled workers, and similar concerns. But there was no question that if you went to Dallas, there was an infrastructure that assured you would not be wanting for companionship during your stay.

The top people in Dallas were the ones who worked together in creating, benefiting from, and using the special district where they tried to keep the clubs. There were officials in the sheriff's office, the police, the courts, and politics, all carefully coordinating what took place. They also protected everyone from the media, for this was an era when scandals could still be covered up. Police conducted their raids away from microphones and photographers' cameras. They would invite the press only when they wanted to make a point, and they would show only what they wanted the people to see. Nothing was left to chance, and if a mistake was made, there was no evidence it ever happened.

The same was true of the intimate affairs of public figures. Adultery was committed on a regular basis. Mistresses shopped the same stores as wives. But no one complained when a relationship ended. No one rushed to the newspaper office to tell about the times they had been kissed. And if someone dared to break the unwritten law, the man's denial was good enough for everyone.

Many Dallas residents remain hostile to anyone revealing the dirty little secrets of the past. (For example, at one point a researcher for the author talked with an employee of the historical society about this period in Dallas's history, asking for whatever information might be in the files. There was none because, she was told, they didn't like to talk about the negative aspects of Dallas history.) Joe Ashmore was one of the few sources present in the era who was forthcoming without a request for anonymity. Ashmore also told of the city his father and uncle had known, the older men having shared their knowledge, enthusiasm, and wisdom with the then youth. It was something he never forgot.

He explained that there was a special district set aside for the clubs no one admitted patronizing. "Everything was all downtown," said Ashmore. "The downtown locations were all controlled by the 'boys.' If you wanted to play, you went down there to play. There was very strict zoning."

When Ashmore said "the boys," he was not speaking solely of organized crime. Not that Dallas was immune from that. The Kefauver Commission found a number of players connected to the mob, most of whom moved on to Las Vegas. Instead, the former judge was referring to a group of politicians, high officials in the police and sheriff's office, businessmen, and the like. They had to approve what was taking place or nothing would happen.

A liquor license would be pulled from or never issued to an uncooperative restaurant or nightclub operator. The top liquor distributor would sadly explain that he was unable to sell your spot any more liquor. If the club had slot machines, as many did despite their being illegal, the owner would find that his club was being raided without warning. And because the newspaper reporters had no idea how the corruption actually worked, they bought into the show of a beefy police officer destroying equipment and supposedly putting the bad guys out of business. They happily photographed the patrons of the uncooperative restaurant or bar when it was raided, never realizing that the people who mattered had already been alerted as to what was going to take place.

Even when matters became unusually brutal, as when a Greek restaurant owner refused to take the vending and slot machines and had his tongue cut out, the press accepted that the person responsible had not been caught. There was no pressure for a crime to be solved. Even when

Benny Binion, a man at the top of the Dallas gambling operations who was ruthless in his handling of others and believed involved in at least one murder, was finally brought to justice, it was justice Dallas style. Binion was forced to leave Dallas, settling in Las Vegas, where he became an entrepreneur, establishing a gambling empire that remains in the family today. The press never questioned why he wasn't arrested and brought to trial. Banishment from Dallas was what the authorities wanted, and that was what they got, the media accepting what anywhere else would have been a clear sign of probable corruption.

The police captains and lieutenants and the sheriff's office hierarchy looked out for prominent people. "If the mayor was in a stag party that was raided, it was not going into the paper," Ashmore said. "Everyone would be hustled off. [Officially] it never happened. Then they might have a bust with people who weren't players just to get them out of the way.

"Back then [the 1950s] the biggest operator of illegal slot machines was the city of Dallas. And they had them placed in restaurants and different places. They had some placed in my uncle's restaurant. They were owned by the city."

The exact ownership was not the city per se but rather the leaders of the city. The police hierarchy would work through a third party in order to keep their distance. Then they would arrange raids to create whatever end they wanted. Sometimes the raiding party was meant to come up empty. At other times, the older businesses would be asked to switch from the regular equipment they maintained to old equipment that still worked but was in storage. "My uncle would get a call and say, 'Get rid of them, there's going to be a raid.' Or 'Don't get rid of them. Put the old machines out.'

"And then you had in the papers the next day where this place got raided and you had some guy with a sledge hammer busting up slot machines. I mean, they were really terrorizing the underworld and putting all these gambling people out of the operation. Well, hell, when I was growing up, it wasn't fifteen minutes later that they were bringing the slot machines in the front door."

An outside third party would handle the slot machine action for those members of law enforcement and the government who were involved. Joe Ashmore, who was working in the Texas Bank while going to Southern

Methodist University (SMU), remembers that his uncle had four slot machines at one time. One day, while Ashmore was in his uncle's restaurant, he saw people he knew from both his work and reports in the newspapers, "people from the city of Dallas," he recalled, who came in with burlap bags, bundled up the slot machines, and took them out the back as a task force came in the front door. "Where are they?" the members of the raiding party asked.

"Don't have any!" Ashmore remembered his uncle telling the raiders.

The officers checked the back of the restaurant on the assumption that the units had been hidden. Not finding anything, they left. "Fifteen minutes later the machines would be back," carried back in those same burlap sacks, recalled Ashmore.

Yet the public perception was that "there was no corruption in the police department, because everyone was well paid. You didn't have a situation where you'd pick up the paper and find out that the police chief was involved in this, that, or the other, because the police chief was one of the players. And the sheriff's department. They were one of the players." Friends did favors for friends. Money might pass hands, of course, but money was not a critical concern. Sometimes the reward was as simple as being allowed to participate in a less-than-reputable activity or enjoy free food, drink, and sexual favors from one of the club owners.

The downtown club district where Abe Weinstein had the Theatre Club was a region with its own rules. It was located near the luxury hotels and ostensibly an attraction for tourists and other visitors. The "good" people of Dallas never went there. Or such was the myth perpetuated by the regulars, the Baptist ministers, and the long-suffering spouses of secret philanderers.

Dallas officially had no gambling of any kind, though the gambling opportunities permeated the city. Unofficially, "You had slot machines and you had these shuffleboard tables, and they [the customers] were betting on that. And the café owners, [keeping everything] under wraps, were paying cash for the rewards." No one complained to any great degree until the first racetrack, Arlington Downs, was opened, operated for a while, then put out of business.

"My uncle would make $200 a week out of his restaurant, and his place stayed packed. He had a good crowd. Beer and stuff like that. No mixed drinks at that time. It was all brown bag. Yet by the same token, he'd make $900 on that goddamn shuffleboard machine."

The shuffleboard machine was like a miniature, self-contained, single-lane bowling alley with small bowling pins at one end. Instead of a ball, you would take a smooth disk and slide it toward the pins, trying to knock them all over. "My uncle made more out of that shuffleboard machine than he made out of his whole goddamn business."

The volume of money each machine generated was enormous. The restaurant and bar owners were allowed to take only a small percentage of the revenue. The rest went through the middleman to whoever in the city was involved. To personally clear $900 a week, as Ashmore's uncle did, meant that huge sums of money were being paid.

"I think at that time it was like twenty-five cents a game, but when four or five guys got together, they were betting with themselves some big money."

There was other gambling as well, because of the popularity of the Southern Methodist University football team and the massive Cotton Bowl stadium that held 80,000 people. The official price for tickets was $3.50 each, though depending on the game, scalpers earned as much as $500, with the Notre Dame–SMU tickets selling for $3,000.

Everything had a price, whether sports, gambling, or women. That was the mood of Dallas when Candy Barr made her way to the Colony Club.

SEVENTEEN

From Burlesque to Stripping, and Candy's Little Book

"Ring-a-ding-ding! Ring-a-ding-ding! Come in and watch girls take off their things."

> —A burlesque barker's chant outside the El Morocco Club
> on Bourbon Street in New Orleans while a
> second man stands by, ringing a bell

Ignoring her uniquely brilliant skills when she first began dancing in 1952, Juanita Phillips cynically came to think that any woman could have become a burlesque stripper. To a degree she was right. Certainly the way in which many of her contemporaries entered the field was as much about a willingness to take off their clothes on stage as it was their ability to move to music. Most worked in the chorus or were among the early acts in the bill, sandwiched between a singer and the comics. They were serious performers, but they were interchangeable, an attitude generally held by everyone from the owners of small clubs using local women to those who ran massive theaters and regularly featured the biggest names in the business.

It would only be years later that burlesque and stripping were corrupted in the public mind so that the women who performed were
presumed to also be sexually available for a price. "Private dances" offered by some contemporary "gentlemen's clubs" seem to imply that the
women were prostitutes and their dance gigs were really for advertising
the merchandise.

That a girl could go from the Capture to the clubs was a seeming
impossibility at the time. Both the victims and the performers might
come from similar backgrounds—small communities where they were
estranged from their families—but the Capture was meant to be an end
in itself. Surviving was hard enough. The idea of a show business career
after being a part of what amounted to assembly-line prostitution was
never contemplated.

Linda Brooks, who played many of the same clubs as Candy Barr, was
more typical of the women who loved burlesque. She was talented enough
to work steadily throughout the year, but she never was a dancer who
would move into the star's position. The high point of her career came
when Gypsy Rose Lee caught her act, tipped her $20 when it was over,
and told Linda that she reminded Gypsy of herself when young. The difference was that Gypsy improved until she starred, while Linda, who at
first danced under the name Honeydew Melon, remained just another
competent professional throughout her career. Her story is thus typical of
the women Juanita encountered and with whom she competed for billing
when she became Candy Barr in 1953.

Like most of the dancers on the circuit, Linda was extremely intelli-
gent. Also like so many others, including Candy, she felt the need to leave
home while still a teenager, thus limiting her formal education. Unlike
Candy, though, she did not experience the sexual abuse or violence from
the assorted men in her life. Her decision to enter burlesque was based on
curiosity, wanderlust, and a love of show business discovered the first time
she was asked to perform.

The job came by chance. Linda and her boyfriend at the time were
walking by the El Morocco Club on Bourbon Street in New Orleans on a
night when there was labor strife. For reasons she never learned, most of
the performers had quit or were on strike. Dancers were desperately

needed, and the attractive Linda was perceived as having the right look for the stage.

"I wore a lot of mascara, the false eyelashes, [and my] foundation was darker than what my normal skin was. I looked normal but the stage look. At that time—I don't think I was a blonde then—I wore [my hair] in what they call the beehive."

The manager, who was standing outside, asked if Linda danced. She said she did, never mentioning that her training was in ballet and tap. She had had the kind of classes many schoolgirls took in the 1950s. They were the equivalent of boys trying Little League baseball in order to learn the basics of the game. She had been an apt pupil, but she had never attempted to perform outside of class recitals as a child.

Before she could think clearly, the manager said that they paid $250 clear, meaning in cash. She would walk home each week with more money than she could have made if she had gone to college, almost five times more than many laborers earned to feed their families.

"So I went into the club and the guy handed me pasties, full bottoms, a net bra, and a little bitty little outfit. It was a skirt and a blouse.

"He told me how to do it. He told me to take the skirt off first, then the blouse. Then I was down to the mesh bra and the pants, and the only thing that came off next was the mesh bra because the pasties were underneath that. And to me, those things didn't make a damn bit of sense because they didn't do anything. These [pasties] were big babies, too. This wasn't anything like the small things they began getting into as time went on. These were big babies!" The pasties had to be glued on with spirit gum, the same adhesive used to attach beards and mustaches to actors' faces.

"I know after the first time when I tried to take them off, it was like good god! It felt like everything was coming off at the same time."

The manager had Linda choose three 45rpm records. In the 1950s, a 45rpm record contained one song on each side, and the time for the song was always approximately two and a half minutes. The songs were written to be played on the radio, and there was a belief among radio programmers that if a song lasted much longer than two minutes and twenty-seven seconds, the average listener who disliked the song would change the station. Shorter than two and a half minutes and the listener would stay tuned for the next song. Thus most popular songs were written to the length the radio stations would air. By using recordings instead of a live band or orchestra, the club assured that all the girls would have almost identical sets of three numbers for stripping. Costs were reduced as well, though this was not a major consideration. Young, non-union local musicians anxious to gain experience were a low cost factor for many clubs.

"I remember putting on this costume," said Linda. "And all of a sudden reality hit me.

"As I was walking up the few flights of stairs to get to that stage, I remember this guy telling me . . . I got nervous . . . and he said, 'Don't worry about it. They'll see you but you won't see them because we have a lot of bright lights.' And I thought, 'What the heck?'

"But as I was walking up the stairs, I started getting like, 'Uh oh, I've got to go to the bathroom.' Nerves set in.

"And all I remember is the sound of that song starting and I went, 'Oh, my god, I'm going to pee right here!' I got through that, though, and I went on stage and all I remember is these bright lights. . . . There were like three spotlights and you really couldn't see the customers. But there really wasn't anything to see because it was just a bar and you had bar stools. But to me, that was a lot of guys.

"I danced, and all of a sudden the applause. Oh, geeze, I ate it up.

"All of a sudden the tap, toe, and ballet came into my mind. The rhythm was always there so I knew how to swivel. And I went and swiveled to the rhythm. Not a big thing. Maybe doing the Hawaiian—putting your arms up.

"The ballet came out in me more so than the tap, toe. I had danced, of course, periodically with other people at parties and such, so I knew how to do that jitterbug and kinda, sorta, stuff like that. And it all came together, and all of a sudden I was doing it. I just went from one type of dance to another while trying to find me in two and a half minutes [of the song].

"I fell in love with it."

The records Linda selected were ones she knew, so she was able to estimate when she was coming to the end of each song. This was important, because the stripping was timed so that whatever was going to be revealed occurred at the end of each song.

"The first record would have been the skirt. The second record was the top, the blouse. The third record was the mesh bra, and that was towards the middle of the record. You waited until you were about three-quarters of the way through before you took off the mesh bra.

"They got a glimpse of you, the record ended, and you were off [the stage]."

Only later did Linda learn that the reason she got hired was because "they didn't have more than maybe one girl left. I talk about timing. I hit it just right!"

Linda developed her act by watching the other strippers as she began getting jobs in different cities. Fortunately she was good enough to get by where she was, and soon Linda and her boyfriend became friends with the master of ceremonies at the New Orleans El Morocco, a comic who performed using the name Johnny Q. Nut. "He was a black guy who was small built," she said. The friendship led to her suddenly learning a harsh lesson about the business. No matter what your position in burlesque, from chorus to star, there were social constrictions that could cause you serious problems. For Linda, who never enjoyed top billing, they were a nuisance. For Candy Barr, the star wherever she appeared, they would be a factor in retaining her freedom.

As Linda and her boyfriend became friendly with the comic, it was natural to socialize. He seemed to be no different than they were, just another struggling entertainer who had been fortunate enough to get a long-term gig that allowed him and his wife to buy a home in the area. He was so soft spoken, so subservient to the customers when he wasn't on stage, that they thought success had eluded him. Instead, when he offered them a ride in his car, they discovered the negative attitude many whites had toward blacks in show business. You could be enormously popular and well paid on stage, but you didn't dare look or act differently from the lowest paid, poorest educated black when you walked about the streets.

"Johnny would put us in the back of his Cadillac. He [said he] always wanted to make us feel good. But whites just did not ride up in the front with black people, so he had to seem to be the chauffeur.

"When we went over there, Johnny Q. Nut hid all his money under the rugs in the house. Under his mattress. He was making good money, well paid, respected. Louis Armstrong was there [in New Orleans]," said

Linda. Johnny was of similar status, though as a comic. And in addition to the white audience, there was a black carriage trade who had the money to regularly take in the various entertainers.

What Linda and her boyfriend did not realize was that hiding the money was not an eccentricity. Banks frequently made clear that the financial business of blacks was not wanted. The only alternative to hiding the money was to be humiliated in bank after bank until some institution agreed to accept what amounted to more money on deposit than they received from most of their white customers. Johnny had learned to live with the irrational racism that made him wealthy for his time on stage and a pariah in other areas of his life. Friends like Linda adapted.

The stars were quite different. Performers such as Sammy Davis Jr. bridled at being treated differently in clubs and on the street. Juanita likewise refused to be a part of the evil based on skin color. She was willing to be seen with Sammy or any other black man in public, walking as a friend, an equal. She saw nothing wrong with taking his old silk shirts and using them for nightclothes when he decided to give them away. She looked below the surface and accepted anyone who did the same for her. But such friendship invariably resulted in gossip-column items and news stories that fueled the disdain already held for a woman who had been a prostitute and participated in stag parties. This was made worse when Juanita, as Candy Barr, became a headliner. Prominent Dallas leaders who had paid to enjoy her when she was a young teenager realized that her sordid past, and their involvement with her, could hurt their reputations.

Juanita understood none of this. She moved from day to day, grabbing at burlesque to take the ride of her life.

From the time she was first forced into the Capture until around 1953, "I was arrested so often for prostitution and vagrancy, I can't remember all the times. I couldn't understand those vagrancy charges. I always thought vagrancy meant you didn't have a job. And here I had a great job, being paid to dance. That's all I ever really loved. Anyway, I'd just go to jail and somebody would put up bail and I'd sign something I never bothered to read, and I'd be out again.

"Oh, I did know that I was being paid particular attention to, more so than anyone I knew stripping or partying, and I began to see a familiar name on those papers I signed. Gannaway, it was. Pat Gannaway. He was captain of the Police Department's Special Service Bureau, and the resident vice squad fanatic. I was told he always was furious because I didn't drink [an issue when she was under age for working in clubs that allowed alcohol] or smoke or use any drugs.

"But I was naïve and innocent. I had no idea that he was acting under orders which came from the very top. Those high society ass-grabbers were getting worried.

"Vagrancy? Bullshit! I was becoming a threat to some very important people who must have thought I would hurt them in some way. Never in my life did I threaten or blackmail anyone. Why would I? I couldn't see anything wrong with prostitution. For me, it had always been that way. But for the city fathers—well, I was a clear and present danger. They couldn't tell the difference between sex as joy and sex as danger."

And Candy had no idea the panic she was causing with her little black book. Joe Ashmore recalled the times: "She had a book because everyone looked for that book. And I can remember some old newspaper stories that would relate to the fact that that book was going to surface or somebody had that book. Candy Barr had no diary but she had an address book of all the who's who because that's the one she'd get calls from. She and our other girls would get a call for a high-priced call girl." It wasn't a record of anything, but it had names in it. People who never used her had nothing to worry about. She couldn't have had their numbers unless they did know her.

"They wanted to get her happy ass out of circulation. They were becoming federal judges and people like that and they couldn't have their name known. Developers, builders, city council members, etc. Candy Barr [was] not putting a bite on them. They were scared." Some believed that girls around her were putting ideas in her head, that she was becoming dangerous. "A minister would be ridden out on a rail if he messed around," Ashmore noted. No one dared get caught in Candy Barr's address book.

What no one realized was that Candy was not being influenced by other dancers. She was not being influenced by a husband or boyfriend. She needed to have names and telephone numbers when arranging her party appearances. She had no intention of blackmailing anyone. She had no interest in compromising anyone. Even if she disliked the customers, the men had families and Candy was sensitive to the ways in which innocent relatives could be hurt by the actions of one guilty party. She had endured enough as a child to not want to cause needless pain to others.

She had sex at stag parties because that's what she had to do to get from day to day financially. All she really wanted to do was what she did so brilliantly. Candy Barr wanted to dance.

EIGHTEEN

Stags and Frat Boys and Cops on the Take

Juanita gained more than a new name and a chance to make more money than she ever thought possible when she went to work for Abe Weinstein. She was also able to divorce Troy Phillips and escape the nightmare world of white slavery. She was at last free, though only while on the stage. She would sign management agreements with the club owner that allowed him to dictate where she performed, when she performed, and how much money would be paid. She went from bondage by rope to bondage by contract, and she found them both almost unbearably constricting.

Abe Weinstein's Colony Club was famous for giving an opportunity to rising singers and comedians, though he would never book an act without first seeing it. That was why he turned down a performer he was told was a comer but whose skills he had not personally seen. That entertainer was the fast-rising singer Johnny Mathis, who would soon become an enduring recording artist.

Abe realized his mistake and agreed to take a chance on another little-known singer, this one with a unique style that was unusually appealing. The contract was for the then astronomical sum of $750 a week, but before the contract could be signed, the singer's first record began climbing the charts so rapidly, his manager wanted ten times the money. As a result, Elvis Presley, fresh from his single hit "Heartbreak Hotel," never sang at the Colony.

The Colony Club, like many of the South Dallas area nightspots, had a secondary business involving sharing the female talent with eager young men about town. Joe Ashmore recalled that enclosed party areas were available in locations such as White Rock Lake and Bachman Lake. "They had little rental places that the city owned. We used to rent the one out at Bachman for our fraternity stag parties. And I'd call Pappy Dolson or Abe Weinstein and get the girls. And so, you know, sitting on the front row of the stag party so we wouldn't worry about getting raided was the president and the registrar of Southern Methodist University. I mean, that's the way things were done.

"And if you struck the right nerves, and you knew these people and they liked you, they'd do anything in the world for you."

Working for Abe Weinstein meant that Juanita had the potential to earn more money than she had ever imagined, to dance, and to experience the stag parties. After what she had endured in the Capture, nothing she was asked to do seemed out of line. It was all more of the same.

The police were regularly hassling Juanita when she first went to work for Abe. The police did not respect pimps, but they were not hassled. The pimps weren't turning the tricks and thus the pimps weren't committing crimes under the vagrancy laws. The majority of the officers also had no interest in the underlying causes of the problems, including the Capture. They would prosecute for kidnapping, but only if it was a one-time act clearly about ransom or rape. They did not care about the psychological and physical damage that led a girl into the type of prostitution Juanita endured. The fact that the girl was alone on the street was enough in their eyes to make her a willing participant. This meant they would arrest her. This also meant that they could fantasize she was a willing participant when they "invited" her to their own stag parties.

As Joe Ashmore explained, "She got picked up. She got arrested for this minor stuff. So what she did as a favor for the police and the sheriff, she would do stag parties for those guys—the chief of police group. And they would invite their friends. They'd invite this person and that person from the city council to come to the stag parties. And they'd all drink and have a good time, smoke cigars, and then, if there were some favors—'Hey, I'd sure like to go to bed with that.' They'd arrange it, and they'd do it in such a way that she was given a deal she couldn't refuse."

Juanita wouldn't get paid, but she wouldn't do time, and she'd walk away after one night. She turned tricks to stay out of jail, though it was just chance when they picked her up and requested such an arrangement.

There were also times when someone connected with the police, mayor's office, or some other government agency would be designated to put together a party. "He'd call her and say, 'I'm going to need a dancer.' Then he'd call the club owner where she was working and tell him that he was going to need her for Saturday night," said Ashmore.

The club owners worked together to provide any of the popular girls they knew, regardless of whether they worked for the owners. Typical was Jack Ruby. Juanita never worked in a Ruby-owned club, neither under her own name nor as the dancer Candy Barr. And the friendship the two developed when she was still a young teenager out for a night on the town did not change the fact that she was a good looking "piece of ass" and he was part of the meat market.

Years later, when President John F. Kennedy was assassinated in 1963 in Dallas and Jack Ruby thereafter shot Lee Harvey Oswald, the prime suspect in the murder, there would be talk of close friendship between Juanita and Ruby. There would be talk that she worked for Ruby in some capacity even though there was no record of her employment in his clubs. The confusion came because, always eager to help the local power figures, he had provided her services for some of the stag parties. Anyone who knew he was familiar with Juanita would ask him to get her for a stag. He would then call the people for whom she did work, helping make the arrangements without Juanita's knowledge or approval.

"Ruby would arrange it even though she didn't know it. Ruby, Dolson, Weinstein . . . they handled the supply. [They] charged $200 for a night [for a girl] to perform. No tips," said Joe Ashmore. Usually the group would rent the Bachman facility from the city for $20. Then the windows would be covered with sheets so no one could see in from the outside. Anywhere from sixty to eighty men would attend, often with just one girl for partying. This meant that dancing and stripping were the primary entertainment. If the girls were expected to have sex, and many of them did, that was a separate arrangement Abe and Pappy knew nothing about. The people who hired the girls paid only a flat fee. "Any problems, the girl was

149

blacklisted," explained Ashmore. "The girls got nothing other than what Abe or Pappy were paying."

Juanita remembered those days of subtle prostitution and how she felt. "In my young days I didn't give by choice so the penetration and the ejaculation was the two most exciting things of sex to me. I can't take these long-distance runners. I mean don't try and impress me with how long you can stay on, Baby. See, I was never trained for longevity. I was trained, in all sexual experiences, it's a hit and run situation. So you get your excitement from the penetration and the ejaculation because the sooner they can penetrate and ejaculate, they're through and they're gone. And I don't care what anybody says, when a dick goes into a pussy, it feels good. I don't care what anybody says."

The people who ran the stag parties had their pick of the dancers who were brought into the clubs from out of town. No matter how famous the stripper might be, she would likely be asked to participate in the stag parties. There is no way to check out who said no and was allowed to return. However, it seems likely that burlesque stars who refused to participate in stags were not booked in the city after their two-week run, no matter how big a crowd they drew.

Candy was confused by the world she unknowingly was beginning to dominate. She had no sense of the history of burlesque. It would be several years before she traveled to New York City to dance in a theater on the circuit where she could view the traditional show. But what she did see in Dallas confused her.

"It puzzled me a lot why there were stars in that field. People who became stars," she said. "I could never understand why people would come and see it, and get excited. I'm telling you the truth. All the time I was in it I could never understand it. Why those places would fill up, and people would scream and holler because those girls didn't do anything.

"Me, I was hired to dance. That was a big difference. I couldn't understand why they would come and see me. I wasn't giving them that much. That's the truth.

"I was always puzzled when there were so many people out there. I figured they may come to hear the singer, but they always [shouted] 'Yes, Candy!' So I would go out there and dance my heart out for them. But I never understood.

"I wouldn't pay to see burlesque. I could care less [about] seeing girls strip, or men strip. So I probably will go all my life not understanding it."

Candy Barr had rules that were never to be broken when she danced. One of them was that no one was to touch her. "She'd pop them," Abe Weinstein recalled. "Many times. Nobody could bring charges on that."

As Abe commented in a 1983 interview, her popularity transcended gender roles, and this seemed to encourage the physical reaction to Candy Barr. "If you saw her, if you sat in the audience and watched her perform as a man, you would immediately say, 'Oh, I'd like to lay her.'

"She had a baby face. . . . How can you pass it up? And that's actually the way she looked. And I named her Sugar and Spice Girl. At first she was introduced as the Sugar and Spice Girl, but the name Candy Barr soon dominated on stage and off."

Burlesque dancing, even in the less reputable clubs, was not the interactive entertainment of a contemporary strip joint. The least talented among the women were still trying to be show girls, entertainers, women who had achieved a measure of success in show business in the nearest big city to where they were raised. Even those who turned tricks on the side would have been insulted and hurt if men stuffed money in their G-strings, as is encouraged in contemporary strip clubs. This was especially true for stags, the reason Juanita sharply delineated her life as Candy Barr, the virgin dancer, and Juanita Phillips, a woman involved in prostitution.

"I was dancing, and this man was sitting ringside, and at that time the floor was even with the tables—not like it is now," Juanita said about a time when a man in the audience misunderstood what the show was all about. "And you dance around, and I knew he was drunk, and he kept reaching for me and I said, 'Please don't touch me.'

"I had to work the area around the door, and it's where you go off and come on, and no one was being bounced.

"They [the bouncers] saw it, and he knows that we can go to jail for the very thing. And the man kept making an effort, and I just kept dancing.

"And I told him if he touched me I would slap him. I told him not to touch me or I would slap him out of that chair.

"Well, that's all I had to say. . . . I came around and went 'whop,' and he sailed out onto the floor and I just finished my dance.

"They took him out cussing, and they thought I was looney tunes. I had asked him nicely not to touch me. They really thought I was a violent person."

Candy did not realize how critical it was to maintain the edge over her customers. Her image, as a tough, hard bitch who would take on anyone who hassled her, helped keep her safe from an extremely rough crowd who filled the Colony every Sunday. Dallas had laws that covered every aspect of vice. Technically prostitution was not legal in Dallas. Practically, the only serious crackdown came on Sunday. Professional sex was forbidden on the Christian Sabbath. As a result, the Sunday audience of the Colony Club and other nightspots was filled with prostitutes and pimps enjoying their day off. Eventually Abe Weinstein found he had to remove several of the pimps who looked as disreputable as their profession. But they filled the seats on the one day that families tended to stay home.

Candy could not dance closer than three feet from a customer. The trouble was that if the man crossed the boundary and the bouncer did not stop him, it was the dancer who would go to jail. Candy's aggressiveness was her best defense if she was ever arrested for being touched. Even sitting with a guest "was against my rules," said Abe. "That's why I stayed in business for forty-four years. It wasn't a hip joint or a hustling joint or anything else."

"I did a lot of stags," Candy said. "In between shows I was out making me two or three hundred dollars. They were paying like crazy for me. I worked all the time." Candy was also being watched by the police.

She recalled one performance at a VFW stag. "We were out there working on the big stage, and I always have to be last. And by the time I get out there, everyone is moist crotches and slobbery lips.

"I come out after all the girls finish, and this guy is sitting where he is not supposed to be at all. And I know the house is full of lawmen just waiting for someone to touch us. . . . They were on me then. . . . I knew it, but I can't be responsible for what the other girls do.

Photo taken about the time Juanita became Candy, in her late teens. Courtesy of Mardi Rustam.

Juanita Dale Slusher post makeover;
Candy Barr in costume

Black Book .151

Candy Barr at the height of her career in the 1950s. Courtesy of Mardi Rustam.

Candy striking an angelic pose. Courtesy of Mardi Rustam.

Candy poses with roses. Courtesy of Mardi Rustam.

On trial for marijuana possession, February 2,
1958. Tom Dillard, *Dallas Morning News.*

Being escorted to jail. Courtesy of Mardi Rustam.

Barr behind bars, 1958. Courtesy
of Mardi Rustam.

Jack Ruby (lower right) a split second before he shot Lee Harvey Oswald on November 24,
1963. Candy Barr was one of the first people authorities sought following Ruby's arrest. Jack
Beers, *Dallas Morning News.*

Back to being Juanita, in a
photo taken in 1970.
Dallas Morning News.

Juanita relaxing at her home in Brownwood, Texas,
January 11, 1972. *Dallas Morning News.*

Juanita and producer Mardi Rustam, who at one time proposed doing a film on Juanita/Candy starring Farrah Fawcett. Courtesy of Mardi Rustam.

Juanita found comfort late in life through poetry and religious faith. Years of smoking and poor eating habits eventually caught up with her and she died of pneumonia on December 30, 2005, at the age of seventy. *Dallas Morning News.*

"He's sitting there on the side and he tried to grab my panel once, and I said, 'Don't you do that.' So, I mean, there was nowhere I couldn't go and he was there.

"He reached up and grabbed my panel with force. And don't ask me how I see things, but I had seen the beer bottle beside him. I came around and picked up his beer bottle and crushed his skull. He was in the hospital for three days.

"I cut my fingers. I wrapped a handkerchief around my bleeding fingers, and when I finished my dance, I ran out of there because I knew those men would be out there waiting for me because I hurt that man.

"They couldn't do anything about it. The law was just waiting for someone to touch me, and one did, and I cracked his skull. But I knew the guys from his group were going to be out there for me.

"I grabbed my valise and my clothes and lit out. But I finished my dance [first], knowing that they would think I would go backstage and change."

Juanita's troubles with the law carried over into the world of Candy Barr. One of the men on the police force, Captain Pat Gannaway, truly was hostile to vice. He hated prostitution. He hated the image of women taking off their clothes to entertain an audience. He was a man who lived in a black/white world, looking only at the person who seemed to be the primary criminal, never caring about the pressures that led that person to whatever actions broke the law.

Gannaway was an expert wiretapper who had served in army intelligence. From 1956 through 1968 he ran the Special Services Bureau of the Dallas Police Department and focused on narcotics and aspects of vice such as prostitution. After his retirement, he would be quoted in the magazine *Texas Monthly* as saying, "It was always a good feeling to see someone on those juries you recalled being at one of those talks. We always told our audiences if you got rid of an addict or pusher, you were also getting rid of a burglar, a thief, or a robber." Over time, Candy Barr became what seemed to be an obsession, the embodiment of all that was evil in the entertainment district of Dallas.

The captain did not realize he might be used one day. He did not know that his actions were ones that would help the corrupt officials find a way to silence a growing potential problem for the higher ups who had once had sex with an underage victim of white slavery. If the captain could legitimately put Candy Barr in jail, they would not have to worry about facing the penalties for their own actions. Their families would never know about their adultery and, in some instances, sexual deviance.

At the same time that there was an effort to catch Candy Barr acting illegally, she was desperately trying to figure out how to get rid of the people who had been hurting her. Just as she had once considered adding cyanide to Shorty's chocolate-covered cherries, so she thought about other forms of violence.

"I used to lay down at night and ponder how could I remove these people. They weren't dreams. They were just thoughts and questions within myself. And I thought about black widow spiders 'cause I heard they would kill people, and I thought gasoline because I heard about people burning people up in beds. Other than that I never thought about shooting or cutting or poison. I thought about that very conscious.

"But while I was having the feelings, I'd be laying on my back in the bed. Christ on the cross would come plummeting out of the air, and it would be so real I would catch myself covering my face like it was going to plummet me to death. So that kept me in a balance, because without knowing what I was realizing, I was realizing that was not right. I really didn't know what to do.

"My subconscious was driving me. The devil was driving me. If it hadn't been the devil, Jesus wouldn't have been falling from the sky on that cross to smash me or to smash the evil that was trying to take me. That's how I look at it, 'cause it was evil trying to get me.

"Devil's been trying to get me all my life. And boy, he hits me at my weakest point and he's hard to fight off. Anybody can call it whatever they want to. It's the devil. It's the eleison [mercy, from kyrie eleison—Lord have mercy] and the amen. It's in the voice. It's the point of hostility. It takes off the energy."

Candy may have been pugnacious when riled, but she never expected to have to use deadly force on anyone. That was why she was unsettled when her ex-husband, Troy, came to hurt her, making it necessary for her to defend herself in a way that could have cost him his life.

The divorce from Troy was supposed to end their relationship. She took her own apartment. She lived on the money she earned as a dancer. She stopped being part of his prostitution ring. She had won her freedom from white slavery. Yet he did not have the sense to leave her alone. He followed her from time to time. He harassed her at work and at home. There were times he would come up to her and strike her, a reminder of who was the more powerful of the two of them. Worse, the situation continued after he married someone else.

One night in 1955, Candy was alone in her apartment when she spotted Troy hanging around outside her building. She suspected Troy had been drinking. She knew he was going to cause trouble.

Candy had few weapons at hand. She had long ago learned what street fighters know, to turn anything at hand—a knife, a kitchen pot, even a shoe—into a weapon. But Troy was also a street fighter, and he was bigger and meaner than she could handle if he lost control. She needed a better weapon, and she knew a student at SMU who had a rifle. She called him and asked him to come over immediately.

The youth grabbed his .22-caliber rifle, made certain it was loaded, and rushed to the apartment. He passed Troy, who apparently ignored the weapon, livid that his ex-wife was apparently seeing this youth. He was certain the boy was having sex with Juanita. He was mad. He was jealous. He was going to come inside even if he had to batter down the door, something he started to do after she had locked the door and instructed the student to hide.

The fight was between Juanita and Troy and did not involve anyone else. The kid was nice, bright, someone not raised on the streets. He did not need to be in the midst of whatever was going to happen. She needed him for his gun, not his muscle. She ordered him to hide in the closet with the rifle until whatever was going to happen took place.

"All I was wearing was one of Sammy Davis Jr.'s white silk shirts he had given to me," she said. Davis, the young black performer who was doing a solo act after growing up on the vaudeville circuit as part of the Will Mastin Trio, liked Candy Barr, the dancer from the hardscrabble background. Neither had enjoyed a stable childhood, Davis living on the road as far back as he could remember. They became friends, seeing each other periodically, exchanging small gifts, but never becoming romantically involved. However, even though he was yet to gain the fame that would come with Broadway, movies, Las Vegas, and the "Rat Pack," he was still noticed in areas where a black man and a white woman were not considered appropriate companions. The innocent wearing of one of the shirts was a potential for trouble with Troy beyond everything else Candy had already endured.

"I went then and opened the closet where the poor kid was quaking from all the commotion, grabbed the rifle from him, and flew to the doorway. There I was, standing at the top of the stairs like Annie Oakley, with the rifle resting on my hip. Troy began moving up those stairs again. I said, 'You come past that third step and I'm gonna shoot you.' "

He did, and she fired.

Troy was not badly hurt. The bullet missed all vital areas, though it took the fight out of him.

The police arrested Candy, for once because they had to do so, not because they wanted to harass her or enjoy her favors in the back seat of a patrol car. There was no question that the issue was one of self-defense. That was why bail was set at $5,000, a readily affordable amount relative to the normally higher fee for a crime of violence.

Candy's attorney was Oscar Mauzy, who went on to become a Texas state senator. He knew that the grand jury would not indict his client. The facts were clearly on her side. Troy had a history of violence against both men and women. He was drunk. There was at least one witness. And Candy had done the minimum needed to avoid being hurt.

Abe Weinstein saw matters slightly differently. He wanted to boost his audience by milking the shooting for all it was worth. Candy the martyr would generate press, and press would bring people to his club. It did not matter if Candy suffered. She'd be fine in the long run. For the moment, publicity was critical in Abe's mind.

First, Weinstein telephoned Sheriff Bill Decker. He had long done the sheriff's department favors, and now it was time for law enforcement to return the kindness. He asked to arrange for Candy's bail to be raised to $100,000, an amount guaranteed to gain headlines in the press. He assured the sheriff that he would pay the money immediately, which he did. He didn't want Candy languishing in jail. He wanted to make a major publicity event out of a relatively minor domestic problem.

Abe picked up Candy and had her dress in a cowgirl outfit, complete with cowboy hat and two toy revolvers. Then he took her to a press conference he had called to protest the "outrageous" $100,000 bond. It was inexcusable. There was no crime. Candy had acted in self-defense as everyone was aware.

Juanita never understood the double standard of Texas justice that required a declaration of moral outrage combined with little or no punishment, because murder was just the Texas way. Houston had more murders per capita than any other large city in the nation. In addition, any Texas husband could legally shoot another man if "he has reason to believe the man is committing adultery, has just committed adultery, or is about to commit adultery on his wife."

Women were treated more harshly by legal statute, but juries did not like to convict them. The best-known criminal defense attorney, Percy Foreman of Houston, had a particularly busy year when he defended thirteen different women who killed their husbands. Twelve were found innocent, though they did kill the men, and the thirteenth received what was usually the harshest sentence given by a jury which also decided the fate of the person convicted. The woman was given five years in jail—suspended.

Candy had little risk of jail time even if she had carefully plotted her ex-husband's murder. Shooting him in self-defense and using a single round of ammunition so it was obvious death was not her intent meant that she was under no risk at all. She was arrested. Bond was set. But Candy was never indicted and never would have faced a trial.

Reporters drooled over the "cowgirl" with the shapely legs, the small waist, and the big breasts. They delighted in the image of her fighting off Troy. And they gave the story extensive coverage normally not warranted for a domestic shooting, especially one where the victim admits his guilt and refuses to press charges, as Troy did. He knew that he was the aggressor and that pursuing Candy might lead to his being criminally charged.

Candy was horrified by the aftermath of the violence. The shooting itself had been necessary. Even Troy admitted that. He would have hurt or killed his ex-wife had he reached her in the rage he had been in.

Abe Weinstein's getting the bail raised to increase headlines, well, that was business. He was a promoter and she was his star attraction. Not that she understood the headlining as yet, but she did know that her pay had been increased as the crowds kept coming. She was earning close to $1,000 a week, and her pay was a small fraction of what Abe was taking in. Of course he would do anything necessary to keep the people wanting to spend their time in the Colony.

What troubled Candy was the way she became a folk hero for the shooting. "What sickened me and still does is that I was defending my very life. Troy would have killed me that time for sure. And yet, men, women, and even kids stood outside my door waiting for my autograph. They all criticized my way of life, and then they wanted my autograph for defending my right to live it."

The Weinstein brothers were delighted by what had taken place. They worked to get her jobs that would keep her—and their clubs—in the public eye. She acted in a Little Theater production of *Will Success Spoil Rock Hunter?* They arranged for her to model lingerie, and they had her pose for artists and photographers producing calendars.

The lingerie modeling did not help Candy Barr's image. This was a time when clothing models had a hierarchy of jobs. At the top were those who modeled for designers at various shows, and not far behind were women who modeled for department store shows. Sometimes the models worked a runway or stage in a section of an upscale department store. Sometimes they moved among tables in a restaurant located within the department store so the women at lunch could see what they liked, then go to that department to buy it.

The least respected models wore bras and other undergarments, usually *over* their clothing. Somewhat more respected, but still considered the low end of fashion modeling, were those who modeled lingerie. There was extra pay for the women, but such modeling was considered a sure way to not be given better assignments.

The Weinsteins did not care, though. They wanted Candy Barr to be famous, not only to attract men to their clubs but also to enable them to get top dollar for her services when they sent her to work for other clubs around the country.

Candy did what she was asked, but the public reaction bothered her. She did not question the more sinister reality of Dallas, the one that caused her bail to be raised and allowed the media circus to take place. Yet it was a revelation of a darker side of Dallas than even she knew, one that would soon have more serious repercussions.

NINETEEN

Three Joints Could Get You Life

"I said, 'This is the marijuana that Virginia gave me. Would you please keep it until I can go home and then come back?' And she told me that I should get rid of it, but that she would keep it until I could get back from changing clothes. I had to go to work."

—Helen Smith, testifying as to how Candy Barr came to have marijuana in her apartment

There are few people in Dallas, Texas, today who remember Jack Newton. He was a man of little importance to the city's political, social, and financial elite. Even the cops who arrested him around 1955 probably would have forgotten his name had he been convicted. The trouble was that he was an innocent man, and arresting an innocent man was always an embarrassment.

It was bad enough for the innocent party and his family. It was worse for the police, because this was a time when an intense public relations campaign by FBI Director J. Edgar Hoover and a number of large city police departments were working in conjunction with television and radio producers to create programs such as *Dragnet*. In the *Dragnet* series, first on radio and then on television, Jack Webb narrated what seemed like a documentary-style program in which the crime was committed and the bad guy was sought, identified, captured, and sentenced (along with commercials) all in thirty minutes. Police were heroes, not humans, and when a large city police department did not measure up to the fantasy image being broadcast, the men in uniform were severely criticized.

Some of the Dallas police higher-ups would have preferred sending an innocent "nobody" to jail, hoping he had previously been guilty of something, rather than publicly admit that the initial arrest had been a mistake. Such was the case with Newton, and rather than accepting responsibility for what took place, the police chose to damn the messenger, the person who helped prove his innocence. The individual, a woman of great integrity who nevertheless had a history of immoral behavior and was a witness to the hypocrisy of some of the most powerful individuals in the city, was Candy Barr.

In a 1983 interview with Muriel Davidson, attorney Charles Tassmer related the events that brought together all those individuals in Dallas who wanted to permanently remove Candy Barr from the streets of Dallas. "A long time ago I defended a man named Jack Newton who was charged with murder," Tassmer explained. "He was not guilty of the murder. The reason he was suspected was [that] the man who was killed was a strong-arm muscle man for another gambler who Newton had beaten that day out of a lot of money in a card game." The gambler and the strong-arm man "grabbed Newton, and they robbed him. And this associate [the strong-arm man] was staying at the Blue Top Inn out here on Davis Avenue. It was then a nice place."

According to Tassmer it was late, about 10:00 or 10:30 at night, when the man who had robbed Newton heard a knock on his door and had his head blown off. "So naturally Mr. Newton was a logical suspect," Tassmer said.

Newton was picked up by the police but had an alibi. "Well, it turned out that he had spent the evening barhopping with Candy Barr, and she came forward and helped us and they did not indict him. It was also against her interest to do this because, at that time, she was seeing George Owens socially. (Owens was then married to Maureen Owens, later the wife of John Dean, who was on President Richard Nixon's staff in the late 1960s and early 1970s.)

"It was against her [Candy's] interest to help us, but she did. At that time I warned her that the police were very much interested in her and was taking a long look at her constantly. She was then in her heyday at her dancing at the Colony." But Candy stayed with the truth as she knew it. "She'd been with him all week. He could not have committed the murder. Somebody else had to do it.

"People in that business losing, then having a muscle man take your money back for you, have many enemies. It could have been anyone.

"That case never reached trial, just a preliminary charge for which I had to get him out on bail. He was 'no bill'—that means exonerated by the grand jury primarily on her testimony."

In the culture of the times, a "nobody" had walked because a young woman of ill repute had stood up for what she knew to be the truth. Prominent people were embarrassed that the case was not quickly solved. Some were more concerned with the bad publicity from the inappropriate attempt at prosecution than they were with the innocence or guilt of the accused. For them, it was easier to hate Juanita, seeking to take her off the streets, than it was to look in the mirror and admit they had erred over Newton.

Dallas, Texas, had gone from being little more than a cow town to a cosmopolitan city whose residents found social status in their work with their churches, the charities they supported, and the money they spent on luxury items. Some wealthy residents traveled the world. Others felt it was easier to simply buy the city of their dreams, as though shopping in boutiques that offered extraordinarily luxurious clothing, jewels, and other items was the same as being a sophisticate. Civic leaders had spotless reputations even if they had to create them using White Out, bribes, and friends who would lie for them.

The men who had enjoyed young women in one of the whorehouses or through an outcall from one of the upscale hotels never thought such experiences could come back to haunt them. Prostitutes were old before their time, often addicts, and often dying young.

Juanita was different. She had been beaten. She had been raped. She had been restrained for sexual violence. Yet instead of becoming emaciated and disappearing from the streets, she had become an entertainer who was bringing record crowds to area clubs. She was giving interviews to the press. She was becoming "somebody," and if she ever told what she knew, the façade of the Dallas elite would be torn away. Women would have to leave their lovers to stand by their husbands. Men would have to abandon their mistresses and spend time with their wives. Church leaders would be exposed as hypocrites. Judges would be seen as engaging in criminal acts, and all of this was because the unnatural blonde with the big tits and tiny waist was too feisty, too determined to live, to fade from view. They wanted her dead or locked away. They didn't understand she just wanted to dance.

It is impossible to say that there was a conspiracy to get rid of Candy Barr. Not then. Not in a climate where there was no gray area for Dallas residents. The police, the prosecutors, and the good, upright, uptight, wealthy white citizenry knew the difference between right and wrong. They determined who was guilty of a crime and, for that matter, exactly how to define a crime. This was the power of the How Dare You squad, the men using their perceptions of intent to determine guilt, then forcing a conviction without regard to the facts.

No large city today has the kind of morals-keeping that the people of Dallas used against those they felt were inferior. A "good" man, married, a father, respected in business, a churchgoer might get sexually aroused looking at a demurely dressed Juanita Phillips walking down the street. His interest could not have come from within the purity of his soul. He had to be the victim of a seductress, a whore, a woman of no good intentions. Juanita had to be arrested for the actions taking place solely in the mind of the accuser. That was the reality of the How Dare You squad, and their moral avenger, if there could be said to be one, was Police Captain Pat Gannaway, a by-the-book cop if you didn't mind that he was writing the book as he discovered a previously unlisted "crime."

John Bainbridge, in his book *The Super-Americans*, quotes a lifetime Dallas resident who understood the women who were the unofficial arbiters of social and moral propriety. "Besides Candy Barr's fancy dancin', the chamber-of-commerce ladies were disturbed by what they called her gross impudence." The man says that he didn't know her, but that they frequented the same hotel coffee shop. "I guess she was just about as impertinent as she could be to everybody, includin' the cops. The worst of it, as far as the chamber-of-commerce ladies were concerned, was that she was getting away with it. She was showin' her bosom and bein' snippy to anybody she pleased, and all this time she was goin' up in the world—getting her picture and write-ups in the paper and makin' a fat lot of money. She wasn't sufferin' at all, the way the chamber ladies thought she should, and they began sayin', 'That Jezebel has got to go.' " And the champion of the bigoted community was Captain Pat Gannaway.

Gannaway was the head of the Special Service Bureau, a unit that would later be described by Lieutenant Jack Revill, a specialist in criminal intelligence who worked directly under Gannaway. At the bureau, Revill explained, "our primary responsibility is to investigate crimes of an organized nature, subversive activities, racial matters, labor racketeering, and to do anything that the chief might desire. We work for the chief of police. I report to a captain [Gannaway] who is in charge of the Special Service Bureau."

It was in 1957 that Captain Gannaway decided he needed to eliminate the scourge that was Candy Barr, and it was his unit, answerable only to the police chief, that was the vehicle for his assault on her freedom. The Special Service Bureau, like other special units in police departments around the country, was built on the idea that certain activities were crimes and being associated with those activities made you a criminal. Juanita had been a whore, and the fact that she was taken in the Capture, that she had been traumatized and brutalized, did not matter. A decent woman, an innocent woman, would not have been so involved.

Likewise, when Candy Barr was dancing and would occasionally return to activities that involved sex for pay, she was still a whore. Then she had the nerve to be in a dirty movie that, to his credit, Gannaway and a number of others involved with the criminal justice system apparently had not seen, but they knew all the details. *Smart Aleck*, it was alleged, included scenes with a black man (it didn't), a large animal (it didn't), and was the first of seven or eight movies she made (there was only one). She was obviously running wild in the streets, damaging the image of Dallas, and needed to be put away.

The focus was on finding a reason to arrest Candy Barr once she avoided jail for having the bad grace to shoot Troy Phillips in what everyone agreed was self-defense. Worse, there was extensive publicity that made law enforcement look foolish even though the impetus for raising her bond and implying a more serious crime came from Abe Weinstein working with Sheriff Bill Decker and against the wishes of Candy and her attorney, Oscar Mauzy.

Juanita had no idea how many people were out to get her, nor did she care. She was morally upright when it came to making the choices for her own life, and determined to act in a manner she could live with. She never volunteered to be put in the Capture. She could not help it if prominent Dallas citizens not only couldn't keep their pants on but would pay to have her forced to act out the darkest desires of their souls. She had always tried to do what was right wherever she was in control, but control was rare in her young years. That the good people of Dallas felt the need to destroy her and would use a rigid, no-nonsense, moralistic police captain to do it was not something she could imagine.

Candy's lack of awareness about the danger was reinforced by the crowds that turned out at the Colony Club. For the next few months, the Colony Club's business was greater than ever before. Men and women came to see Candy Barr, and she reveled in what she was certain was their enjoyment of her dancing.

Another concern also kept her from being fully attentive to all that was taking place. The relationship with Troy Phillips had left her pregnant, a fact she did not like to discuss, even in her later years. By the standards of the "good" people of Dallas, Juanita, both as a teen and as the young adult Candy Barr, was a slut. Juanita, by contrast, considered herself a Christian, steeped in the idea of Jesus' love. She had known him as a child in the Pentecostal church. She believed in his love for what the Bible calls the least of his people. She felt her faith fortified when she never contracted a sexual disease in the Capture and was able to have a healthy infant in 1956.

The baby, a girl named Troylene, was proof of the blessings that endured despite the actions of others. She kept the child, whom she called "my little parcel of love," with her when possible, and left her with Doc and Etta when caring for the baby would be too difficult. Etta and Juanita may have been at odds over the years, but Juanita saw that the older woman could be a kind and loving grandmother. More important, the entire family closed protectively around Troylene, making certain she would rarely be heard about and never exploited, regardless of what happened to Juanita as her Candy Barr alter-ego became famous.

One person who would make herself known, if only in Dallas, was a teenager named Helen Smith. She was nineteen years old and had become Candy's friend when both were in the Dallas Little Theater play group back in February 1957.

It was spring of 1957 when Helen Smith decided to become an exotic dancer, the term she used for the work Candy was doing. Like Candy, she took her first job at the Theatre Lounge, supplementing her income with club dates. For several months she lived with Candy, but in October, Candy was living alone and Helen, by then known as Pixie Lynn, was back with her family though still working at the Theatre Lounge, rising to be one of the featured dancers in the earlier, less well attended shows.

On Saturday, October 27, 1957, Pixie Lynn was featured in the early shows, left the Theatre Lounge for a break, and returned to work the evening shift at 8:30 p.m. She drove her car into an alley connecting with the back entrance for the Theatre Lounge. She had worked at another club the night before, and since the Weinsteins had booked her, they also let her borrow some gowns she normally used when performing in their club. She planned to wear them again that Saturday night and wanted to be certain she could get them inside without damage. The back entrance made the most sense.

An acquaintance named Virginia Strom and another woman were waiting in the alley outside the Theatre Lounge when Helen drove in. Virginia called her over to her car and said she had something for her. "She gave me a Prince Albert can of marijuana," Helen recalled when eventually testifying in Candy's trial. Helen took it with her into the lounge and went to work. "And then I went over to a girlfriend's house where I left it. I didn't know exactly what to do with it, never having used it before."

Helen and the friend, Maxine Williams, met at the Artist's Club, drove to Maxine's apartment, and then went to a party. On Sunday, at about a quarter to 6:00 in the evening, according to Helen, "I called Candy and told her that Virginia had come over and given me something, and that I had to go home and I couldn't take it home. Could I come by there and leave it with her, and as soon as I went home and got dressed again to go to work that I would come back and pick it up."

Had Helen arrived at Candy's apartment on Saturday, she would have been noticed by a man sitting in a car about three-quarters of a block away. He sat there for more than three hours before taking a dinner break around 5:00 p.m. He returned four hours later, keeping watch until 1:00 a.m. Sunday, October 27.

The man returned sometime after 1:00 p.m. that Sunday. This time he stayed until 4:30 p.m. before going home for the next two hours.

The previously inconspicuous observer had friends when he returned Sunday evening. The observer, Lieutenant J. M. Souter of the Special Service Bureau, was accompanied by Detective Revill and Lieutenant Frazier of the Narcotics Squad.

But by the time Souter and his companions arrived, Helen had come and gone, unnoticed. Helen had reached Candy's apartment at approximately 6:00 p.m. Candy was in suite 24-A in a small building at 4328 McKinney Avenue. "This is the marijuana that Virginia gave me," Helen told Candy. "Would you please keep it until I can go home and then come back?"

As Helen remembered, "She told me that I should get rid of it, but that she would keep it until I could get back from changing clothes. I had to go to work."

The only special request Helen made was asking Candy to take the marijuana out of the Prince Albert tobacco can and place it in a different container. Candy agreed, though what she would use or where she would put it was never discussed.

Helen left Candy's apartment at approximately 6:15 p.m. She went home, changed her clothes, and went to work. But she never made it back to Candy's apartment.

Candy was not concerned with the small quantity of marijuana with which she had been entrusted. There was no reason to be. She certainly did not connect Helen's request with James Daniels, the new tenant three doors from her suite. Daniels had rented apartment 28-C approximately three weeks earlier. However, he was quiet, kept to himself, and she could not remember ever seeing his face.

There would have been far more concern had she known that his real name was Captain Pat Gannaway. He used the alias Billy Paul when he requested gas and electric service from the Lone Star Gas Company. According to the utility company's records, the bills for 28-C were to be sent to Billy Paul at 3527 Monte Carlo Street, which happened to be the home address of Captain Gannaway.

It was 9:00 p.m. Sunday when Candy heard the doorbell. She was dressed to go to the movies after she finished talking on the telephone with George Owens, one of the few men in her life with whom she had gotten close. They met when he was still married, and the relationship had grown in intensity more than either of them had expected. Their conversations were frequent, and he stayed on the line while she went to the door. Her visitor was a Western Union man with a telegram for her.

Knowing she would have to sign for the telegram, and not wanting the messenger to see the container of marijuana on her table, she picked up the container and put it inside her blouse. "What was I going to do, run to the bedroom and stick it somewhere, or in the cabinet? So I put it in my blouse and opened up the door."

As soon as Candy opened the door, Lieutenant Souter "stepped inside the apartment," he later stated, "and told her that I was an officer; identified myself and told her also that we had a search warrant and handed it to her." He had two other officers with him, and they informed Candy that they were going to search her apartment. None of them was Captain Gannaway. None of them would later claim to be aware that they knew Captain Gannaway had taken an apartment two doors away, using an assumed name and wiretapping her telephone.

The search warrant had been issued by Judge W. E. "Bill" Richburg, a justice of the peace for Precinct 7, Place 1, that was believed to not have jurisdiction in Dallas County. That issue did not matter, though. The only issue was what might be found when the raid took place. The warrant read:

Lt. J.M. Souter do solemnly swear that heretofore, on or about the 26th day of October AD 1957 in said County and State, one Juanita Dale

Phillips and unknown persons did then and there unlawfully possess a narcotic drug, to wit marijuana and I have cause to believe and do believe that said narcotic drugs are now concealed by Juanita Dale Phillips and unknown persons in an apartment, #24A situated in Dallas County, Texas at (8) 4328 McKinney Avenue, City of Dallas, Dallas County, Texas which said Juanita Dale Phillips and unknown persons occupies, possesses controls and has charge of.

MY BELIEF AS FORESAID IS BASED ON THE FOLLOWING FACTS:

(A) I have been informed of the existence of the foregoing set out facts by reliable, credible and trustworthy citizen of Dallas County, Texas.

That was the warrant. No names had to be revealed to the judge. No facts had to be presented. Not even the specific judge mattered. The vague application was legal in 1957 Dallas, and Judge Richburg signed the order.

George Owens had been talking with Candy on the telephone when the police arrived, and he rushed over to her apartment in time for the search. Soon after he reached there, he saw Souter pick up a chair in Candy's living room, look under it, pick up something, and then say, "Well, well, this looks like a joint."

Souter immediately placed Candy under arrest. He was about to take Owens to jail as well, if only for being her friend, when she said, "Please, he's just a square John and doesn't know anything. If you'll let him go, I'll give you what you came looking for." With that she reached into her bra and handed the officer a small Alka-Seltzer bottle in which she had placed the tiny amount of marijuana Helen had brought.

Owens was innocent of any involvement, but the threat to arrest him in addition to Candy caused her to give up what she had been asked to hold for Helen. In the end, Souter carefully noted what had been found and taken from the apartment:

A large quantity of Marijuana
One (1) Marijuana cigarette
Two (2) books of cigarette paper
One (1) empty Prince Albert tobacco can
One (1) Automatic pistol, MAB Brevete brand, Model C .32 calibre,
    Serial #11742 which said property was found by me (we) at the

place designated and described in the warrant; and I (we) also, at the same time, arrested in obedience to the command of said warrant.

The alleged "large quantity of Marijuana" was actually not enough for two cigarettes, which the police undoubtedly knew, because they did not list the weight or volume.

TWENTY

A Brief Note

The arrest of Candy Barr created an odd situation in her life. She was angry, convinced she had committed no crime. She was also scared because she knew that, in Texas, she could face as much as life in prison. The sentencing structure was outrageous, the bigotry was daunting, and the hypocrisy was almost a matter of civic pride. However, before the four days that would decide her fate, and after the trial, when she was out on appeal, Candy would be exposed to a world she never knew existed, a world of mobsters, entertainers, and fans who might fantasize about marrying the beautiful dancer, but they could not imagine participating in the brutality of the Capture.

Before looking at Juanita's life after Dallas, it is necessary to examine the February 1958 trial.

TWENTY-ONE

Judge Brown Had a Camera

BE IT REMEMBERED, That on the 10th day of February, 1958, the above entitled and numbered cause came on for trial before the honorable JOE B. BROWN, Judge of Criminal District Court No. 3 of Dallas County, Texas, and a JURY; WHEREUPON a jury was duly impaneled and sworn; the Indictment was presented and read to the Jury by Mr. Alexander to which the defendant plead 'Not Guilty;' The Rule of Evidence was invoked by both the State and the Defendant, and the witness instructed and cautioned as to the Rule of Evidence and excluded from the courtroom; whereupon, testimony before the jury began on February 11, 1958.

Juanita Dale Phillips, called Candy Barr by most people except her friends, and with her marriage to Troy not yet legally over, entered a packed courtroom. Her bright blonde hair was pulled back in a demure ponytail. Her baby face was unsmiling, and her green eyes were sparkling defiance. She was being framed because of a life others had forced her to live, then were embarrassed that she might reveal their complicity in the horrors she endured.

Juanita took her place at the counsel table, flanked by her two attorneys, Lester May and William Braecklein. The trio faced the Honorable Joe B. Brown, who some five years later would preside over the trial of Candy's friend and sometimes mentor Jack Ruby for killing a former part-time employee, Lee Harvey Oswald, President John F. Kennedy's assassin.

Judge Brown was typical of Texas oddities. In other states, a man or woman practices law before being considered for the bench. Judge Brown made a career out of being a judge, never bothering to practice law in the conventional manner. He was a railroad rate clerk when a friend registered for night courses at the Jefferson Law School in Dallas. Brown, then twenty-two, decided such classes might be fun. He studied for three years, graduated, then ran successfully for election as justice of the peace in the Oak Cliff section of Dallas. By 1956 he was on the Dallas County Criminal Court. Three years later, after convincing at least one hundred others, including Jack Ruby, to join the Dallas Chamber of Commerce, he was given the honor of becoming a lifetime member.

On the bench, Judge Brown was known for both dignity and a lack of formality, the latter resulting from his having spent no time in traditional courtrooms. But he understood how the game was played in Dallas. He knew how often Candy Barr had upset the sensibilities of the people who mattered in the city. He knew her past, knew that she had gone so far as to gently mock the sincerity of both the patriotic eccentricities and a cultural icon of the community.

For example, there had been times in her act when she had taken off the Stetson she wore on her head and placed it solemnly over her heart. Then she would let go and the hat would stay where it was, her breasts keeping it up.

Candy Barr thought the Stetson trick was funny. Perhaps had she used a Bailey or other perfectly serviceable ten-gallon hat also worn on ranches throughout the Southwest, no one would have minded. But a Stetson! The Stetson was synonymous with Dallas. It had a history of being a cowboy's best friend, protecting him from the sun as he herded the cattle and filtering the water taken from a stream when he dismounted to get a drink. It served as part of Dallas's formal wear. It served as part of Dallas's casual wear. A Stetson brand ten-gallon hat made a man complete. And Candy Barr used it for laughs.

District Judge Brown expressed the moral outrage expected of him. Then he thought about what he had undoubtedly seen in the clubs where he was just another customer and decided that he needed a personal souvenir of the trial over which he was presiding. He borrowed a movie camera from one of the television cameramen and then proceeded to shoot at least one roll of film of the woman some referred to as "the shapely defendant." He allegedly brought his own camera the next day, taking Candy into his chambers for some additional pictures.

The national press was amazed not only by the way the trial was being handled but also that Candy Barr had been arrested at all. They felt there was an obvious miscarriage of justice, and as the story of the arrest unfolded, their perception seemed an accurate one, at least if you weren't a Dallas, Texas, resident.

The defense counsel began the trial with what proved to be a bad judgment call. The jury was eleven men and one woman, selected because it was believed that the men would be more sympathetic to the dancer. They would not want to send her to jail and risk her being hurt by the experience. What was not considered was the fact that the male jurors were married, and the "good women" of Dallas wanted to eliminate what they perceived as the bane of the community. The men had to go home and proudly tell their wives that they had done their part in improving the living conditions of their beloved city. Otherwise their wives would question their actions with the woman they despised.

To the amazement of the reporters covering the story for papers outside Dallas, the Candy Barr arrest was an obvious miscarriage of justice. According to the testimony, on October 7, 1957, the apartment down the hall from Candy's was rented by a detective from the Criminal Intelligence section of the Dallas Special Service Bureau. Then on October 15, a telephone repairman checking to see why Candy was having trouble with her telephone found that it had been wired (with a "jumper" attachment) to the detective's apartment. However, the detective had never legally applied for a telephone and there was no record of his having one. The same day the electric company found that electricity was being used in the detective's apartment. Again there was no record of a legal hook-up.

On October 26, Judge Richburg issued a search-and-arrest warrant for Juanita Dale Phillips, ordering her to be immediately arrested and brought before the judge. The warrant demanded that the action be taken without delay. It did not allow for the surveillance that subsequently took place while the stripper friend of Candy's brought her the tobacco tin of marijuana.

On October 27, with the warrant expired, the arrest was made. It was after 9:00 p.m., and George Owens was credited as the "person" unknown from the original warrant, though he had nothing to do with what was happening. As for the marijuana, Candy had hidden it in an Alka-Seltzer bottle placed between her breasts. The next day, the detective tenant, who had claimed he worked for a bank, terminated his lease with the landlord.

As the trial began, it was obvious there was going to be a show. The prosecution team of Bill Alexander and Jim Allen were skilled in the courtroom. The defense attorneys were also skilled, but they made the mistake of being on what Dallas insiders knew would be the losing side. Justice was frequently not blind in Dallas. She peaked from under the cloth supposedly covering her eyes, checking the temperament of the community before replacing the blindfold and ruling whatever way the "good" people seemed to desire.

The often outrageous testimony (in the ears of legal experts in other parts of the country) was carefully presented so that Judge Brown could rule favorably for the prosecution. The defense stated that the warrant had been illegally obtained, executed, and registered, all based on an illegal wiretap that was used to allow the street surveillance team to know when they should be out and watching. In addition, both the marijuana cigarette and the marijuana in the Prince Albert can had been planted. These were all logical conclusions, impossible to fully overrule in courtrooms outside Texas. In Dallas, well . . .

The initial warrant used to justify the arrest was signed by Judge W. E. "Bill" Richburg. On February 11, 1958, the first day of the trial, when defense attorney Braecklein questioned him about whether the police officers requesting a search warrant had any evidence of a problem, Judge Richburg responded, "Nothing more than the fact that he [Lieutenant J. M. Souter of the Dallas Police Department] stated that he believed, that he had reasons to believe that there was some marijuana at this particular place."

Attorney Braecklein: "That's all he said, he had some reasons to believe."

Judge Richburg: "Yes, sir."

Attorney Braecklein: "And you didn't ask him if he had seen it, anything like that?"

Judge Richburg: "No, sir, I didn't."

The questioning revealed that the warrant was issued from the wrong jurisdiction, was never properly filed, and was based, in part, on the statement that a reliable citizen had provided information of a crime. The judge was never told the name of the reliable citizen, nor would the police officers involved reveal the name. The illegality of the matter should have resulted in Judge Brown throwing the case out of court. However, this was Candy Barr, and the Chamber of Commerce ladies, the How Dare You squad, and the other "good" people of the city did not want a few facts to impede their getting rid of the greatest moral danger the city had apparently ever seen.

Neither Judge Brown nor, in January 1959, two judges on the Texas Court of Criminal Appeals cared about the niceties of the law or the facts in the case. Only Judge Lloyd W. Davidson, in a dissenting opinion, noted what the journalists had seen when covering the trial. He wrote of what everyone agrees was an illegal search warrant: " So the time has come in this state when peace officers can kick in the door of one's home and search and ransack it at will and without any lawful authority to do so and in total disregard of the law, and the owner of that home, upon trial for possessing property found therein, must submit to such outrage and deprivation of her constitutional right against unlawful search before she can show that she was innocent of any unlawful connection with the property so found. If that is equal justice under law, I want no part of it. If a conviction obtained under such circumstances is due process of law, then there is no due process of law."

But truth and justice were not desired for the woman who dared to defy the Capture and live to dance.

The case unfolded in a way that would have been comic if used in a movie. According to the prosecution, there was no communication between the head of the Criminal Intelligence Division and the member of his six-man team living in the apartment near Candy. There was no wiretap. Even though the illegal connecting cables were not of a type the telephone company had ever used, the court held that the jumper was simply left over from a party line (a shared line).

Finally, it was stated that an unnamed informer, at some unstated time before the warrant was issued, assured the special unit that Candy "did then and there unlawfully possess" the marijuana, although it was not even delivered until the day after the warrant was applied for. Judge Brown never sustained any of the defense counsel's objections to such outrageous evidence.

The judge enjoyed his days in court with Candy Barr, though. As he periodically filmed the defendant with his camera, the prosecution was probably as nervous about the outcome of the trial as the defense. There was always the chance that he would not go along with their presentation of seemingly questionable evidence, but he did.

The defense team's efforts included a lengthy statement of objections to the admission of evidence they said came from an illegally obtained search warrant. Defense counsel Lester May, for example, raised the issue that "nowhere on the face of the affidavit is there probable cause shown, that having been left blank until much later," and he called it "defective upon its face, for the reason that the address described in said affidavit is a private residence and, being such, a search warrant may be issued only upon the affidavit of two credible persons."

May continued that "it does not comply with the Constitution of the State of Texas in that they must show probable cause.

"And the Court, in looking at that affidavit, cannot see any probable cause shown, any facts set forth therein. All they did was just say, 'I believe' and did not set forth any facts which would show any probable cause for the issuance."

May concluded with: "And we object to it as violating her constitutional rights."

"Are you through?" Judge Brown asked May.

"Yes, Your Honor," said May.

Judge Brown then replied, "The court overrules your objection and admits the search warrant into evidence."

Bill Braecklein, apparently playing to the crowd, rose to his feet and said, "We accept the court's ruling." Unfortunately, her case for appeal would have been stronger, according to some legal experts, if he had said that, for the record, he objected to the admission of the evidence. There were also no objections to the admission of the Alka-Seltzer bottle.

The prosecution team put Candy's character on trial. They asked one witness to explain what it meant to be an exotic dancer. Another witness was asked by what name he knew the defendant, making clear that Juanita had been married more than once. This was extremely shocking in Dallas, where the proper people stayed married to the same spouse until death. They might use prostitutes, of course. They might have a lover on the side. But a woman could hold up her head and brag that she and her husband had never so much as considered divorce.

Then there was the "shocking" action that occurred at the time of her arrest. "I'll ask you if the defendant pulled any object *from her bosom* . . . "

"Is the person who pulled the marijuana *from her bosom* and gave it to you present in the courtroom?"

"From her bosom." "From her bosom." "From her bosom." It was a refrain repeated five times in the course of the trial.

The container of marijuana was placed on the rail of the jury box, a reminder of both the crime and the location where it had been secreted. Then the prosecutor asked the obviously white George Owens, the man who had visited Candy that day, whether he was a white man or a Negro. It was a reminder to some of the jurors and a horrifying suggestion to others that Candy had more than a nodding acquaintance with black people. To many in the courtroom, such behavior was worse than any crime on the books and certainly helped seal her fate more than the question of drugs. It also helped turn the jury against the defense team, no matter how effectively they did their job. It was time for Candy Barr to stop polluting the city of Dallas. Or such was the conventional wisdom. The jury sentenced her to fifteen years in jail.

"Sometimes people make me sick," Juanita stated to the press on Saturday morning when she was released on bond from the county jail. "I'm calm. I'm all right, I guess. But people make me sick. . . . They were prejudiced."

Juanita continued, "I feel fine. But I burn when I think that some of them wanted me to get twenty-five years. Marijuana? I don't even smoke. Narcotics and my ulcers won't mix. I'd die."

When asked about her future, Juanita replied, "Future? The nearest thing I can see is they'll run me out of town.

"But my preacher told me to have an unbroken spirit. That will help some. But still, some people make me sick."

Juanita was freed on $15,000 bond, pending appeals. She would have to leave Dallas if she wanted to dance, but there were no objections to her leaving the state of Texas. She was free to travel to Los Angeles and Las Vegas, anyplace where they had never heard of the Capture and where no "nice" Texas leader would have to face his past. The result was that Candy Barr's career truly began to soar.

TWENTY-TWO

Mob Action, Vegas, and the Sunset Strip

"Good ole white Texas gals just didn't consort with coloreds. The hooker-with-a-heart-of-gold wouldn't play in Dallas. That kind act really cost her."

—A Dallas attorney, concerning Candy Barr's friendship with Sammy Davis Jr.

It was December 1957, still weeks before the trial. Juanita Slusher Phillips had all but disappeared from the public's mind. In her place was Candy Barr, an alter ego she was never happy hearing about, not when the dancer was being sullied by the same people who used her in the Capture.

The past had been hell in many ways, but she believed that the good Lord had given her the strength to endure. She had escaped the Capture through dancing. She had found a way to be free on stage, to dance in a manner that had never been seen before, improvising with her musicians in a way that made her physically the equivalent of Duke Ellington, Billy Strayhorn, and other jazz greats. And now she was being railroaded into jail as fast as the law could move. Fortunately, even for the "good" people of Dallas so anxious to rid themselves of this mirror of their own misdeeds, the law still had a few values.

Candy wasn't a danger to herself or others. Her "crime" was no more serious than spitting on the sidewalk, despite Captain Gannaway's rigid

morality, and it certainly wasn't going to take precedence in the courts. Instead of bringing her quickly to trial, the judges decided to let the murderers, robbers, and strong-arm thugs first have their day before the bench. Candy Barr was simply ordered to not work in a Dallas club until her trial. However, if she wanted to work outside the city, preferably outside the state, that would not be fought. That experience, before and after the trial, would change her forever.

A man named Joe De Carlo, then working as the manager of entertainers Louis Prima and Keely Smith, learned of Candy Barr and decided he could benefit from the notoriety. He had the sensibilities of Abe Weinstein, figuring any unfavorable press would bring men and women flocking to wherever Candy was dancing. The management of Larry Potter's Supper Club in California's San Fernando Valley agreed, flying her out to perform.

Suddenly the world was at Candy Barr's feet. Chuck Landis owned the Largo Club on the famous Sunset Strip and hired her to perform the moment she was free from the contract with Larry Potter's Supper Club. The money was huge and the acclaim beyond anything she could have previously imagined. What she did not understand was that her appearance crossed several lines. First there was the dancing, for it was in the Largo that she developed the routine with the wall. Second, there were the behind the scenes (and not so behind the scenes) players on the Strip itself.

The Sunset Strip was mob territory. It was an unincorporated area outside Los Angeles proper where businesses that were considered criminal enterprises in the city could openly operate. Mickey Cohen made the Sunset Strip his base while reporting to Bugsy Siegel and Meyer Lansky, as much as it could be said he reported to anyone. He was an independent operator who recognized the need to work with the East Coast mobsters who were moving aggressively into Las Vegas and the West Coast.

Mickey's activities were known to law enforcement officers such as Fred Otash, who later became the chief private investigator for *Confidential* magazine, and people like Nick Sevano, the longtime manager of Frank Sinatra. They and others who were on the scene during that era explained in interviews that Mickey Cohen helped many young actors and entertainers get started. He did them favors without asking anything in return, knowing that when they were successful they would feel a debt of gratitude. That was why, when the Los Angeles Police Department forced him to leave the area under its jurisdiction in 1947, he was able to go to Charlie and Sy Devore and arrange to have his office in the back of their Slapsy Maxie's Café on Wilshire Boulevard.

Slapsy Maxie Rosenbloom had survived sixteen years as a prizefighter, and his success in boxing made him popular in Los Angeles. He was paid for the use of his name by some friends who opened the club and had him hang out, drinking and eating for free while greeting his fans. However, the owners were inexperienced and the club folded. When the Devores wanted to reopen it, keeping better cost controls, Cohen supplied the cash in exchange for a room for his office. Mickey could not be touched by the LAPD, because Slapsy Maxie's Café was in an unincorporated section of the Sunset Strip, a location policed by the sheriff's office. Moreover, the sheriff was believed by the LAPD to be on the take.

Cohan arranged protection for various criminals, charging them a weekly franchise fee. In 1948 local bookmakers had to bring him $250 a week to be able to stay in business in the Sunset Strip, where LAPD could not arrest them and the arrangement Cohen had with the sheriff meant they would not be arrested.

The Devores proved they could be successful, so when they wanted to bring in more expensive, yet still-rising entertainers, Cohen agreed. He advanced them $4,000 per week plus airfare to bring in Dean Martin and Jerry Lewis, a duo just beginning to be successful on the East Coast. Locals had not heard of them, but Cohen not only took a chance, he called on prominent friends to attend opening night. Martin and Lewis stepped onto the stage, and there were the biggest names in Hollywood. Fred Astaire had a table, as did Jane Wyman, Clark Gable, Humphrey Bogart, Joan Crawford, Grace Kelly, Loretta Young, Gary Cooper, and numerous others. That exposure was the break Martin and Lewis needed to reach the next level as entertainers, and soon they were among the biggest names in both nightclubs and movies.

Martin never forgot the favor and did not mind associating with Cohen when others turned away in 1952 after Cohen went to jail for four years for income-tax evasion. He remained friends after Cohen's release, when Mickey worked to take control of the rackets, though not his taxes;

Cohen would return to jail in the 1960s. Martin and the other entertainers were never part of the mob, never connected with any of the rackets. They were simply loyal to a man who believed in them when no one else thought they could succeed.

Frank Sinatra was another friend because of Mickey's favors. Jimmy Tarantino convinced Sinatra and Hank Sanicola, one of the singer's managers, that Hollywood needed an entertainment weekly. This would have stories about the entertainers, the clubs, and the industry. Mickey Cohen was an investor, so the other two felt they should put up their money as well. What went unsaid was that Tarantino gathered extensive personal information about the stars, then explained that he would print it unless they bought large advertisements in the publication. He did not tell his investors what he was doing, and he did not blackmail Sinatra, who was cheating on his wife, Nancy, every chance he could get. After all, Sinatra was an investor. But the truth came out when Tarantino later went to jail for extortion.

Cohen liked Sinatra and began publicly supporting him in early 1950 when the singer's career was at a low point. Other entertainers were more popular, and Sinatra could see the end of his career. Hit movies and successful recordings were in the future, not yet seen as a possibility for resurrecting his image. Cohen, determined to help Sinatra, threw a testimonial for the singer at the Beverly Hills Hotel. He invited everyone who had been important in Sinatra's past and would prove important in the future, as well as others who went more as a favor for Cohen than for Frank. Only the "nobodies" showed, a fact that convinced Sinatra to be loyal to anyone, including a mobster, who stood by him when times were difficult.

Cohen moved heavily into the nightclub business because he saw the clubs as giving a license to steal. He went beyond skimming from the gambling and food business. He would buy a cheap painting for $50, then declare that it cost $5,000 and deduct it as a business expense. He could run showgirls as prostitutes. He could move illegally gained money from drugs and other criminal activities onto the casino and nightclub books, claiming they represented paying customers. A club once making $2 million a year would suddenly report $3 million, paying the taxes. No one investigated to see if the money was earned by the club or earned illegally, then laundered through the club's books. The Feds were happy so long as the taxes were paid.

Clubs along the Sunset Strip and in Las Vegas made voyeurism and losing money a respectable way to spend a weekend. Shows were elaborate, had mild sexual titillation, and introduced entertainers that patrons might not feel comfortable seeing in their home communities. The chorus girls, often topless, were presented in a way that seemed sophisticated, slightly naughty, but enjoyable for both men and women. And it was in this world, while waiting to go to trial, that Candy Barr became more famous than in the past.

Exactly when Cohen became aware of Candy Barr is uncertain. Most likely it was early in her time in Los Angeles, both because of Joe De Carlo, who later went to work for Cohen, and because of her relationship with Sammy Davis Jr.

From the time Candy arrived in Los Angeles before her trial, and then again when she was out on appeal, she began involving herself in the world of up-and-coming entertainers. In the next few months she would date men ranging from Bing Crosby's son Gary to actor Vince Edwards, who became a close friend. But the relationship that mattered most, the one with Sammy Davis Jr., was the one that led to her vilification in the racially charged 1950s.

It was natural that Juanita Slusher and Sammy Davis Jr. would become friends. They were both outcasts of sorts, welcome on a stage but often shunned when their performances ended. Juanita had the stigma of her past, as though it was her fault that she had been a victim of the Capture. Sammy had the stigma of his skin color, people assuming that if he had any sense, he would have been born white.

Juanita had a few more options than Sammy when she reached Las Vegas. She was allowed to enter the casinos to gamble. Sammy had to look in from whatever corner he could find, hiding from security just long enough to see a gaiety among the gamblers and revelers he was denied. At the time, a black man was not allowed to set foot in the casinos, even if he was able to star in one of the shows. Later, when he was working with Frank Sinatra at the Sands (in which Sinatra had a tiny percentage of the ownership), Sammy was allowed on the casino floor. However, a white man, frequently Peter Lawford, with whom he regularly appeared, was required to handle the slot machines for Sammy. The town was more liberal by then. They took pride in the fact that a black man could look at the action, and they were privately relieved that he was not allowed to touch.

Just as Juanita would forever be defined by the childhood hell she endured from the hands of everyone from pedophiles to the Dallas elite, so Sammy was defined by a series of racist moments. Perhaps the most outrageous incident occurred at the Copacabana nightclub in New York City in January 1957, the year in which Juanita would be arrested.

Frank Sinatra had been booked as the star of the Copa's show for a two-week engagement. Sammy, both a fan and a friend, arranged with manager Julie Podell to get a ringside table for ten people every night of the show. Davis planned to run up a tab, then pay it off at the end of the two weeks. But on January 14, when Sinatra's friend Humphrey Bogart died, Sinatra asked to be excused from one night. Jerry Lewis agreed to step into the early show, but the more popular later hour needed a stronger talent. Sammy Davis Jr. was asked to fill in.

Davis, whose performance brought thunderous applause, was one of the few people in the country who could substitute for Frank Sinatra and not have customers leave disappointed. A grateful Podell, who otherwise would have lost extensive business, paid Davis handsomely. He also was given the best seats in the house, the very center of ringside, free champagne and scotch for his guests, and the tab he had run up over the previous few days was eliminated. It was star treatment richly deserved, and the staff, including the maître d', rushed over to congratulate him.

Then he sat down to enjoy his steak and heard the man directly behind him refer to him as the "little nigger in front of me." As Davis later related, when the waiter and the maître d' could not silence the customer, the captain came over, at which time the man said, "Maybe you can do better than your flunky here. You look like a man who knows right from wrong. It's obviously some kind of mistake. I come in here thinking I'm spending my money in a first-class place, so you can understand my surprise when I find my wife and I seated behind that little jigaboo." The customer was immediately half-walked, half-carried from the nightclub. The entire staff was outraged. But that did not lessen the pain.

It was not the first time Sammy Davis Jr. had been exposed to such hatred. It certainly would not be the last. What hurt so much was that even in the rarefied world at the top of show business, Davis would always be branded as something less than fully human because of his skin color.

Other performers, both white and black, went to see Davis on stage in order to learn dance steps, attitude, song phrasing, and style. He had no color when he moved about the stage, a master of everything he tried. He was an original, as was Candy Barr. But just as she would often be viewed as white trash, good for nothing but being a receptacle for whatever sexual act they wanted her to endure, so he was forever branded a "nigger" when he left his "place" in the club.

Candy had been traumatized by blacks when a young teenager. To the end of her life she referred to the "nigger porter" who broke her into prostitution for Troy. But the relationship with Sammy transcended color. They didn't date. They weren't having sex. They were two people in show business who understood what it was to be hated for superficialities.

"Sammy and I were such good friends," said Juanita. "Now I don't know about outside races and that. I had my thing with blacks early in life. But in show business, to me, people who entertain . . . it's a whole different thing."

Candy would prove to be a true friend when Sammy got into trouble, but the initial relationship was the result of shared professional interests. "I think that Sammy and I were attracted to each other as human beings because I loved to dance and he did. He loved his work and so did I. He'd come in the club and play the drums. He wasn't a drummer. We'd make a spectacle of ourselves. Everybody thought we were [lovers] and we weren't. And I had a boyfriend. Believe it or not, when I have a boyfriend, I have a boyfriend."

According to Candy, her having a boyfriend truly frustrated one of Sammy's friends. "You know," she related, "I had an opportunity to be with Frank Sinatra." But Candy had a boyfriend visiting from Dallas. "My sweetheart was in town and I just could not do that, and I've kicked my ass ever since. I said, 'Looky here, you could have been Mia Farrow.'

"He pursued me for several weeks, 'cause I heard about his bed jumpin'. Don't know if it was true, but that's what I heard. I wasn't going to be one of them, and besides, I had a boyfriend. He would have heard about it. How naïve can a human being be on the stages of Las Vegas? Nobody would believe it 'cause they couldn't see behind my face."

The relationship with Sammy mostly involved going to his home to watch movies and talk. Sometimes they were together. Usually they were with others. The problem was that Sammy had become high profile because he desperately wanted to be accepted by white society. Davis had never been a civil rights pioneer. He simply resented being held back from anything by the color of his skin. As he would later be quoted as saying, "Long before there was a civil rights movement, I was marching through the lobby of the Waldorf-Astoria, of the Sands, the Fontainebleau, to a table at the Copa. And I'd marched alone. Worse. Often to black derision." Sammy wasn't out to prove anything. He had already done that. He simply wanted to be allowed to live his own life any way he desired, and that included dating anyone in whom he was interested.

The only reason Candy Barr's friendship with Sammy was rarely mentioned in the press was because higher-profile women caught the attention of the media first. For example, he had a very casual acquaintance with actress Kim Novak. For some reason the media decided the two were having an affair when they weren't. Fed up with what was happening, and both performers recognizing their image problems, Sammy finally called Kim and suggested they date for real. The dating led to passion, and both of them eventually admitted they had consummated the relationship just to see what the taboo was like. But there was no long-term intimacy sought or desired by either of them.

Years before meeting Candy there had been not-so-subtle warnings to Sammy. One seemed to catch up with him in November 1954. He had been in Las Vegas, where he, his father, and his uncle—the Will Mastin Trio—were working at the Last Frontier Hotel, earning $7,500 per week and having the unusual request that they eat, gamble, and socialize there. A decade earlier the three men had played the same hotel and been given $350. They were allowed in their dressing room, on the stage, and at the back of the hotel, where they were to wait for a cab to take them to the part of the city where blacks were welcome. However, by the end of 1954, the hotel found that when a popular star, regardless of color, went from the stage to the casino, betting heavily, others were encouraged to do so. There was a financial benefit to the casino that overrode the bigotry, though in those years the Last Frontier was the exception.

In addition to the Las Vegas stint, Sammy was commuting to Los Angeles, where he was doing recording work. He was also being romantically linked with Ava Gardner, a relationship that existed only in the minds of some members of the media yet was widely believed. There were people who claimed that studio executives had a contract out on him, and on one of his trips to Los Angeles, some people believed it was fulfilled.

On the night of November 19, 1954, Sammy was driving alone in his Cadillac convertible from Las Vegas to Los Angeles, listening to a radio station playing his hit single "Hey There," when a car made a U-turn in front of him. Sammy swerved to avoid it, running into oncoming traffic and crashing head on. This was the days before seatbelts and airbags, and Sammy's head hit the steering wheel. The Cadillacs back then had a stylized chrome piece sticking out of the center of the wheel. It smashed into Sammy's left eye, destroying it.

Davis was rushed to a hospital near Palm Springs, where his life was saved, his broken bones were set, and he learned he would always be blind in one eye. It is not certain exactly how much later he also learned that the car crash was probably not an accident. Men in high-powered positions both in Hollywood and in organized crime made clear that the incident was an attempt on his life that could be repeated. Perhaps they were taking credit for a genuine mishap. Perhaps it was a set-up. What is certain is that Sammy ran both scared and angry the rest of his life. And when he befriended Juanita, each was watched by Jewish mob figures such as Harry Cohen, Italian gangsters, and the Dallas current and former players. The problems would increase after Candy's trial.

In 1958, according to the story that was put out at the time, Sammy was fed up with being called an "Oreo"—black on the outside and white on the inside—by the black press. He was tired of being unable to have an intimate relationship with a woman without being scrutinized based on color. He was tired of friends like Juanita being unable to be seen with him without comments being made that would not be made if he was white or she was black. And Sammy was being threatened by organized criminals, though exactly which ones and the reasons why have not been determined. What is clear is that he was told his other eye would be removed if he did not stop pursuing white women.

Sammy was drinking and gambling heavily at the Silver Slipper on the Strip one night in 1958 when he asked dancer Loray White to marry him. According to friends of hers at the time, there would be a one-year contract, though he did not announce that fact when he had pictures taken that night. He had dated Loray, who was black, but there was never a spark. She was a convenience, nothing more. There were several problems with all this. Not only did he not love Loray, but he found that the black press did not quit attacking him. They understood the engagement was a sham. In addition, his father and uncle were upset. However, Sammy felt the need to complete the deal, having one of the men who worked for him arrange how Loray would be paid to endure what proved to be both abuse and neglect.

During this time, as well as when Sammy was involved with Kim Novak and Swedish actress May Britt, Candy felt the need to stand by him. She was willing to be seen and photographed with Sammy and his often taboo women. "I stood by Sammy when nobody else would during the period when I was on trial for my life and it was a 'no-no.'

"My lawyers knew it. They already cautioned me, this is not how you handle it. This is a frame. He's a nigger, is what they said. So be it. He said, 'You know they'll crucify you.'

"My remark to them was, 'They've crucified me.' What more could they do to me? They were sending me to prison. Turning against a friend in need is not going to make me go to prison.

"To me, none of us were big stars and all that stuff. We were entertainers. We were friends. We were show business. Sammy and I were quite damn close. He would come in and get a bongo and say, 'Can I play for you tonight?' and I'd say, 'Yeah.' But that meant the show would go to hell, but he was an entertainer down the street, and everybody was aware of Sammy Davis and the Will Mastin Trio, and Sammy came into his own. He played drums in his act, so he'd get up there with me and I'd dance. No big deal.

"And then, all of a sudden, he moves into a [new] category and we're not friends anymore and I don't pursue it. It would have been different if we had been lovers, but what I felt was the right thing to do. But that's one thing about Sammy and that's kind of sad."

Candy never did understand the racism of the times. She was incapable of such emotion and never looked to find it in anyone else. That was why she would do what others were too frightened to do, including standing up for Loray White when she married Sammy Davis Jr. She was black and thus okay. But everyone knew that, given a choice, Sammy Davis Jr. was interested in white women. Candy Barr standing by his side at his marriage went against all they felt was decent. As one Dallas lawyer commented, "Good ole white Texas gals just didn't consort with coloreds. The hooker-with-a-heart-of-gold wouldn't play in Dallas. That kind act really cost her."

Sammy also did not fully understand the mood in the country. So much of what was taking place in his life could be directly related to the outrageous egos of the studio moguls, organized criminals, and club managers that he was often out of tune with the nation. Yet hate filled the land. In 1956, for example, entertainer Nat "King" Cole was the victim of an attempted kidnapping in a nightclub. The racists who went after him, being stopped at the last minute by sheriff's deputies, felt that he was corrupting the nation with his black music. Anyone listening to the beautiful voice and stylings of a Cole song would place him in the same category as Frank Sinatra. But in the 1950s, the fact that Cole was black was enough for hate groups to see a conspiracy in his merely being alive.

Sammy faced a certain amount of bigotry even within his own home when he married May Britt. "All the white furniture she covered with plastic," said Candy. "She told him, 'Don't sit on the furniture,' 'cause he was black." May was nervous that somehow his skin color might rub off, a little like the black polish on shoe leather. "God, she tortured that boy."

Yet always Sammy and Candy rationalized what was happening, based on the person involved with an incident. It was a mature way of looking at the world, yet in the 1950s, it was naïve. The individual incidents of hate they encountered were part of a larger attitude in the land. And in Dallas, when stories of the indicted Candy Barr were reported, including mention of her friendship with Sammy Davis Jr., there was outrage. Just how much it cost her she would learn in February 1958, when she at last went on trial in Dallas before eleven men and one woman, the so-called jury of her peers.

TWENTY-THREE

Last Fling

"For the record, with all of my lovers in California with no disrespect to any of them, I've got to say this: Rod Steiger was the manliest man I had. He was such a fine lover. He really was."

—Juanita Phillips, about working in
Los Angeles prior to going to prison

The woman who had become notorious as Candy Barr went a little wild in Los Angeles while awaiting her trial. She had limited freedom, but she was enough in control of her life to begin thinking of herself and what she would enjoy. This included finally being able to relax and reveal her sense of humor.

Juanita had always been able to laugh. It was the only way she had survived the hell that had been her childhood. She delighted mocking the seriousness and expectations of the audience, much to the occasional horror of a club owner. For example, when she was headlining at Abe Weinstein's club, there was a night when the audience consisted mostly of young men connected with the Southern Methodist University homecoming celebration. Being in the club and watching the famous Candy Barr was seemingly a rite of passage. However, none knew what to expect except by reputation, and that was often a fantasy.

The film *Smart Aleck* had made the rounds of some of the fraternities, and while the action on Candy's part was relatively tame, the "memory" of those who had not seen it led to rumors that in the film she had sex with a goat, among other perversities. The young SMU men looked forward to encountering the most beautiful, most notorious, most sexually liberated woman the nation had ever seen. What they did not expect was a bag lady.

Candy deliberately reached the club very close to the time she was to go on, so Abe Weinstein could not see what was about to happen. She had blackened enough of her teeth to have a mouth that looked like that of an aged crone whose breath was foul and body decayed. She had done up her hair in an unattractive manner, and she wore an old trench coat that looked as though a thrift shop might reject it for being too ugly to meet its standards. And when she came on stage, she used the stoop-shouldered, shuffling walk of someone whose body had been ravaged by time, alcohol, and harsh living. When she slowly raised her head and smiled, the seeming gap of her teeth and her disreputable appearance made the young men gasp and Abe want to explode. Then, as the music started, Candy briefly turned her back, rubbing the black from her teeth, letting down her hair, and slipping off the trench coat to reveal her costume. When she turned around, the young men saw the exquisite body and brilliant dancing of a woman whose reality was greater than any legend. And Candy was laughing harder than any of them.

While still in Dallas, she was asked to appear in a Dallas theater's production of *Will Success Spoil Rock Hunter?* The George Axelrod play, which originally opened on Broadway on October 13, 1955, was a brutal satire of actress Marilyn Monroe, a woman Axelrod had come to despise when he wrote her movie *The Seven-Year Itch.* The original production starred actress Jayne Mansfield, a woman who had blonde hair, a tiny waist, a genius IQ, and a bustline that was one of the most admired superstructures of the 1950s. Her character, Rita Marlowe, was a woman whose "golden curls and fantastic behind have endeared her to moviegoers the world over." The play had all the characters in Marilyn's life, including an athlete in the mold of baseball great Joe DiMaggio, Marilyn's second husband. By the end of the play, the pretentious Rita, who moved from Hollywood to New York to prove her intelligence (as Marilyn did), is shown to be nothing more than a bimbo.

Candy was hired to play Rita Marlowe in the Dallas production. The man who ran the theater was a friend of Abe Weinstein. His show was running in the red and he hoped that the presence of Candy Barr would help him. Not only was she sick at the time, but the idea of a play didn't sit well with her. "I didn't want to do a stage play 'cause I don't care about acting. I'm a dancer, and that's it.

"I said I would try, and I would go to work, go to rehearsal, and go to the doctor.

"I didn't go in there to do an excellent job. I went in there to sell some tickets.

"We had a cute little play, and it was dumb to me, and dumb things never interest me. I knew my lines. Of course a couple of times I had to pull an antic or two. Like at the end where the guy would pick up the lady [Rita] and whisk her off her feet. I told the little guy, not tonight. I told him, I'll carry you off, so he didn't know what I was going to do. So when it came time to sweep me off my feet and carry me off in my negligee to the bedroom, I threw him over my shoulder. I thought it was funny as hell. To me, it was great. That's show biz. I didn't know how anybody was going to take it, but I got the people out of the red and that's what I went there to do."

At the Largo, the Los Angeles club where she developed some of her unique dance routines, Candy used humor when things went wrong, rather than planning practical jokes. "I was dancing and doing some kind of step where I bent over backwards and my hair touched the floor. I said I was going to do it one more time so I'd get it down right. Well that last time I fell off the stage, fell on a table in the audience. Usually I would have said, 'Well fuck my dog,' but I didn't. I said, 'Well, my goodness gracious!' 'Cause I'm in public, you know.

"Well, I was covered with candle tallow, and when I got back on stage, I knew I'd better kick those [high heeled] shoes off. So that led to my being introduced [on other nights] as the Barefoot Contessa." (The audience would have enjoyed the joking reference to Ava Gardner's starring role as a Spanish dancer in the 1954 film *The Barefoot Contessa*.)

Next up for Candy Barr was Las Vegas, where she worked at the Desert Spa, Silver Slipper, and El Rancho. All the great musical acts of the jazz age and big band era were there—Cab Calloway Revue, Red

Nichols, Lola Falona, and numerous others. Sally Blair entertained, as did her much more famous son, Lenny Bruce, the comedian.

The El Rancho management "sent me to California to a wardrobe person," Candy recalled. "I wish I could remember his name. He really deserves mention. They made me some nice attire to wear [form-fitting gowns, for example] and dress out. Get to my full potential. And with my music, I was beautiful there."

This was the era when Las Vegas choreographers created production numbers reminiscent of Busby Berkeley musicals. Berkeley was the motion picture choreographer who created song and dance numbers in which hundreds of beautiful chorus girls would dance on massive grand pianos or make elaborate entrances on spiral staircases that seemed to stretch to heaven. The Las Vegas productions were scaled down, dozens of elaborately costumed women replacing the hundreds in the films. All were relatively tall, with good figures, and powerfully built in order to support headdresses that could weigh seventy pounds.

Candy Barr was a star who did not have to appear in the production numbers, but she managed to occasionally get in trouble whether alone or with a cast of dozens. For example, there was the time at the El Rancho when she was working alone on the large stage. "They have those little holes [in the floor]; they can put microphones in them. Well, who gets in it but my heel. And I've got on my great white gown, you know, and here I am, my heel breaks. I fall on my butt, and I got up, and I took my shoe off, and I held it up, and I said, 'Well I can't do this one lame.' So I just took the other one off and never missed a turn. Everyone thought it was wonderful. I liked it so well, I wished I never had to wear shoes again."

Most times Candy chose to be a part of the production numbers because she felt a part of the entertainment world, a feeling shared by others. Even her friend Sammy Davis, along with Dean Martin, Frank Sinatra, Peter Lawford, and Joey Bishop, liked to put on a special performance after the normal lounge and stage acts were over. That performance, often at 3:00 or 4:00 in the morning, was solely for the chorus men and women, the dealers, and others who worked the strip and never had the time to see the shows. No matter how self-centered an entertainer, there was camaraderie in Las Vegas that Candy shared.

In Las Vegas, she auditioned drummers for her act, she recalled. "There was a newspaper article talking about my dancing in Dallas, saying I was losing the beat. This might not mean anything to some people, but it meant a lot to me because it's an insult, because it wasn't true." The music was in transition at the time. In the previous ten years, the interstate highway system had gone from a dream to a reality. Small communities with their own music traditions had become accessible to young travelers. New sounds and combinations of sounds, such as the rockabilly of Buddy Holly and Elvis Presley, were being introduced. Traditional musicians who had developed their skills in nightclubs and theaters were considered passé by younger, far less skilled musicians. And Juanita had encountered far too many drummers who failed to understand her work and her music. Since she was so carefully attuned to the musicians, their failings reflected in changes in her dancing that were not for the better, something the Dallas critic had noticed.

"It was a time when the music wasn't playing anymore, and the new sounds . . . the beat wasn't going anywhere. All kinds of beats, and all these young people with their bullshit." At the time, the "old pro" Candy Barr was in her early twenties. When she finally quit the business, it was because of the new sounds and the inability to get drummers who could work with her body as another instrument in a jazz piece.

"I take a lot of pride in how I feel about my music, and anyone who watched me perform will tell you I am on time [right with the beat] and I do everything on time. To me that was a total insult. They could have said anything else about me [and it] wouldn't have bothered me. [What he wrote] was a cheap shot. I really knew my business and that was my artwork. I was able to excel at the El Rancho [because of] the quality of my talent and that I was torrid."

The stages in Las Vegas were perfect for Candy Barr's dancing. At the Largo in Los Angeles, she had worked on what she called "a postage stamp stage" and concluded "I couldn't work in that small a space." But the people in Las Vegas offered to build her a stage if she would come out there to perform, so "I said yes. I auditioned the drummer and he had a sax player. He loved that horn. To a musician that instrument is his sweetheart. I could look at a musician play and I could tell you exactly how he would stroke me."

And so Juanita gained control of the world in which Candy Barr would be a star.

Those were heady days in Las Vegas, yet they could not erase the knowledge that jail was to be the future of Candy Barr. She would never touch alcohol or hard drugs, but when someone offered her marijuana, she saw no reason not to indulge. In her mind, it was different from smoking. It would get you high without doing harm, and while she would not buy it or sell it, when a close friend offered her a chance to get high between shows, she took it. The result was often quite humorous.

"One night I was at the El Rancho and there were two girls from the chorus line I hung out with when I wasn't with the guys, and we decided we'd sit in the back of a car and smoke a joint. We were living dangerously. So they've got this big bird number where they wanted me to come out in this big bird costume and do an African dance. So all the girls were standing on pedestals with those big-feathered headdresses, and I know they weighed a hundred pounds with all that stuff. We came out and I'm doing my job. I had to come down off the birdcage. A ladder from the birdcage I came down. It was very strenuous. I came down, did my job, and I had to go back up." As Candy started back up the ladder, however, one of the dancers leaned back, the weight of the headdress sent her off balance, and she fell over backward.

"Everybody else got so tickled, three or four girls fell over [laughing]. And I got so tickled, I missed my cue and couldn't get up there in time. By the time I got to the cage, the cage was coming down, I missed my cue, and it caught my tail feathers. And I'm up there laughing, and they're laughing, and I'm calling, 'This caught my tail feathers!' The audience went crazy. They loved it." The boss was not that pleased. "We were always getting into trouble," Candy said.

"One of the chorus girls, Carla was her name, she and I would once in a while get a little wild and we'd go out and smoke a reefer. Hide in the car and do it, like kids. So anyway, we had this big New York scene." They had cutouts of Manhattan buildings and perhaps two dozen men and women in the production. "I had this elegant, elegant gown, so when the boy dancers stood up to open the door, the chorus girls were parading in a big fashion show. Then they'd open those big New York street-scene doors. I'd walk out in this [costume with] a white hood over the top—it was beautiful. It had a gold lamé midriff. It was a gorgeous gown. The doors would open and I'd step out, and that would be the introduction to do my number.

"Well one night Carla got totally lost on stage. All the girls had gone off and she's out running around out there. She couldn't find her way so she came through the damned door and knocked Seth [the male holding the door for Candy] down, knocked me down, but we just went ahead and did the show anyway."

New people entered Candy Barr's life in Los Angeles and Las Vegas. Some were actors on the way up. Others, like Gary Crosby, were the off-spring of famous parents, a situation that, for some of them, created serious problems.

Bing Crosby was the most popular entertainer of the 1940s, the one singer Frank Sinatra both wanted to emulate and was most jealous of early in his career. Crosby was obsessed with his work when first on the rise, creating a home environment that caused the sons to later feel they needed to constantly prove their worth to their father. The three brothers tried to have a singing career of their own, but it was never very successful. And one of them, Gary, sank into heavy drinking for a while. It was Gary with whom Candy developed an intimate relationship, though one she found she had to leave because he drank too much.

"I had that with Troy and everybody, and I couldn't handle it. He had gone too far before he met me and he didn't know how to handle it.

"I really did like Gary. My heart hurt for him a lot, but more than that, I just liked him. He did act strange when he was drunk, but he was just a decent guy.

"That's another one of those possibilities. We could have had a good life, 'cause we understood one another. We didn't convict or condemn, but I just couldn't handle the drinking."

There was another problem as well. Gary "couldn't handle the girls hitting on me all the time. We had a scene in the club one night. The girls and guys hit on me equally as much."

The issue of lesbian and bisexual women being interested in an erotically charged entertainer was not something new. Candy Barr's sensual appeal was the same whether it was in a heterosexual or homosexual setting.
She had no interest in the women, did not try to understand her appeal,
but accepted the reality of what took place. Gary, on the other hand, had
trouble, though perhaps that was partly because of Betty Grable, a friend of
his mother, Dixie Crosby.

Betty Grable, an actress twenty years older than Candy, had become famous as one of the sweater-girl pin-ups popular with American servicemen during World War II. Only after her death in 1973 did many of her
Hollywood acquaintances mention that she was attracted to good-looking
women.

Candy knew none of this until one night when Betty Grable came
into a club where she was performing with the Ritz Brothers, who were
extremely popular in the 1950s. "We were sittin' at the table. I only went
down because the Ritz Brothers were at the table. I was not impressed by
Hollywood, but they were Gary's friends. We were sittin' at the table and I
feel this hand on my dress and I didn't know what to do. I didn't want to
embarrass anybody. I didn't know at that time the Hollywood scene was
girls, boys. I really wasn't broken in to all of that.

"Then we went to Gary's for a get together, and she got up on the
chair in front of my face, and I told Joe De Carlo, 'I can only handle so
much of this with dignity. If you don't take this lady off my hands, I'm going to hurt her. It's just a matter of time. I can't take any more of this.' "
Candy didn't like the insinuation that she would have sex with a woman,
and she also thought it showed disrespect to Gary.

The actress had been drinking heavily, but as Candy said, "It didn't
make any difference. She knew what she was doing. She used being drunk
to do it. Maybe I brought out stuff that nobody else brought out. And
Gary got upset. That's the last time I was ever with Gary."

The one intimate relationship Candy has never forgotten is the one
she enjoyed with actor Rod Steiger around the time he was first married
to actress Claire Bloom. "For the record, with all of my lovers in California, with no disrespect to any of them, I've got to say this: Rod Steiger was
the manliest man I had. Oh, he was such a fine lover. He really was.

"I have to tell you this because it has to be known. He had his sickness [Steiger suffered from clinical depression] and that took away a lot of his stamina. . . . I don't know how he was with anybody else, but he got my attention, and he kept my attention all these many years. I will never forget, 'cause it's not easy to make me feel to a place of expansion. For whatever he did, it was great, and if he hadn't been married, I have a feeling we just would have hung in there. We liked each other.

"Isn't that amazing? I know you know when it's right. They know when it's right. But Hollywood and commitments and movie stars . . . "

TWENTY-FOUR

Mickey, Mexico, and What Passes for Love

"I called myself a self-made multiple schizophrenic. I didn't know who I was going to be that day."

—Juanita Phillips, discussing the time of the
Capture and fleeing for her life

The money in Los Angeles was excellent—$2,000 a week at the Largo, which was ten times what someone who considered himself successful would make. Candy Barr drove a Cadillac and moved into the Garden of Allah apartments on Sunset Strip, where the famous had long enjoyed homes. Sammy Davis Jr. lived there, and it was near where Gary Crosby and rising young actor Vince Edwards lived. Years earlier she might have seen John Barrymore, Marlene Dietrich, or W. C. Fields. It was a location of status that also had a tolerance for show business people regardless of their color or the aspect of the business in which they were employed.

In the midst of all this, Candy became pregnant. The child was as desired as Troylene, but the pregnancy was not normal. It was a tubal (ectopic) pregnancy. There was no way the fetus could come anywhere near to term, and Candy's health and even her life were in danger. She was immediately placed in Cedars of Lebanon Hospital for an abortion. The procedure was unavoidable. There was no choice in the matter.

Abe Weinstein, Joe De Carlo, and other promoters of Candy's career tried to spread the myth that she had been briefly hospitalized for hepatitis. When the truth came out, she suddenly found herself without friends. Even a legal abortion for critical medical reasons when there was no way to save the baby's life was shocking at the time. Candy's body seemed to have joined the conspiracy against her.

It was in this time of glamorous success and intense loneliness that mobster Mickey Cohen made his appearance. There are any number of stories about how this occurred, including the one he told about being approached by Joe De Carlo, who wanted to find a way to keep Candy from going to jail. He thought that Mickey Cohen might have enough influence to either ensure that the appeal would go favorably or find a lawyer who might have more clout. The trial lawyers apparently had made some mistakes that affected the appeal. Reviewing the trial, the Texas Court of Criminal Appeals found that when the marijuana cigarette and bottle containing marijuana were offered by the prosecution as exhibits and were admitted as evidence, the defense attorneys had not objected that such evidence was unlawfully obtained, so they had waived any objections as to the fruits of the search at Candy's apartment.

According to Cohen, when he heard De Carlo's account of Candy's being railroaded through the legal system, he agreed to help. He had seen her dance at the Largo two or three times and that also influenced his feelings. When she got out of the hospital, he took her to a restaurant called Puccini's, which was partially owned by Frank Sinatra and Peter Lawford. In Cohen's mind, he and Candy were mad about each other and began living together immediately. In fact, Candy did not have such strong feelings.

"Mickey Cohen to me was no stranger," said Candy. "And I was working at the Largo Club—that's when I had the ruptured tubal pregnancy and I went into the hospital. I was fighting my case still—this was in 1959 evidently. I don't remember Christmas with him—the first part of the year it must have been—and while I was in the hospital, Joe [De Carlo] and I had an awful lot of problems 'cause I wouldn't stand in line, and he knew I was going to prison, and he didn't want to get shortchanged. He'd become acquainted with Mickey and he mentioned to me he knew some people I knew. He was acquainted with Mickey because he went to work for Mickey, he quit me."

As Candy recalled, "Mickey sent me this glass, this champagne glass with an orchid and a note in it that said, 'Don't worry little girl. You have friends. Mickey Cohen.' So when I got out, Joe told me about Mickey and I should go out when I got well enough and have dinner.

Joe De Carlo indicated that Cohen could help her, but Candy didn't ask how or what Cohen did. She only knew that Joe said "organized crime and he was powerful. I knew what powerful meant. I had powerful gangsters in my area but they weren't big time. But later on when I found out who he was in the newspaper, it kind of backed me up a whole lot. I spoke to his friends about it and all this stuff, and I wondered what I was getting into.

"Nobody really knows except me and I know it. My daddy always said it was in their eyes. . . . No matter what they said about not having an involvement, they ended up having an involvement. It just happens."

Cohen was "exceptionally bacteria conscious," Candy recalled. "Evidently he had abstained from being with a woman since his last relationship. So they said you don't have anything to be concerned with anything.

"I went into it because these people worked for him, 'cause I figured Joe's trying to get me in bed with him to make a big thing and get in with the mob after I learned who he was.

"So I went out and had dinner a couple of times. And we talked a couple of times, and he offered me some money and I told him, 'I don't want your money,' 'cause I knew what that money meant to me. It meant he wanted to buy my body. Whether he was or not, that's how I saw it and this caught his attention. He really became impressed with me.

"'Cause if I knew who he was or who his bosses was, I might have been different. Most likely I wouldn't have. But anyway, that's what got his attention. And he started to become interested in me in a different situation. Like they said after our war's over, he said, 'One thing I've got to say about you, you're a moxie little chick.'

"So I became Mickey Cohen's girlfriend, and it caused me a lot of problems. I was livin' with a guy at the time. And I liked him quite a lot. In fact, I was content with him. We danced. He played music and we danced. I needed a good dance partner, see, 'cause I had to have that. He used to be in a group. We had a good relationship."

The boyfriend, Buddy, was originally from Philadelphia, the son of a Polish American family. He fell deeply in love with Candy and wanted to take her home to meet his family. She thought about doing just that. She realized that this was becoming serious and she was enjoying the growing intimacy. However, he was straight, and Mickey Cohen had his own agenda for anyone who got in the way of whatever he desired.

"It got to the point where Mickey wanted him out of my life, and he forced the issue. It was either/or, so I had to make a decision right then. And I knew that I had to give Mickey the attention he wanted so Buddy wouldn't get hurt. Wasn't anything the matter. I had to compromise at the moment 'cause I knew that he would, and that's how my capture began.

"When I say 'capture,' I mean my inner spirit, my energy, my time. That big, black car right up there at night would go to the drugstore. Sometime I spent some time with him, sometime I wouldn't. I had family there. My little brother and sister were going to school part of the time that I knew him there. I was sending them to school—Travis and Kathy— and I had a nice little life going I thought, even though I knew I was going to prison. I was takin' every second. Then this happens."

Cohen and his attorney, famed criminal defense lawyer Melvin Belli, became backers on her bond with Dallas attorney E. Colley Sullivan. Sullivan's name on the bond was being withdrawn in April 1959, at the same time that Candy was working at the Largo. Then, on April 29, sheriff's deputies H. Fife and E. Gabriel went to the Largo, spending two hours watching Candy finish her last show before arresting her. Cohen was present and immediately began making calls. As he raced to see both Candy and the reporters at the Los Angeles County jail, he announced, "This shows what an injustice they've done to this girl. They've pulled her bond right from under her."

Candy knew very little. She told the press, "The bail bond was repealed. That's all I know. I shouldn't be here anyway because I'm not guilty of anything."

When Cohen told the press, "I'm going to make her my wife," Candy would not comment.

Candy spent eight hours in jail. From then on she was free while appeals on her behalf were being made to ever higher courts.

Although she had no idea whether Cohen loved her, he would later write in his autobiography that he did. She later tended to agree with that assessment. "I feel like he did, and sometimes it makes me feel bad. Let me tell you, you'll never hear me say in my life that I regret many things at all. If I do, it's a regret somewhere along the line of one of my extreme loved ones, 'cause I don't." But Candy considered herself "captured" once again, this time to the point of constant surveillance.

Despite Cohen's obsession and violence, "He was a very clean person," Juanita recalled. "When he bathed, it was over an hour. Then he would come out and . . . talcum himself. And he used lavender cologne." He'd take the clothes that had just come back from the cleaners, and "he'd lay them out on the bed, and he'd take this lavender and sprinkle it throughout the room so it float down [on] his clothes. He was extremely immaculate."

Mickey had to completely possess Candy. She was constantly watched. Her friends were threatened to make them stay away from her. She had her work. She ostensibly had her life. But Mickey overwhelmed her. "All my life I've been able to handle a lot except when they start persecuting other people. [That's when] I really become really emphatic. I don't become angry. I just feel responsible."

As for Mickey, "I didn't really feel. You see, once I realized what the situation had to be, I didn't have any feeling for him."

Candy began traveling with Cohen, who took her to Philadelphia to see newspaper columnist Drew Pearson. In the 1950s, syndicated columnists such as Pearson held enormous power in American politics. Television was in its infancy; radio commentators such as Walter Winchell (who also wrote for newspapers) and columnists could sway the public as well as government officials. Most cities had morning and afternoon papers, each with several regularly updated editions. Larger cities had three or more newspapers vying for attention. Someone like Pearson could reach millions of people every day in large and small cities throughout the nation.

Pearson was what was known as a muckraker. He liked to write about scandals and injustices. Cohen felt that with Pearson behind Candy Barr, she might be able to avoid jail. The problem was that while Pearson was sympathetic and the injustice was clear, she was a woman whose plight would not tug at the heartstrings of the average American. Ultimately she was seen as a burlesque dancer with an unsavory past rather than a scared, hurting, naïve kid whom men had tried to victimize her entire life.

Candy tried to create one bright spot out of the Philadelphia trip. She decided to sneak a call to Buddy's family. Mickey "had my lines listened to. It's this kind of thing. Then he got upset 'cause I called Buddy, but Buddy was a dear part of my life and I wasn't concerned. I knew I could call my friend and be sure he was alive." But she felt that part of her life was chopped off. "You hear no more, you talk no more.

"It's painful. If it's just a friend, it's painful. But your sweetheart at the time . . . "

Cohen had an apartment in the Brentwood section of Los Angeles, and Candy maintained an apartment on Switzer. She was not living with him, nor was she being kept. He was generous, though, giving her a couple of pieces of jewelry that seemed valuable, but she never had them appraised or insured. The gifts were nice, but she was not in the relationship for a reward.

The first hint of the problems she was going to have came when there was a break-in at her apartment. Candy had no idea who might have broken in. It might have been someone sent by Mickey Cohen, assuming he wanted to be known as being generous without it costing him too much to do it. Or, she thought, it might have been Joe De Carlo, either acting on behalf of Mickey or acting for someone else in the mob. Or it might have been members of the mob trying to send a message to Mickey. Whatever the case, the only items stolen were items either given to her by Mickey, such as the jewelry, or items that people would presume were gifts, such as a fur coat.

As the years have passed and more information concerning this time is available, it seems clear that the thefts were a warning to Candy, a warning too subtle to be understood. Mickey Cohen was working for men who wanted him to lead a lower profile life. The move of the mob into Las Vegas brought a legitimacy they had long lacked. Cohen was important for operations both in Los Angeles and Las Vegas. He was an independent operator, but he always had the sense to follow what the mob bosses currently in power desired. So long as he was respectful of their wishes, he was allowed to maintain his independent rackets, including extortion.

According to Fred Otash, "If I had to pick a man whose actions most affected the men and women who ultimately would find their lives shattered as they were on their way up or down from the pinnacle of power and success, I would probably say Mickey Cohen." Cohen had long been a target of the LAPD, and Otash had worked with an electronics expert to "unofficially" wire microphones into the home Cohen built in the early 1950s. He would later work against Cohen and some of his men after he retired from the police department to work as a private investigator.

"There had been any number of attempts to kill Mickey Cohen over the years," Otash said. "His home was bombed twice, and there were several attempts to shoot him. Eventually he remodeled his home for security, keeping weapons strategically placed near all points of entry. There were floodlights on the grounds, multiple alarm systems, and a number of bodyguards including John Stompanato who I investigated."

Stompanato, originally from Chicago, moved to the West Coast and married Helen Gilbert, a wealthy widow, in order to bankroll what became a string of affairs with popular stars of the day—Kathryn Grayson, Ann Miller, Ava Gardner, and others. "Some he dated," Otash related. "Some he married after divorcing Gilbert. But always he caused them trouble, either physically or financially. His playground was the Sunset Strip, and I periodically had to investigate Johnny's activities when they spilled over into the city while I was still a cop. I knew he had become Cohen's boy, so I let Mickey know when I had a problem and he would give Stompanato a wrist slap, which was better than nothing. However, I personally hated the guy because he always liked to bully the weak."

Stompanato, working for Mickey Cohen before he met Juanita, had a carefully orchestrated affair with Lana Turner. He was working for Cohen as a bouncer, though others thought he was serving as bodyguard. The idea was to get the actress in a compromising position, then blackmail her as he had done others. There were morals clauses in studio contracts, and any scandal could damage a career. The problem with Stompanato was that he was too violent, and when Lana's daughter, Cheryl Crane, heard Lana fighting with the gangster, she grabbed a knife. Stompanato was stabbed to death in the ensuing struggle, generating headlines.

The general public did not know about Cohen's connection with Stompanato, but the mob did. Since Cohen had worked for Ben Siegel and was connected with everyone from Meyer Lansky to Sam Giancana of Chicago, being lowkey was important. The blackmail operation had a high risk of going public, and Cohen never stopped.

Suddenly, after meeting Juanita, Cohen was faced with another high-profile woman. Whether he was in love with Candy Barr or was considering extortion in her time of greatest notoriety is unknown. What Candy did know was what Mickey told her years after the fact, when she was out of jail and he had gotten out of prison after being convicted of tax evasion. He explained that someone, to whom he referred only as "the big man," had "called him in on the carpet and told him that he had to quit seeing me. That I was . . . they said, 'She's too bad.'

"Mickey says, 'Bad? Jesus, man, we kill people and you say she's bad.'

"And they said quit seeing her; she's too bad. And he wouldn't do it."

This was not the romance of the century. Juanita did not want to have the involvement with Mickey that he insisted on. The mob leaders who were angry with Mickey for his involvement with Candy Barr did not understand that she was not encouraging the attention.

Part of the concern had to do with what happened to Bugsy Siegel. He was murdered because of the $650,000 of mob money that was either removed from the sums allocated for the Flamingo Hotel or misspent. He had been given the opportunity to quietly repay Meyer Lansky and the other backers. He had been given a chance to leave his girlfriend, Virginia Hill, the presumed cause of his financial indiscretions. But Bugsy could not stay away from a woman whose moral character was suspect at best. He lost his life because he sold his soul for a woman instead of remaining loyal to the mob, and it was feared that Cohen had come to look upon Candy Barr the way Siegel had looked at Hill. Before matters went too far, Candy would have to die.

Juanita knew none of this at the time. She just knew that she did not want to continue the relationship. "Nothing I did would make him quit seeing me," she said. "I wanted him to stop seeing me because I was getting a different kind of silent harassment, such as drugs put in my dressing room at the club, but for the grace of God I was one up on all of them. And I knew Joe [De Carlo] was part of it. I knew that." She also suspected Beverly Hills, a dancer who was another of Mickey Cohen's girlfriends.

Candy believed that Beverly Hills was being set up to replace her in the clubs. She believed that Joe was going to be rewarded by being given the management of the dancer as she was moved into the high-paying jobs that were increasingly being given to Candy Barr. De Carlo, now dead, cannot speak for himself. As for Beverly Hills, it is doubtful that she was part of a plot. However, she was as ambitious as all the dancers, and Candy resented her. "I threatened her two or three times," Candy remembered. "Somebody always interceded."

Candy was constantly blamed for the newspaper publicity Mickey Cohen was causing. As she explained, "I didn't make 'em [headlines in newspapers]. He made 'em. I wake up one morning and there's a newspaper, and my friend's knocking on my door. The paper said, 'Mickey Cohen to wed Candy Barr,' or something like that. And this hadn't been discussed with me. You see, I really got upset and I made a spectacle of myself, you know, naturally, which is a no-no.

"I went looney tunes after that happened."

This was not the first time Mickey had seen Candy riled. She once slapped him "because he threatened the little colored girl that worked for me—Gloria—that he would put her eyes out if he found out that she was bringing me drugs, because Joe De Carlo had told him that Gloria was bringing me drugs, which was a lie! And she came to me scared to death. I was very upset.

"Now I'll jump on anybody or harassment of any innocent human being and that's just how it is with me. So what I did happened to come into his view. That's why he got hit in the mouth." She understood that most people thought it was because she was jealous over another woman. But "I just wanted to go about my life until it was run out, until I had to go to prison. That's why he got his mouth busted."

The hostility toward Cohen may have helped him feel comfortable with what happened next. Candy Barr was to be taken out of the country. That much he knew. Her appeal was about to be denied and her removal from the country would keep her from going to jail. What is unknown is whether Cohen was aware there was supposed to be no return trip. Candy Barr was to be either isolated or killed, her proposed fate varying with whoever is telling the story.

Mickey Cohen's official version is a seemingly loving one. "One of my right hands, Roger Leonard, was married to a Mexican girl named Blanca. Blanca's father was with the Federalistas in Mexico, and he was a hell of a guy. So Roger Leonard made arrangements through his father-in-law that Candy would be well taken care of down there. We got her a very beautiful apartment in a brand-new building in Mexico City. With her little girl there, they had it real nice."

There was some truth to what Cohen said. There was a nice apartment in which Candy and her daughter would live for a while, but it wasn't the destination to which they were originally taken. It was a place Candy apparently found on her own.

There was a man named Bobby (not his real name) whose girlfriend, Betty (not her real name), was to drive Candy and Troylene south of the border. Candy would be disguised for the trip, and Mickey would give her money to make certain she could travel without problems. Betty knew that Candy and Troylene would not be returning, but it is unknown whether any of them knew she might be murdered.

What research can be done this long after the fact reveals only one outcome for certain. Candy Barr was not to return to the United States. Her taking her daughter may have been to keep her trust, to ensure the child would stay with her mother, or to eliminate both mother and child, a less likely scenario. Organized crime has never been so honorable as television and movies like to romanticize. However, in the 1950s, children who were too young to act as witnesses were not harmed. Troylene was an innocent of no danger to anyone. It must be assumed that if Candy was to be murdered, someone else would care for the child.

There were two possibilities for Candy Barr. One was a new life in Cuba, an island nation ninety miles off the coast of Florida, then dominated by organized crime. Meyer Lansky had the greatest political and economic clout in Cuba, controlling the casino operations almost exclusively. Men such as Sam Giancana, Carlos Marcello, and others also had interests there. Ironically, Jack Ruby was occasionally involved with Marcello's Cuban interests, employing one of Marcello's "lieutenants" as well as the lieutenant's nephew. The latter, who worked briefly in the clubs as little more than a "go-for," was a youth named Lee Harvey Oswald.

Some of the men who controlled the Havana casinos and nightlife would have been in a position to use Candy any way that was desired. They were capable of murder of course. That was a normal part of doing business. They were also capable of forcing her to work in the clubs or return to prostitution. With her daughter there, she would be compliant. Thus it is quite possible that she was to begin a new life as a dancer in Havana, starring where the law could not touch her.

The other possibility is that Candy was to be murdered, a decision that might have been made by people in Dallas working through Cohen or some other connection. The person who made the connection, such as Cohen, might not have known that was the plan. Whatever the case, Candy's trip was intended to be one way. Only the intended final destination—Cuba or an unmarked grave—is unknown.

First came the disguise. Candy was too well known to risk going as she normally looked. Among other changes, she had her hair dyed brown. "I'm the one that suggested Jackie Sahakian," Candy said of the hairdresser selected to do the work. "He'd lived down the street from me, and we'd become acquainted during this period. I knew he was a beautician, and he's the one I suggested doing it because he'd be the most trustworthy. So Jack came up and dyed my hair, and he really wasn't sure what was happening. He just knew they were taking me out of the country because my appeal had been turned down."

Actually the official news of the judicial turndown had not been reported. The mob was able to learn what had taken place three or four days before the information was released to the newspapers.

"They sent me to Mexico. They gave me some fake papers. They dressed me up as a pregnant lady. It struck me funny.

"They wouldn't let me take a weapon. I couldn't take a knife or gun or anything. They wouldn't let me go in my old car. And all these things struck me odd because they're putting us out on a highway that was really desolate in those days—two lanes and whatever across a rugged country in Mexico City.

"We were supposed to meet a man in Guadalajara, and that was a long damn drive in an old Cadillac car, so that struck me funny," by which Candy meant she thought it was odd.

"So we headed out, and I paid attention because I wanted to know what was going on. I paid attention at the border. When I figured once they started searching us they'd never let us through, 'cause I knew what they did at the border. I'd heard stories and I'd never been over there, but I knew." But a bribe took care of the border official.

As Betty drove along, however, Candy became aware of another possible danger. "Being raised around criminals like I had been, and always running and escaping and getting captived, I was very aware. I saw this black car all the time at a distance. It was like a little French car with two people in it all the time. And I became very concerned. And so, when we got to Guadalajara, I told her that."

Candy had been told that they needed to pick up a man in Guadalajara, but she did not trust what would happen if she went into the motel room when they stopped. She knew they had been followed, and she assumed that everyone was involved with whatever fate was meant to await her. She had been overwhelmed, tied up, and raped in too many hotel rooms to not have a touch of paranoia about them. Moreover, they had been followed by two men in a car over such a long distance that the men could not have any concerns other than her. There was no way she was going to get out of Betty's car.

The woman was surprised. The Cadillac convertible's cloth top had become damaged and ripped in places. It was raining hard, and water was leaking inside. Candy had to keep Troylene dry as best she could, and she was miserable from the weather. But she was not going to get herself in a position where whatever might happen would have no witnesses.

"I told her, you go get that man because I'm not going to that room. And he came down, and got in the car, and we left. In that kind of weather, in that car, in that condition."

Candy began analyzing all that had been taking place. Mickey had given her money. But she had not been given an opportunity to see a newspaper while she was traveling. She was unaware of current events, unaware of anything else that might be taking place. She knew that Mickey was in some way involved with organized crime and that there could reach a point where, no matter what your personal feelings, what the mob wanted would determine what happened to you.

"So, we got into Mexico City and he's had this place [ready for us]. I don't know if it was a hotel or motel. They already had the rooms."

The building was small, just two stories, but that was typical of motel construction in those days, whether luxury or low cost. The massive hotels and high-rise motels were relatively rare in the late 1950s.

The man who had accompanied them left, saying he would return. Candy, Troylene, and Betty went inside to the room. "And she got on the telephone, and she's calling the airport to get her trip back," Candy recalled. Betty made a reservation for herself. Then she called a used car lot to arrange to sell the Cadillac.

"And I said, 'You're not going to stay here a couple of days and help me get situated?'"

"She says, 'No! We got to get back today.'"

"I said, 'How come?'"

"And she said, 'Well, I just have to get back today.'"

"I said, 'What are you selling the car for?' I could have used the car, you know.

"And she said, 'I have to.'

"And all of a sudden I just said to myself, I want to know what's happening.

"What they didn't know is I had an old knife that when it opened up, it was this long [several inches], but when it was closed up, it was much shorter. My step-grandfather had given [it to] me when I had run away before so I'd have something in my boot."

Candy had no idea what Betty was thinking, as she made no effort to hide that she was selling the car. Candy suspected that Betty knew everything except what was ultimately planned for her. "So I walked over to her and I said, 'What's going on? What is all this?'

"And she said, 'I can't tell you.'

"That's all she had to tell me. If she had just said, 'I don't need to guess anything, I just need to get back and give them your reason,' but it's no fair. So I just came around with my handy dandy little weapon and my

217

normal way of doing things and put it at her throat. I said, 'Well, it's like this. I'm confused about it.' And I did say I'm very confused. And I was very tired, too.

"Well, for me, I would rather go on to prison than to live any kind of life like that going outside of the country.

"So she said, 'I can't tell you now. You know what would happen if I tell you.'

"And I said, 'Well, it's just like this. You know what's gonna happen to me, and if you didn't, it was gonna happen to you anyway.' I would have cut her throat, because I knew I had to leave, and if she didn't tell me and let me leave, then I knew I would have to do that very thing. And God knows I would do that very thing.

"See, I was feeling the pressure of captive too strong and I had to escape. I've never driven to that point till it's possible to do anything else, and just by the grace of God. He takes care of it.

"She said, 'Well, you're supposed to not come back from there.' That's all she said.

"I said, 'Oh, you know. Okay, you know, I'm gonna tell you what I'm gonna do. I'm gonna leave and you fall asleep. You didn't have any idea that I was gonna leave. And I'm gone. Otherwise, they'll hurt you. Now if they hurt you, it's because you didn't handle it right.' "

Candy grabbed Troylene and left. She knew she did not dare try to return to the United States immediately. She had no idea where the greatest danger might exist. She later realized that Mickey was unaware that whoever had arranged for her disappearance had no idea where she was. They acted as though they had someone observing her every move, so Cohen believed that Candy was dancing and spending money. They wanted him to feel she was betraying his love, trust, and assistance when she was actually on the lam from everyone.

Would Cohen have wanted her killed? There was a theory that Cohen had given her a large sum of money so she could live well until he could join her in exile, perhaps marrying her. The problem with this idea was that Cohen did not seem interested in marrying anyone right then, especially Candy. He was closer to the stripper who danced under the name Beverly Hills.

Whatever the future might have held, the present meant her taking a suite in a high-rise Mexican apartment house, where she hired a Mexican woman to help her with cooking, cleaning, and Troylene. This was a time when the dollar was worth so much more than the Mexican peso that retirees on budgets at or below the poverty line would often get a home in Mexico. Given the favorable exchange rate, a couple could live well in Mexico, eating out frequently and having paid help. Candy's several thousand dollars from Mickey was more than enough to keep her comfortable with Troylene.

Although she did not know it, there was a search taking place for Candy, presumably from members of organized crime working in Mexico. She was living in Mexico City, though she paid no attention to the section of the city or what was around her. "I was quite sick. Most of the time [the Mexican woman she hired] would take the baby to the park and stuff like that. I started trying to learn to smoke, and I'd be sick."

The cigarette smoking came from seeing too many movies. "You know that's what I'd seen. When you're locked up in a room somewhere, everybody always smokes a cigarette." She stopped quickly, though. The smoking alone made her feel sick, but she also was unwell. With illness racking her body, the combination caused her to quit almost immediately.

Candy called Jack Sahakian—the hairdresser who had dyed her hair to disguise her appearance—and told him that she was going to try to get away from Mexico City. She never did learn how they found her. "They approached me in the middle of the night at a drugstore and someone walked up and said, 'Aren't you Candy Barr?'

"I said, 'Who?' I said, 'I don't know. I've been asked that many times.' See, I had brown hair and I was in pregnant paraphernalia. Whenever I went out, I went out in pregnant paraphernalia, brown hair, like a little pregnant Mexican girl with green eyes. But it was the middle of the night. And then I knew. I knew that they had found me, so evidently they had had a screen around the city, watching to see when I would surface, and knowing I would have to surface just like I went under."

The men did not try to kidnap Candy or go back to her apartment. However, they knew the area where she was living.

Cohen later claimed that he was always aware where Candy was living. He said that he received telephone calls from the Mexican father-in-law of his assistant Roger Leonard, complaining that Candy was going out to places to dance. She was so famous that she was recognized and announced in the clubs. She was also, according to Cohen, spending money "like a drunken sailor."

"So I'd call her and say, 'Hey, Candy, what's the matter with you? Lookit, you're not on a vacation, you're a lamster. You've got people down there in your corner, they look at things in a broader fashion than you do here. But for Christ sakes, they can't carry ya under these kind of conditions."

According to Cohen, they had a fight on the telephone, during which she announced that Jack Sahakian was going to come down to see here. She said she wanted to marry him. "And here I'm being called to task by the organization people back East about going with her. They thought I knew nothing about Candy Barr. I was always kind of like a fair-haired, clean-cut guy, clean habits and all that. And they made a big stink about it."

Candy did call Jack Sahakian, and they met in Tijuana, Mexico. The trip was fast and frantic. She was so terrified that she blocked all memory of whether they drove, flew, or found some other way. "I have no idea how I arrived in Tijuana. I have never been able to remember, and I've been try-ing to remember twenty years. I don't know what transpired. I keep trying to see myself doing this or this or this to this, but knowing I wouldn't know how to do that or this or this in a strange place. I don't know how. . . . I really don't know how I got there.

"The first thing I can remember in Mexico with Jack is being at the zoo. This is the first thing I can remember. Not him picking me up or finding me . . . or nothing. But being at the zoo, walking around with the animals and the baby, and us walking around, and me in brown hair. That's the first thing I remember after leaving Mexico and being with Jack. Evi-dently every time I had to make an escape, I went into blackouts."

Jack and Candy drove to a motel outside Los Angeles, from which she called Mickey Cohen. "I said, 'Guess who's back?' Warfare to me is warfare. If you escape you should be free.

"And he said, 'Get over here right now. I want to talk to you.'

"And I said, 'Oh, no, I'm not going to come anywhere close to any of you all. I'm going to get myself a job and go to work until I have to go.' And that's when they put the ban on me. I couldn't work anywhere."

There was another problem more pressing than the issue of work. Candy and Jack flew to Las Vegas, where Candy, though blacklisted by the mob and in trouble with the law, still had a chance to return to the work she loved. At the same time, she was told that her bond had been forfeited and she was considered a fugitive from justice. Uncertain what to do, she decided to marry Jack Sahakian and let him handle her personal affairs.

Candy may have been blacklisted by the mob and in trouble with the law, but one man, Beldon Katleman, the owner of the El Rancho Vegas, was intrigued by her potential. He ran what he claimed was the only hotel and casino "without partners." This meant that there was no organized crime involvement in his casino, no hidden interests or skimmings being passed on to others. Eventually it meant that the El Rancho would be mysteriously destroyed in a fire, but for the moment what mattered was that no one could object when he offered Candy a job. He paid her $5,000 per week.

The job was brief and pressured. Famed California lawyer Melvin Belli, who later would be involved with the defense of Jack Ruby after the shooting of Lee Harvey Oswald, had sent a telegram to Sheriff Bill Decker explaining that he and Mickey Cohen were rescinding their guarantee of the $15,000 bond posted by Dallas attorney E. Colley Sullivan. Sullivan had allegedly backed out after Candy went to Mexico. The exact nature of the finances has always been confusing. Apparently there was a three-way support involving Sullivan, Belli, and Cohen. When one of the three dropped out, neither of the other two would step in with the extra money or property needed to secure the bond.

Another story, probably more accurate, has the problem resulting from Belli's reaction to a feud between Candy and his client Mickey Cohen. On November 21, 1959, Candy angrily spoke of Cohen to the press, saying, "He bugs me. I never want to see him again."

The outburst should not have been a surprise. Cohen was an unfaithful lover at best. He had misled Juanita concerning where she and Troylene were being taken and toward what end. There was a chance that their relationship was going to get her killed. Enough was enough.

"I don't want any part of her," Cohen responded. "I still say the girl is an ungrateful person and does not know the meaning of appreciation."

Cohen's financial backing for Candy was dropped, though he said it was not his doing. "I didn't withdraw the bail. It was my lawyer, Melvin Belli," Cohen related to reporters. "Belli got excited yesterday when she said she wanted no part of me." He added that the attorney "told me he didn't see the sense of helping her if I didn't have her support and he withdrew the bail himself." Then, after disagreeing with his attorney, he stated, "But I won't back down on her now."

Attorney E. Colley Sullivan, who had acted as Candy's bondsman in Dallas, was through. "This thing has given me enough trouble already. I won't go back on that bond under any circumstance."

Sheriff Decker was fed up. He began extradition proceedings against Candy and said that he would not allow her to continue on bond unless $15,000 in cash was posted.

As the drama continued unfolding in Dallas and Las Vegas, Las Vegas businessman Max Chasen posted a $5,000 bond necessary for Candy to be released from jail in Las Vegas, where she had been placed after the bond was withdrawn. It was obvious that she was ready to resolve matters and would not flee the state, which was the reason her bond in Las Vegas was relatively low.

Sheriff W. E. Leypoldt, however, said, "I don't think she has a good moral effect on the town." It was clear that Dallas Governor Price Daniel would ask the governor of Nevada to return her.

On November 23, a spokesperson for the El Rancho announced that both Candy and the seminude chorus girls who danced in the shows had a "detrimental effect" on the morals of the city. It didn't seem to matter that the city was built, in part, on money from murderers, bootleggers, extortionists, and loan sharks from around the country. The hypocrisy was obvious, though there was an additional pressure on the El Rancho. The Clark County Commission was threatening to take away its gaming and liquor licenses because of the "objectionable" floor show. It was easier to replace Candy Barr with longtime singer Nelson Eddy, famous for his movie musicals.

On November 24, Juanita was granted a divorce from Troy Phillips in District Judge John Mead's court, based on "cruelty" and "desertion." She did not fight the causes listed, because she had shot Phillips and she had fled Dallas. Their turbulent marriage had lasted six years almost to the day, Troylene being the one good result.

Two and a half hours after the divorce was final, Juanita married Jack Sahakian. He was twenty-eight years old, one to three years older than his bride, depending on which of the different birthdates she claimed. They had tried to get a minister to marry them, because Juanita wanted a religious ceremony. The attempt ended after two ministers refused, fearing adverse publicity. Instead the couple was forced to turn to a justice of the peace.

Sahakian met with reporters to explain that his wife was retiring from stripping. He said she had planned to give up that business several weeks earlier but needed the money to help her daughter, younger brother, father, who was quite ill at the time, and her stepmother. "I tried to help her spiritually," Sahakian commented. "I've dedicated myself to her. Believe me, this girl has been misled and misguided, morally and mentally, ever since she was fourteen years old. I only hope someone—perhaps the authorities in Texas—will step forward and do something to help her. Anyone deserves a chance to take a new path."

TWENTY-FIVE

The End of Candy Barr
and the Start of #153781

"She may be cute, but under the evidence, she's soiled and she's dirty."

—Dallas Assistant District Attorney Bill Alexander,
during the trial of Candy Barr

The pressure was building. Not only were the appeals not working, but agents and officers from the Federal Bureau of Investigation, Treasury Department, Los Angeles police, Las Vegas police, and Dallas police wanted to talk with her about Mickey Cohen's activities. They were trying to put him behind bars and hoped that his former girlfriend would have inside information.

The image of the mob and of mob-connected men such as Cohen was that they would never reveal their secrets to a woman. However, it had been just one generation earlier that government agents brought down Lucky Luciano because the crime boss delighted in showing off in front of the prostitutes who worked for him. He would make telephone calls in their presence. He would brag about some of his activities. And he was also foolish enough to mistreat them. The first opportunity they had, they told law enforcement officers all that they knew. Their testimony

allowed Luciano to be convicted and deported. It was hoped that the notorious Candy Barr might do to Mickey Cohen what Luciano's prostitutes had done to him.

Juanita and Jack were living in Las Vegas. They had just gone to bed
one night when they heard a crash, "and it was either the FBI or the Treasury. I don't remember their name. They said they had to put us under arrest, and I don't remember telling us why, but I remember them checking
my car.

"We were following in a car behind them and another car following
us. I didn't care. All I wanted to do was get my kid back to Texas." That
was not to be for a while. Juanita and Troylene would remain together until the law enforcement officers were through with her.

"They took me back to L.A. somewhere. I don't know. It was on the
outskirts of L.A. or it wasn't. I don't really know. It was really like in the
movies. There was a big table in this room," Candy said. "And they did
come out in the middle of the night and question me [about] things that
were really alien to me. 'Cause I just didn't pay any attention. I knew what
I had to know." About Mickey's finances, diamonds, or people and things,
Candy didn't know anything. According to Candy, even if she had known
something at one time, by now she had forgotten it.

Juanita was due to turn herself in to the prison system and decided not
to wait. She was in fear of her life, and when she got through answering
the questions as best she could, she realized that no one could help her in
Texas, especially not some federal government agent working in California. "I said it's me against the law," and the men realized that the danger
she perceived was real. They had no idea who might be after her. They had
no idea if there were corrupt law enforcement officers who posed a threat
to her. All they knew was that they needed to get her safely back to Texas.
"They took me through the luggage compartment [at the airport]. I
mean, they were really protecting me. I had no idea this was so dangerous,
but they knew."

Juanita added, "When all the hassling was over and I knew I was going
to prison, I actually was relieved. Otherwise I would have been lying dead
someplace, or worse, lying on some gangster's couch. But the Texas cops
were more scared of my getting killed while they were trying to deliver

me to Goree Prison [a prison farm for women] in Huntsville. So they spirited me away to San Antonio."

When they boarded the plane that would take Juanita and Troylene to San Antonio, Texas, the first leg of her trip to the penitentiary, "They put me up in front and they put a man right here to see me at an angle at all times. And in the back part section there were some service men. They didn't know who I was at the time. It was very well screened."

The landing was not what Juanita expected. She was certain no one would allow her to simply walk off the plane. She figured she and Troylene should stay seated until a law enforcement officer came and got them. Instead, one of the flight attendants explained that there were newspaper reporters waiting for her. The flight attendants had just learned who their passenger was, though they did not register shock, despite the fact that some of the papers had referred to Candy Barr as Mickey Cohen's "moll."

"I said, 'No. I can't get off until someone comes and gets my child.' "

The mob of reporters was keeping everyone from deplaning. Finally Candy's stepmother, Etta, pushed through, boarded the plane, took Troylene in her arms, and enabled her to get off.

Instead of law enforcement waiting, there was just an attorney. The judge felt that there was no risk of Juanita trying to disappear. The lawyer had been told to take her to the hotel and let her have breakfast with her family. She had a few hours to relax, "Then I went and turned myself in, and way before daylight I was in [San Antonio] jail. The warden [at the penitentiary] had been called and was told there will be an arrival sometime today. I was coming. He was told when I left and when I would be there."

During the approximately four-hour drive from San Antonio to the prison in Huntsville, Juanita was prepared. She had been acquiring expensive, high-quality bras and panties from a fashionable boutique in Palm Beach, Florida. "I didn't go in for the frilly stuff. I went for the ones that wouldn't be seen under my clothes—very close fitting, soft underwear. I had to have a heavy bra because I had heavy tits, and they don't make soft-fitting, lacy [bras] for people with heavy tits. [I got] different colors with a little frill on it."

Juanita took what she thought would be the minimum necessities, including thirty bras, sport clothes, cold cream, and cosmetics all jammed into four suitcases. She fully expected to be in jail for fifteen years and knew there would be no chance to shop. She needed to look her best during that time, and while she couldn't keep up with changing styles, that had never been a concern. She just wanted to look nice. "I don't know what I thought prison was," she laughed years later. "Maybe a country club."

Juanita quickly learned that all clothing was issued by the state and there would be no deviations. She was allowed to bring $20 with her to pay for commissary items, but money was the only thing she was certain she would not need. She also learned that prison did not look as she imagined. She thought the outside would consist of high gray walls, perhaps with barbed wire and armed guards walking catwalks at the top, much like the prison movies of the day. Instead, it was a building made of red brick, a medium security facility that blended into the surroundings instead of standing out. Scared, but determined to joke with the officers driving her, Juanita looked at the building and said, "Just what I always wanted—a red-brick home." Then she fainted.

Juanita was taken immediately to the prison hospital ward, where the doctors discovered that she was pregnant, a condition Juanita had not expected. But the situation was even more complicated than that.

Juanita had been in extreme pain throughout the trip. She was seriously ill but did not know it. Even at this writing, more than forty years later, there remain serious questions about her health and medical history. Her lungs eventually deteriorated to where the lowest lobe on each side would have to be removed to improve her breathing. Her symptoms were similar to those of lupus. And she tired easily, having to plan her day around frequent rest periods. Talking on the telephone was tedious for her, and at times she had to fight to get out of bed. All of this probably started around the time she went to prison, the doctors either not understanding the problems or only able to do the minimum to make her comfortable.

The doctors would later claim that she was suffering from the ravages of the sexual abuse she had endured as a prostitute. Her body was in such bad shape that the fetus was either being rejected prematurely, or the fact of pregnancy alone was seriously endangering her health. Whatever the reasons, Juanita miscarried, after which the doctors performed a hysterectomy. Instead of at least twenty more childbearing years, Juanita discovered that Troylene would be her only child. The knowledge was devastating. She loved her daughter so much, the idea of giving birth to a second child was exciting. Even if she served her entire sentence, and Candy was certain she would be behind bars for the next fifteen years, she would be just in her early forties, still young enough for more children. Until the hysterectomy.

There was no informed consent. There was no discussion. Once again Juanita was back in the Capture, this time in the hands of a doctor, and again the experience was emotionally overwhelming. "When I found out what was done to me, I prayed to go insane. I was so wild, so out of my head, that I was given heavy doses of the tranquilizer Thorazine."

It was impossible for her to suppress her outrage about the unauthorized hysterectomy, even with the Thorazine she had been given. The tranquilizer was one of the strongest available. It had been created to serve as a chemical straitjacket for the sort of patients who usually wandered the locked back wards of hospitals. Society at large would have considered its use in the prison population unethical at best, medical malpractice at worst. But Candy was administered Thorazine and remained in the hospital ward at the prison farm.

The delay in placing Juanita, now known as #153781, into the general population was not caused by her medical problems. Instead, the warden, a powerful, overweight, brook-no-nonsense type of woman named Velda Q. Dobbs (nicknamed "the Hippo"), did not know what to do with her famous prisoner.

Candy Barr had come to Goree Prison Farm with a reputation that concerned everyone from Warden Dobbs to the more aggressive prisoners. Everyone knew who she was. The prison received newspapers every Sunday. It had radio and television. It had magazines. Juanita's lifestyle, her legal troubles, and her career were frequently being reported. There was no way any adult alive in the state of Texas, incarcerated or not, could be unfamiliar with her. In addition, "I had a very tough street name. I'd shot my second husband. I'd been Mickey Cohen's moll. I was no easy score."

A change came because of a movie—*The Ten Commandments*. Goree liked to show movies to the medium security inmates every Tuesday, and Juanita learned that the Charlton Heston film, one she had always wanted to see, was going to be playing the Tuesday after she had spent almost two weeks in the hospital ward. She also knew that anyone in the hospital ward was not allowed to go to the movies.

Juanita sent a note to the warden informing her that she wanted to see *The Ten Commandments* that Tuesday. She stated that the warden had to let her go on campus with the general prison population. "If you didn't have room for me, why did you take me in?" she asked.

"Jua-ni-ta," said Warden Dobbs, carefully pronouncing each syllable of her name. The warden would prove to be a kindly person whose slow, deliberate speech and large body were idiosyncrasies that did not prevent her from running Goree as fairly as possible. "I give the orders."

"Then either put me on campus or give me a release date," said Juanita.

The warden was still uncertain about Juanita Phillips, but she couldn't argue with the request. Two weeks was too long. Juanita was placed in the general population, assigned to a ward of twenty-eight women, each of whom had a bunk bed in a large open room. The ward was not much different from an army barracks, proof that the population was not considered dangerous. Other sections of Goree held prisoners who would be a problem, from lesbians actively seeking relationships with new women to individuals who were so violent they required isolation.

At first Juanita was an observer of the prison population. She needed to understand the culture, the way the women related to each other, the scams and the dangers.

Thorazine was the first concern. It was used indiscriminately in high doses. It was used when someone needed such an extreme tranquilizer. It was used when someone was temporarily out of line and the guards didn't want to either talk or use any extra force with the inmate. And it was used because the inmate was an unknown factor, like Juanita.

While *The Ten Commandments* was the source of the first run-in with the warden, the Thorazine would prompt an encounter that led to the first harsh discipline. Because of Juanita's reputation and her understandably hostile reaction to the surgery, the Thorazine was continued for thirty-five days. Juanita considered it unnecessary. She also knew that she was losing the ability to think. She was beginning to enjoy the drug, to have to force herself to care about anything. It was an unhealthy state, and so she wrote the warden a note saying she was so zonked from the Thorazine, she was going to refuse to take any more.

Warden Dobbs summoned Juanita to her office. The discussion quickly escalated to what the warden felt was a challenge to her authority. She ordered Juanita to spend thirty days in solitary confinement.

Juanita endured. She had been through far greater hell than being left alone in an isolated cell for a month. If anything, she found a great degree of peace within. But that did not mean that the experience "tamed" her as the warden may have hoped. "I had been told by then that if you ever let the Hippo stare you down, you were dead. So, like it was when I was a prostitute, I moved myself out of my own body and stared *her* down. I didn't blink once. When I left her office, she'd given orders to change my medication. It was a small victory, but it helped. After a time, Miss Dobbs even came to respect me some."

Juanita was initially assigned to the night sewing crew. The prison system tried to be as self-sufficient as possible. This meant everything from growing food to making the white uniforms worn by the prisoners. The Goree sewing room made the white male prisoner pants and the white cotton uniforms worn by the female prisoners. But the job offered no pay. At the time, prisoners were unable to earn money from legitimate prison jobs. If they did not have cash for the commissary, or if they lacked someone on the outside who could put money in their account, there was no money for little luxuries such as cigarettes.

In the years since Juanita left prison, men such as Abe Weinstein would brag about their visits to see her and how they helped her. She would always claim the statements were false. She always said that, for almost two years, the people who might have helped her never came to see her. They would not be supplying her with money for the commissary.

Juanita analyzed the prison system in order to find ways to make money. The first project she tried was renting space under her bunk.

There were lesbians in Goree, and accommodations were made for such women. There was a section where lovers could go to find the privacy for sex. Such women were offensive to Juanita. At times she had had to pretend to be involved with lesbian sex when she was in the Capture. But the idea of it was repulsive to her, both personally and watching someone else. She had also seen that the "dykes," the lesbian partners who took the role of the aggressive male, were often the troublemakers.

There were also women who wanted a chance to be close to each other. They wanted privacy and a chance to be close in a nonsexual way. Yet two close friends who on the outside could physically comfort one another in times of trouble were not allowed to touch in Goree. A gesture that was considered normal, gentle, and loving by a heterosexual woman in the "free world" (anywhere not behind bars) would be classed as wrong in prison.

Juanita decided to offer the straight women who wanted time for closeness an opportunity to use the space under her bunk. It was large enough for two women to find privacy, and she learned that the space was worth fifty cents at a time. It was also a violation of the rules that Juanita felt comfortable challenging. She knew in her own mind that she could defend their action and her encouragement of it if there was such a need. What she would not do was rent her under-bunk "bedroom" to lesbians.

"I am not going to be in a position to be in somebody else's lie. I knew what the consequences were if they got caught, and I knew it would be lock-up [solitary] and [good] time lost. So if it had actually been two girls down there draggin' each other's panties off and that kind of stuff, they would have never been by my bunk. I do have a certain amount of ethics, and one of them is not putting myself on the lie. I knew what they were and were not doing. I knew the difference, and whatever they were doin' was just being close.

"You couldn't hold hands. You couldn't walk down the hall and hold hands with your cousin. It was not allowed. And that's hurtful.

"You couldn't sit in the yard and touch. And people have to have human response. It doesn't mean that they're gay.

"Bisexuals has nothing to do with it. You know, kiss a girlfriend has nothing to do with it. No personal contact, so what I did I didn't feel badly about. Had I been contributing [to a lesbian act], then it would be different."

Juanita won the trust of the women by acting as lookout for their rendezvous with "Joe Rita," a made-up name in a ritual some of the women enjoyed on weekends. They would find a time to be in the shower when no one except the lookout was around. Then they would tie a rag around the showerhead and slow the water pressure. "They'd lay on the floor of the shower and let the water slowly trickle down their clitoris until they came to a climax. There were two or three gals that were really strung up on that. We called them Joe Rita. They trusted me and I knew it.

"Every morning we would get ready to go to work and I holler[ed] 'Don't forget to kiss Joe Rita.' And a few of the girls would slap them on the butt as they went. It was really kind of cute."

Juanita was curious about all this. "I tried it once to see what was so good. I told myself, good gracious, honey, this could become a habit. You got to stay away from that. No, I would never take time to lay down on that floor of that dirty shower and get my hair wet to come. There are other ways. You had no privacy. I don't care what anybody else wanted to do. I wouldn't want to fondle myself in a place where everybody could see me. I wasn't that way anyway. Sex didn't rule my life."

The sewing area was the scene of the one instance where Juanita had to defend herself. "It was a disagreement over our work room. See, being regimented like I was in my life, . . . whatever job you do, whether you like it or not, you do the best you can." Juanita was in the sewing room, working to turn out the best products she could as rapidly as possible. "I could put out a hundred pair [of slacks] and Reva could put out a hundred pair. The other group of girls, they put out twenty-five or thirty, just rebelling, just making remarks. I didn't want to go through that in the penitentiary. And one day I had all I [could take]. Janie, one of the other sewing room women, smarted off to me and said, 'I'll see you out in the yard.'

"By the time I got out in the yard I said, 'I don't want to have to go through this.' I know how I am. I go in to remove that bacteria that's makin' me sick to the point where I feel I have to have an altercation. That's not violence. So I sat down on the bench, and she came over, and I told her—her name was Janie—and I told her just leave me alone. I really didn't want to go through this.

"She started screaming loud at me, and I told her, 'Don't loud talk me,' and then it wasn't her anymore. It was back to when my stepmother screamed at me one time about my mother and slapped me in the face.

Anytime a woman screamed at me after that, it turned into that [memory]. I would attack like an animal."

The argument quickly escalated. "I had a carved madonna made out of gold which I always wore. She reached down, and she grabbed my treasure, and when she did, that was it. I said to myself, break her back, and I came up off the bench under her chin, and as she went back, I put her over my knee to pop her back.

"All of a sudden I realized what I was doing. I was close to killing her. I just dropped her and I sat down and waited for them to come and take me into lock-up. What else were you going to do? 'Cause I lost my treasures. They were somewhere in the yard and probably somebody found them."

Solitary confinement was an odd location. "It's a cell where you see nothing but a blank wall. That's all there is in front of you are bars and a blank wall. The person next to you, that's all they have. You [usually] don't have mirrors or a brush. It depends how dangerous you are to yourself. And you have a commode that they can turn the water off once a day and not let you flush it. It's not nice. They didn't do that [to me] the first week, and I don't remember after that [because] I stayed Thorazined out.

"They put Janie in, and her 'daddy' [male lover] followed her in so she wouldn't be nice by herself. And of course they have to put me on the very end where there's nobody on the other side of me. And they'd sit up at night and hug, and they'd been taking Thorazine so long it didn't bother them, so I said, 'Look, we're up here, but a little peace of mind wouldn't hurt a thing. I'm going to have to tell them to increase my Thorazine,' and they said, 'We'll give you ours.' "

The cells were set in a way that the prisoners could reach around and touch, but they couldn't see each other. The other two women decided that they would sleep in the daytime and talk at night. It was a slumber party in solitary confinement.

"So the nurse would bring it [the Thorazine] to you in a little cup, and they would pretend so I would take it. I must have taken nine hits of Thorazine in one day."

The strong drug use had an impact on Juanita's body and mind. "Sometimes when I was in there, I would wake up and see the trees. I really did. I forgot where I was.

"I gained about twenty-five pounds. Thorazine makes you gain weight, and eatin' those starches, sittin' on your ass on a bunk . . . " Solitary confinement was meant to be as unpleasant as possible without being inhumane. There were times when the inmates were fed only bread and water, just enough to sustain life. There were other times when the meals were better, but they were never planned to be as pleasant as the ones eaten when in the general population.

"And I just had so many hallucinations. All I wanted was medicine call. I really began to know what it was like to be stoned. [And I] have to go to prison to have that experience.

"[Janie and her 'daddy'] would pass it [the Thorazine] down and I would say, 'Good night. You all have fun.' And thirty-five days [later] Janie wakes me up and says, 'If you don't write a letter, we're not going to get out of here.'

"I said, 'Why?'

"She said, 'I don't know, but since it's your first trip, they're suppose to let you out in thirty days,' and said, 'If you don't write a letter, we may be up here for sixty days.' So I wrote more of my famous letters to Velda Q. [Dobbs] tellin' her that the system is set up that first offenders [get] thirty days, and it's now thirty-five days, hopin' they were right, 'cause everybody tries to give you wrong information.

"So what happens? Now she comes up and takes everybody out but me. Miss Craig [one of the guards] came back up and said, 'I don't have a release for you,' so I said okay and unpacked my sack. They didn't know that I was so pacified by that Thorazine had gotten control of me so that I just took a nap. So I just unpacked my sack and I laid back down, so Miss Craig went down and told them how I reacted. The punishment didn't affect me. I just turned over and snored. So about a hour later she came back and took me out to this different ward. And that's where I drank my first cup of coffee."

Each time a woman went into a ward, she started in the least desirable bunk. Over time, as she earned privileges, she could move to more private areas. The shift in ward was accompanied by a lighter schedule the first two or three days. The women in solitary had trouble adjusting to normal movement. Their muscles were weak and they needed to move around in order to rebuild. However, before the end of the first day out, one of the women who had been in isolation passed out in the ward.

"We got a matron [one of the guards], but the matron was old and couldn't do anything about it. Never realizing in the midst of a crisis I will react when nobody else will, I picked up this girl who was larger than I, and this matron had the door open, and I headed down the stairs to the hospital with her in my arms, and here comes the warden.

"Here I am, not out of isolation even three hours and we meet 'cause the girl is unconscious and nobody knows what to do."

The combination of physical and emotional toughness linked with compassion for others fascinated the warden. She decided to see just what her new prisoner would endure. She ordered Juanita to be outside in the hot sun the next day, hoeing the ground, something that shocked the other inmates, who knew how she had helped the woman who had become ill. "They said, 'I can't believe she'd do this to you just getting over being in ice,' and the girls would say, 'Candy, get out of the sun. You're going to be sick.'

"I said, 'I'm going to stay right here because I know why she's doin' this,' and they all knew, too. They were tryin' to be helpful to me. She was trying to see what I was made of evidently, 'cause the lady didn't hate me.

"They say what they want to about her, and I know she made lots of errors, but she ran that penitentiary. They didn't have rape, and they didn't have this and they didn't have that. No matter how she ran it, she ran that son of a bitch. You didn't have to worry about one of those matrons hiding behind a barn while somebody else hurt you, because that wouldn't happen with Miss Dobbs.

"I know she made her mistakes and she did some things that probably wasn't [right] but that was the way her supervisor told her to handle it and that's the way she handled it. Regardless if it was shock treatment or what it was. She had to get some approval for some punishments. Let's face it. She had to account to somebody. Anyway, I was out there [in the sun] and it turned out to be a really great day. The little matron, she wasn't without feeling, and I kept on workin' and workin' and workin' and she'd ask me how I was doin'.

"I said, 'Well, tell you the truth, we could use a few more hoe-ers around here.'

"She said, 'Juanita!'"

"And I said, 'Well, that's what they are. They have hoes and that's what we're doin'.'"

"I was doin' it for a joke 'cause I'd done it before I went to prison. I'd seen it in vaudeville. And she had to laugh. She knew the connotation, and we just all fell out. I was sick that night, though."

TWENTY-SIX

Fighting for Freedom

"For the first time in my life I wasn't owned by someone. I wasn't forced into anything. Oddly, as much as I had feared confinement, I became a person because of it."

—Juanita on her time in Goree, the Texas medium security prison for women

Many nightclub patrons thought that Candy Barr, instead of being behind bars, never stopped dancing. This was because some club owners hired young women who were similar in appearance—short, athletic, with blonde hair (natural or unnatural), and a wardrobe that included a cowgirl outfit, complete with toy six-guns. The club owners did not care about the quality of the girls' music or their dancing. They did not care if they followed the traditional approach to stripping or engaged in something more exotic. What mattered was that they bore the name Candy Barr when on the stage, they looked like the public imagined Candy Barr to be, and they kept their mouths shut about their real identities.

Only in Texas was no one fooled. In Texas, self-righteous men smugly showed their wives that they did not tolerate loose-moraled women, at least not ones with a little black book that had their names in it. Candy

Barr, the corrupter of all that was good and decent in Dallas, was behind bars. Amen! Hallelujah!

Juanita thought she might have peace in prison. Neither she nor the men who feared her thought that prison would be one more chance to exploit the name of Candy Barr. However, she entered prison when there was planning for the annual Texas State Prison Rodeo taking place, and to have Candy Barr be the star attraction, fetchingly albeit fully clothed, seemed a way to make even more money than in the past. Self-righteousness was set aside as plans were once again made without Juanita's knowledge.

It is hard for people who are not from ranching states to understand the money spent on professional rodeos. Originally cowboys would get together to compete in contests that related to the skills they used at work—breaking wild horses, running down and roping calves for branding, and other physically demanding activities. Sometimes they competed for bragging rights. Other times there would be a small trophy such as a fancy belt buckle.

Gradually rodeos became community events because the ranches were large and chances for neighbors to spend time together were few during much of the year. Women began participating in such events as barrel racing, a competition that showed how well a rider could control her horse in a series of tight turns around barrels placed at a set distance from one another in the arena. More dangerous activities, such as bull riding, were also added, though bull riding had nothing to do with ranch work. Soon there were rodeo parades, breeders of aggressive riding stock to challenge the cowboys, equipment sponsors, and arenas that could hold thousands. A few rodeos added entertainment apart from the events in the ring. Prize money increased, and some men and women became professionals, traveling from major rodeo to major rodeo throughout the year, making six-figure incomes from prize money and sponsor fees, much like golf professionals.

The Huntsville rodeo was one of the biggest in the nation. It was also the most unusual in that it was held within the state prison, though attended by fans from throughout the state and beyond. There was entertainment provided, usually by major professionals from the "free world." And always it brought money to the state, big money, as though a combination football championship and major rock concert played in the same location. The fact that Juanita was now one of the Goree Girls meant they had their big name, and she did not have to be paid. Candy Barr had to work for the state, or so the warden and others assumed.

Not that Candy would be allowed to dance as she had in the clubs. Bareback riding meant something quite different in a family rodeo. But Candy was multitalented, and to have her sing would enhance the promotion. What was not considered was both her attitude and new problems caused by the prison doctor trying to keep her docile by overprescribing the extreme tranquilizer Thorazine.

"Morning, noon, and night [I was] fighting my way to the medicine line by then," said Juanita. "Thorazine was rotting my mind. It was really something, and if I had not become aware of it, I probably would have been in bad shape now."

As Juanita was fighting the drug abuse, "somebody from the free world came in and told [us] they were broadcasting the fact that I was going to be at the prison rodeo in October. See, I went in in December one year, so October was the first rodeo. But they start ballyhooing and rehearsing one month before. And I said, 'Oh, I didn't know I was,' and they said, 'You don't have to go.'

"I said, 'How come?' and they said, 'It's not compulsory.'

"I said, 'Well, I don't want to go.' "

During this period, Jack Sahakian was visiting rarely. And Abe Weinstein would not start visiting until around eighteen months after she was jailed, despite having originally said he would came regularly. But Candy Barr found someone willing to keep her life in the public eye. A reporter for the *Dallas Morning News* made regular contact. He was sympathetic to her case and outraged by her sentence, though he knew that some women had been given eighteen years for the same offense. The difference was that they were regular users of marijuana. Juanita was not an innocent, but the marijuana resulting in her arrest was not hers, and at least part of it was a planned set-up. That resulted in some of the media people anxious to see justice done and willing to help however they could. The *Morning News* reporter, for example, visited approximately once a month, and though no stories were generated, the warden was aware they could be.

Juanita took no chances. She wanted to be certain that she did not have to participate in the rodeo. "They just wanted me to have an altercation 'cause they knew I had some outside assistance in the newspapers. 'Cause all the way in through then they kept trying to get me to go forward and rebel, and I wouldn't do it. I would only do it quietly in circumstances that required attention, and I did it directly with her [Warden Dobbs]."

This was also why Juanita rarely gave a story to the reporter. "I knew if I gave him an exposé on the prison without due cause, it would be hard for the girls. When you're responsible for other people, you just have to be careful. If you have any conscience, you have to be careful, I think."

Warden Dobbs called Juanita into her office and asked if she'd perform at the rodeo. "I said, 'No, I won't.' And she said I had to, and I said, 'No, I don't.' You always had to be frank or they'd get you on insubordination and put you in isolation."

Juanita's thinking seemed to work because she was only in isolation after the one altercation. "From then on all I had to say is 'I'll beat so and so. If you really want to do this, let's get it over with. I have things to do.'

"I don't really like it. I don't like to portray a violent attitude when you're not even violent, just disgusted with the whole mess that they would put you in that position. It's so dumb. Hostility is so dumb."

As for the rodeo, Warden Dobbs said, "We're expecting you to be there."

Juanita said, "Well, I'm aware that you all said I was, but I am also aware of the fact that it's not compulsory and I do not have to perform at the rodeo, and I don't choose to."

The situation was reaching a crisis point for the prison system. They had too much publicity out to have to explain why Juanita would not perform. Warden Dobbs talked to a Mr. Ellis, whose exact title Juanita does not recall, though she said he was "the big man at the walls" ("the walls" was the name for the main unit where the men stayed). Ellis decided to talk to Juanita, who was summoned to Warden Dobbs's office to meet with him.

"I already had meetings with him when I first came in there to let me know Mickey Cohen wouldn't be visiting me." When she had first arrived, the public assumed Juanita desired the relationship with the gangster and expected it to continue while behind bars. She had explained that she didn't care about Cohen being allowed to visit her, that she just wanted to be left alone. Still, she had the reputation of being "a big-time Mafia broad," and oddly, Ellis's first words that she remembers when they met again about the rodeo were, "Are you afraid of me?"

"Mr. Ellis, I'm not afraid of anybody," Juanita replied. And she again stated, "I'm not going to perform at the rodeo."

Years later, she explained how she felt about the situation. "By then you get to the point you don't have to bullshit anybody. You can just get pushed so far, and you can't get pushed no more by nobody at any point in your life unless it means the life of your child or your loved one or a friend. Then you will let them push you until they break your bones."

With Ellis, she would not be pushed. She was not going to perform at the rodeo. "And he said, 'Why aren't you?'

"And I said, ' 'Cause I don't want to.' So they left and Miss Dobbs came back in there, and she said, 'Juanita, you have to perform at the rodeo.'

"And I said, 'Miss Dobbs, no I don't.'

"She said, 'What can we do to convince you?' "

It was the opening Juanita had been waiting for. She had long ago come to realize the foolishness of packing clothes for the fifteen years she expected to stay behind bars. She had given up hope of being released on some technicality. What she did want to do was lead a productive life, something she felt she could do better behind bars than she could in the free world. She had already started taking advantage of education opportunities, earning a 99.5 average as she completed high school course work. She had begun seriously writing poetry that would eventually be published. And she had come to realize that if she could get a job in the library, she could begin devouring the great works of literature, philosophy, and other areas of learning contained on the shelves. That was why Juanita said that she would do the rodeo if she was taken out of the sewing room and given a job in the library.

"She said, 'We can't bargain with you about things like that.'

"And I said, 'Then I can't do the rodeo.' I said, 'I'm not asking a whole lot and you are.' And these are my words. I remember, 'cause these were encounters that were victories but not victories in any smart-aleckness, but victories in what was right. I didn't abuse anything.

"And she said, 'You're not qualified for the job.'

"I said, 'I'm as qualified as the girl who went in there, and I know there's a place because she's discharging in three days and I know there's an opening for a librarian. I'm as qualified as anybody in here for that job,' and I said, 'I can do the job.'

"She figured I couldn't really." But Juanita bargained for the chance to try, "and then she could remove me if I couldn't do the job.

"So we made a deal. I would perform at the rodeo, that was our agreement, and I got the job in the library and I made a success of it."

Juanita, thirsting for knowledge, mastered the work. "It was a whole new world for me. I read. I studied. I wanted to be in that library. I never had the opportunity to read outside. I knew every book in that library and where every book was. I knew every piece of material I had on those shelves. I did the job so good, she told my matron to leave my business alone, 'cause my matron went to the office two or three times, and I'd slap her hands for getting in my books."

The Huntsville prison rodeo in which Candy Barr appeared has become part of the legend of the notorious stripper. People claim there never was an event more spectacular, nor was there a performer more daring. Candy was a bull rider. She was the star. She was . . .

The truth was different, of course. Her role at the rodeo was much simpler. Juanita, devoutly religious, saw Jesus as a personal friend. She never lost her trust in God, no matter what she experienced. And in prison, there were opportunities to express her joy in a manner she had not previously explored—in song.

Juanita started attending worship services. She had been raised a Pentecostal, but the prison was divided by broader categories—Protestants, Catholics, Jews, and those who practiced one or another of the Indian tribal beliefs. As soon as she was in the population at large, Juanita joined the Protestant choir and the Catholic choir, singing with both groups and at all services. Her voice range at the time was wide, what some professional singers jokingly call "sopralto." This is a voice that can cover the range from alto to first soprano, and Juanita was asked to sing in both ranges, as the choirs needed.

The women sang without musical accompaniment in the main church. Juanita's voice was not as strong as that of some of the other women, but she was able to sing on key, a blessing in the prison. Many of the songs were favorites she remembered from the church her grandparents took her to, such as "My God Is Real" and "I've Got a Friend in Jesus."

At first there were inmates who wondered what Candy Barr was trying to prove. Over time, though, they realized that Juanita was not playing another role. This was the real woman and she was joyous in the Lord. The warden knew the quality of her voice, and so Juanita became part of the Goree Girls who would sing at the rodeo.

The production quality was rather odd. "All Texas prisoners had to wear white at the time, but the Goree Girls' costumes were black.

"They're so against gays and dykes, but we had black motorcycle boots, black skirts with white fringe that was made in the sewing room, cowboy hats, and black shirts with fringe."

For five weeks the women prepared. They practiced Elvis Presley songs. They practiced "Home on the Range." They practiced "Fever," a powerful number that they tackled aggressively. Juanita both sang and played the drums.

The day of the rodeo, the Goree Girls were in great company. Singer Ray Price was there. Bo Diddley performed. And there were numerous other top professionals, the event having talent much like a state fair, in addition to the prison performers.

"I was there for the convicts, not the audience," Juanita stated. As a result, when she was asked to speak a moment before the Goree Girls sang, she said, "Remember, all good guys wear white!" The prisoners in their sea of white uniforms took on a single voice as they cheered the remark. The wardens, fearing what might come next, immediately had Candy's microphone cut off. She had made her point, though, and the rodeo appearance went off without incident.

The microphone was turned back on for the music, and as she did when dancing, Candy Barr could not stop. "I think I sang forever," she recalled. "The girls in the penitentiary just got all over me 'cause I got more applause than anybody in the whole show, outside entertainment and everything. They said, 'You just got out there and fucked them, and I didn't even think about that. I live my stuff. I really do. It just brought the house down. It was five weeks in October you had to perform."

What was not remembered, what was not discussed outside of prison walls, was the real Juanita. She was not changed so much as set free.

"In the morning, at library time, I would go and pick up the books that were due to come in from the wards and the cell blocks and stuff. And then two to three days a week I checked out books. I also took classes in English. I took classes in math while I was in that library. And I got control of the compulsory class."

The compulsory class was for inmates who didn't know how to read, and it would cause a few minor problems for Juanita. Warden Dobbs "took me off of it because evidently they were learning more than they should. I was teaching them how to write home, and they would bring their letters to me and I would read them and teach them how to write their letter back, just so they could write a few lines so that their family could have their letter.

"I really cared, and I'm not just pattin' myself on the back. I truly cared about these people. Like anything I try, [I try] to do my best. I was teaching them how to make out their commissary list, how to get their mail outside that building without begging somebody to do it and then go tell the warden what they're writing. 'Cause I already censored. But families need to hear from people, and if somebody's illiterate, nobody's going to hear from them.

"Prison's like that. So anyway, that's what I was teaching and it's compulsory 'cause it's totally illiterate people that cannot read or write, and I really liked it.

"One day Miss Dobbs called me in and told me that I was spending too much time with it. She removed me. But I knew why she removed me. There were too many illiterate people becoming aware. You don't want illiterate people aware, because if people become aware a little tiny bit, they rebel and they want to make changes in their life. They really began to see. It's amazing what an illiterate adult [becomes when] they begin to form words that start making them ask questions.

"Ask me and I have to give them the answer. I want to be honest with them. This makes them want to do something else. But I wanted them to make out their commissary list so they wouldn't get beat out of their nickels and dimes, and to write 'Dear Daughter,' 'Dear Son,' 'Honey,' a few little words, and then if they needed something else, I'd take time to write the letter."

When the inmates Juanita was teaching received mail, they no longer took the letters to Miss Dobbs or one of the matrons. "They'd keep their letters for me to read for them, because they knew if I read their letter, they were hearing their letter.

"Some of them got to where they could read their own letter. You can pick out so many words. . . . But [Warden Dobbs] made me quit and gave it to someone else."

The library was not all innocence and learning. Juanita still needed a source of money. She could make enough for cigarettes and a few extras by renting out the space underneath her bunk, but she needed more. She started a mail service, finding ways to deliver notes between prisoners who were otherwise not allowed to communicate. And she blackmarketed toilet paper, which was a highly prized item because it was carefully rationed. It was only in the library that the quantity was relatively unlimited. Everyone used the library, and trying to maintain restrictions that existed for each ward or solitary cell was impossible. So long as Juanita limited what she took and sold, an inventory would not show any irregularities.

And always Juanita worked to improve her mind. She read the dictionary to learn words and the meaning of language. She became curious about Swami Prabhupada, the founder of the International Society for Krishna Consciousness, and read all his work. She read and memorized the poetry of Emily Dickinson.

Oddly, life was good. The food was often terrible. There were women who wanted to prove themselves, especially against a celebrity prisoner. There were times when Juanita had to "walk hard, walk cold," adopting an attitude that was foreign to her character. And she found that the parole board was not sympathetic to her transformation, even though there was no question about her sincerity.

Once again she had to endure, but this time there was a degree of control. This time she was allowed to grow as a woman. Others were fighting for her release, but as much as Juanita wanted to be in the free world, Goree was proving a respite in life she desperately needed.

TWENTY-SEVEN

Freedom

Hate the world that strikes you down,
A warped lesson quickly learned.
Rebellion, a universal sound,
Nobody cares . . . No one's concerned.
Fatigued by unyielding strife,
Self-pity consoles the abused,
And the bludgeoning of daily life
Leaves a gentle mind . . . Confused.

—Title poem from *A Gentle
Mind Confused* by Candy Barr

It was impossible to keep Juanita behind bars. She was serving her time too well for that. She had made the honor ward, where most of the inmates were considerably older and seemingly not prone to causing problems. However, as she recalled, "They were aware in that prison what position I could be out front anytime if we ever wanted to have a rebellion. A group of girls there kept trying and trying to get me to go up against the system with them to try to get the attention of the newspaper and get something. They did not know I was quietly getting the best I could do without causing them anguish or making it harder on everybody inside the penal system. [A rebellion] would have been disastrous and we would have only won temporarily. And me, I'm not one to make a spectacle of myself. I do not go out and do things to get my name in the newspaper."

Elsewhere in the nation, the fifteen-year sentence was an outrage. In Texas, it was a just punishment. Yet even in Texas, too many people understood what was happening, too many people saw that the little black book had never been used, that Candy Barr was genuine. An exception was Police Captain Pat Gannaway, a true moralist who may have had the support of Dallas District Attorney Henry Wade. Certainly both men talked as if they were upright citizens.

They may also have felt unspoken pressure from prominent citizens to keep Candy Barr out of the public eye for as long as possible. They had to at least suspect the reason so many rising stars in Dallas politics, business, and law enforcement were concerned about what was locally known as an exotic dancer.

The governor was not beholden to anyone, though. Governor John Connally, who had strong presidential ambitions—and who would gain unwanted fame on November 22, 1963, when wounded in the motorcade where President John F. Kennedy was assassinated—was a man who believed in justice.

Texas laws were notoriously harsh. For example, the state's three-time loser law ensured that anyone who committed three felonies would go to jail for the rest of his or her life. Approximately twenty years after the freeing of Juanita, Connally would quietly arrange for his Houston law firm to provide top-quality assistance at no charge to a "lifer" in Huntsville. The man was a three-time loser for writing three bad checks totaling $229.50. Worse, the third check was not bad. At the time of his trial, however, the defense counsel was ineffective and did not do much for a self-employed handyman of no importance in the community.

The handyman's case brought the wrath of Supreme Court Justice Thurgood Marshall, a man who spent his entire legal career concerned with the issue of justice for all, including the "nobodies." He was irate to learn from the lawyer representing Texas that if the victim of the three-time law was released on probation, he would be returned to jail for life if he so much as got a parking ticket.

Connally's firm ultimately prevailed, and the man, freed from Texas, moved to Michigan to start a new life. But Connally's public concern first came to light with Candy Barr. He looked at the information provided by the Board of Pardons and Paroles and saw that they viewed her as a model prisoner. She had involved herself in the prison rodeo for three years. She had an exemplary work record. She helped educate other prisoners while constantly advancing her own education. She was devoutly religious, the Bible and church a part of her existence, not a scam to get release. And her felony was to get caught with a substance that increasingly was popular with the college-age children of the very rich and powerful. There was no pressure from any special interest or moralistic group that could alter his outrage. On March 22, 1963, Texas Governor John Connally ordered Juanita's release.

On April Fool's Day 1963, exactly three years and ninety-one days after she entered the Goree Prison Farm, she walked out without press or public awareness. The message was clear. Juanita wanted nothing more than to have some peace and, with luck, take control of a life that had seemed free only when behind bars. Toward this end, the state of Texas provided Juanita with $5 in spending money and $5.70 to return to Edna, Texas, where she would be restricted to a radius of thirty-six miles. It was considered one of the harshest paroles ever given any inmate.

The parole board did allow Candy Barr to keep dancing, though in a way that ensured she would not step on the dance floor for a total of eight years following when she first entered prison. The board said she could dance in any club in or around Edna, knowing full well there were none. And in case someone decided to open a club using Candy Barr as a draw, the board also said that she could not work where liquor was served. Since the clubs made their profit on the liquor and the entertainment, the board effectively ended any chance of her earning a living as she had in the past.

A former employer and his wife met Juanita at the prison when she was released. Her few possessions were piled into their Chevrolet Impala and the couple drove Juanita to a motel so she could relax. They took two separate rooms, but while the wife waited in one room, her husband escorted Juanita to where she would be staying, several doors away. Then, when his wife could not see what was happening, he made clear he expected Juanita to have sex with him. Instantly she knew nothing had changed in her life, though she had hoped that the illusion of total freedom would not be shattered so quickly.

Juanita refused her former employer's request, she and the man knowing neither would ever tell the man's wife. But even the request brought great anger, frustration, and sadness.

Next Melvin Belli returned to see what he could do for Juanita. He and two Dallas attorneys drove to Edna, where Juanita and Troylene were living with her ailing father and stepmother. They felt that if they took her directly to Austin to see Judge Brown, there was a chance that he might ease her parole.

The problem was that Judge Brown was quite ill, though he was still on the bench and would soon preside at the trial of Jack Ruby. His heart was failing, and when he had a heart attack during the time Juanita was in Goree, she learned that he had been near death. "I sent word through somebody to please give his wife my compassion and that I really hope he gets okay. I don't know what I exactly said, but I sent him love and caring. It just affected him and I didn't do it for that reason. I had nothing against that man."

When Juanita and her three attorneys entered the judge's chambers, he said, "You know, this is highly unethical."

"So is everything else," said one of the attorneys.

"You have caused me a lot of trouble," Juanita told the judge.

"You're right," he replied. "I could never do this publicly but I will do this right now. I really apologize for the part I had to take."

According to Juanita, "He told me once he retired and started putting his memoirs together he would do the best he could to vindicate me, but he didn't live that long. Didn't make any difference in whether anybody else in the whole wide world knew what he had to say as long as he knew that he had cleared his conscience with me. And that came about 'cause I knew he had a heart attack and I was really in misery for people."

There were others who cared. As news of Juanita's return to Edna spread in newspapers, she began receiving mail from all over the world. There were letters of support from people in England, France, Holland, Syria, and elsewhere. Members of church groups wrote, as did a Jesuit priest, whose letter read, "To you, as a woman, I have a message. A wonderful surge of courage lifts your head fiercely in the face of threats and adversity. You magnificent lady. You'll toil. You'll fight like a tigress. We know. We see it in the courageous lift of your chin."

As she became settled, Juanita instituted divorce proceedings against Jack Sahakian, hoping to end all past connections. But a few weeks into her parole, Troy Phillips arrived with a man named Bill Carson (not his real name). "Troy just showed up one day, along with this man, Carson. The minute I saw Troy's face, I knew there would be trouble.

"They swaggered in, and I could see Troy had a knife on his belt. They barely spoke to me before Carson ripped off my clothes, threw me on a table, and began raping me. It was a sick scene. I could feel my vaginal area tear. I was in mortal agony but I was damned if I was going to give them the satisfaction of knowing that. Also, I was on parole and I knew in my heart that someone had sent these men to hurt me and then force me to try to defend myself. If I'd so much as struck Carson, they would have reported me to Henry Wade and Gannaway, and poof, quick as that, I would have been back in prison. So I lay as quietly as I could and I even reached out and took an apple off a plate and bit into it during the rape.

"All that stopped them from finishing me off was that my sister-in-law, Lois, walked in and saw what was going on. She screamed that she was going to call my brother, Gary, and that he'd come and kill them. Troy believed that and they left. Lois took me to a doctor."

There would be other visitors during those early days back in Edna. One of the men in Dallas, a man who was in Juanita's address book, could not believe she would not try to hurt him and the others who had railroaded her into prison. He was certain that, once out, she would reveal who he was. To protect himself, he arranged for a thug to hit her on the head, plant dope on her unconscious body, and drive her across the county line in her own car. The thug drove her car into a ditch, figuring the police would find it, find the drugs, and assume she hit her head when she left the road. The blow was severe enough to have caused a concussion that would eventually need medical attention.

"Somehow or other I made it back home and told my brother what happened. After three or four days I couldn't take the pain anymore, so my sister-in-law took me to the doctor. I said [to the doctor] I'll tell you what happened but you cannot tell the law. And while we were looking in my purse and all, there were all these drugs. If they had caught me on the highway, unconscious, with all those drugs, I'd have been in prison again."

To Juanita's surprise, the town's people were mostly rallying around her. Some of the men appointed themselves her guardian. They felt bad for the way she had been treated, and several of them, she later learned, had sent letters to the warden to try to get her sentence lightened. They wanted her to have no more trouble, no matter what had to be done to protect her.

A stranger came to town looking for Candy Barr one day during her first few weeks back in Edna. Word got around that the man didn't belong, especially since the locals all knew her as either Juanita or Nita, her family nickname. "A couple of the little guys in town came to my house and said, 'That son of a bitch won't bother you.'

"And I said, 'Why?' And they said, 'We hit him in the head and left him in a ditch. We ain't goin' to tell nobody but you, but we left him in a ditch.'

"I said, 'You're kidding.'

"They said, 'Nope, we aren't. But we're not going to tell anyone but you, but he's out there somewhere in a ditch. I hope he lives because nobody knows we did it.' "

Apparently he did live, because the body wasn't found. The men were her self-appointed protectors, regularly coming to her house to let her know if there was trouble in town. It was a situation that she found deeply moving after what she had endured while growing up.

Despite the neighborhood protection, Juanita's parole supervision was intense. There was a parole officer assigned to meet with Juanita once a month. A second man, a community volunteer who supplemented the workload of the parole office, checked almost daily on Juanita. It was the type of extremely close supervision that was supposed to be used only for those ex-cons at high risk for returning to jail.

As foolish as that may seem today, it was Juanita's friendships that made them wary. This was because, in the early days following her release, the pugnacious club owner Jack Ruby came calling.

"Dear Jack!" Juanita said of that first visit after she left the prison. "He brought me several presents that day. Two of them were AKC dachshunds, a male and a female. He said I should breed them and get wonderful puppies I could then sell."

Ruby was well aware of the parole restrictions on Juanita and the difficulty she would have making money. The puppies were a present that he thought could lead to a thriving business. Her personal love of animals had nothing to do with his thinking.

"He also brought me an air conditioner because he knew how much the humid Texas heat bothered me. And then he gave me $50.

"He spent the afternoon with me, and that night I fixed dinner for him. We talked for hours. Mostly he and I agreed how much we adored President Kennedy—that he truly was a savior for our country. It was very touching, the way Jack felt about that man."

Ruby had come to believe that there was going to be an American Holocaust. He never mentioned who he thought might be leading such a cataclysmic event. He never explained why all the Jews would be targeted for death. He was certain it would happen, though, and he was equally convinced that Jack Kennedy was destined to be the person to prevent it.

Others who knew Jack Ruby felt there was another reason for his strong interest in the president. In 1963 little was known about Kennedy and his family. They were extremely conservative, Kennedy's sister Eunice having dated Joe McCarthy during his notorious days of attacking communists. And while that conservative streak was liberal compared with the politics of Dallas, they were very much an accepted part of the era that honored courage against the perceived "red menace," heroism in wartime, and compassion for the underdog.

The marriage between Jack and Jacqueline was seen as a strong one. They were viewed as glamorous, good looking, and patrons of the arts. No one knew they had long been estranged, Kennedy having frequent sexual encounters with other women. Instead, Ruby and others saw the couple in much the same manner as idolized movie stars. These were people with glamour and power, the combination Ruby knew he would never possess. However, with his friend Juanita, a woman who had known what it was to be attacked for actions outside her control, Ruby discussed only his feelings about anti-Semitism and what the president was going to do to protect the public.

"Always before," Juanita recalled of Ruby, "he'd referred to himself as 'a black Jew.' I think he meant that he and his people never really had been accepted by so many Americans.

"He felt the anti-Semitism strongly. Like, in his clubs, anybody in the nightclub business could always come to his places and get in free, drink free, not pay anything. But when he visited *their* clubs, they always made him pay for everything."

What he did not say and Juanita did not know was that Ruby was considered unethical in the way he ran his club. He would go to people standing outside Abe Weinstein's club and give them passes to his Carousel. He also had raffles of turkeys, dishes, and other desired items to bring people into his clubs. Such promotions had been common in movie theaters during the Great Depression, but the other Dallas nightclub owners did not view them as appropriate business practices.

Ruby did have a good heart, though. He may have been a cutthroat competitor, but he genuinely cared about the people who worked for him, including the strippers. Abe Weinstein pretended to care but commented, "Do you know a moral, Christian, God-fearing girl who'll stand up there and take her clothes off?" It was a question he never posed to Juanita. If he had, it would have further soured her opinion of him.

As Juanita explained, Ruby "said that with Jack Kennedy he could sense the change in religious attitude in this country. He said that President Kennedy would see to it that no one was discriminated against. After all, Jack [Ruby] said, Kennedy had to fight all odds because he was Catholic. And yet he got elected to the highest office in the land.

"I remember how Jack told me that day about Al Smith being a Catholic and yet he was governor of the state of New York twice. And how, in 1928, Franklin Delano Roosevelt helped Al Smith win the presidential nomination of the Democratic Party and ran against Herbert Hoover. He said what a tragedy for this country that Smith lost the race. When Jack left, he said he'd see me real soon."

There would be one telephone call to Juanita. It was a call Juanita would barely remember because it did not seem all that important at the time. He was trying to get in touch with Mickey Cohen or some other mobster Ruby was certain Juanita would know. He had bought into the myth of her relationships with violent, wealthy, powerful men and hoped that, through her, he could find a way to borrow money to pay the back taxes he owed the Internal Revenue Service. Had the call happened at any other time, it would not have mattered. By taking place shortly before President Kennedy was shot, Ruby was inadvertently bringing the notorious Candy Barr back into the public's mind.

But in the weeks after Ruby's only visit, Juanita took his advice and kept encouraging the dachshunds to have sex whenever the female was in heat. Her efforts were unsuccessful. "They just didn't like each other that way, I guess."

Then, on November 22, 1963, "I had the radio playing some soft classical music, trying to get them in the mood, when a bulletin broke in announcing that President Kennedy had been shot. I stayed glued then to the TV for the next several hours. I tried to telephone Jack to console him, because I knew how devastated he'd be, but I never did get him."

Juanita did not know what was happening to Ruby during the time when Kennedy came to Dallas, Texas. The city was intensely conservative and hostile to the president. Before the initial investigations into the assassination were complete, Peter Lawford and his wife, Pat Kennedy Lawford, Bobby and Ethel Kennedy, and other members of the Kennedy family tried to decide who had arranged the murder. It was their feeling that it was coordinated by two well-known Dallas businessmen who did not like Jack Kennedy's politics. There was a strong logic to the thinking and even a certain amount of circumstantial evidence—several of the people known to be involved with the murder had been in and out of the businessmen's office building in the two weeks prior to the assassination. The fact that the family believed the possibility, never justified by facts, reflects what they knew of the city's reputation and the deadly frontier mentality believed to be an integral part of the citizenry.

The night before the assassination, Jack Ruby was demonstrating a twist board, a new product he was trying to sell in his club. You stood on the board and twisted in a manner similar to the popular dance craze known as "the twist." You could use it while watching television or listening to the radio. As Ruby said, "Even President Kennedy tells us to get more exercise." When someone in the audience referred to Kennedy as "that bum," Ruby grew hostile. He did not tolerate such disrespect toward the president of the United States. The incident would eventually add to his intense emotions after the assassination.

Ruby was placing an advertisement for his nightclubs at the *Dallas Morning News* when he heard of the assassination. Horrified, he called his sister, then changed the ad so there was a black border and a notice that the clubs would be closed in tribute to the president. Then he went over to the Dallas police headquarters, where he helped the press by identifying the various members of the homicide unit and other detectives in whom the reporters had an interest.

As the afternoon ended, Ruby went to a nearby delicatessen and bought sandwiches and soft drinks for the police. He knew the action might not be proper, so he called headquarters before bringing over the food. When they thanked him but said they could not accept it, the food was taken to an area television station for the people working there. Ruby continued to work from the police headquarters, finding ways to help the out-of-town reporters who had come to Dallas for what they originally assumed would be the typical dull assignment to cover the president on a mostly political journey.

The next morning Ruby insisted that George Senator, who lived in the same home as Ruby, accompany him to take Polaroid pictures of a billboard reading "Impeach Earl Warren." Earl Warren, the liberal chief justice of the Supreme Court, was widely hated in conservative Dallas. Ruby seemed to link the billboard with an advertisement attacking President Kennedy that had appeared in Friday's newspaper. He was hell bent on proving a conspiracy in the assassination, though he did not seem to know what that meant.

The "investigation" seemed to end when George Senator, Ruby, and a young Carousel Club employee stopped by the Dallas post office to try to learn who owned the post office box number listed for replies in the anti-Kennedy print ad. They were not told, though they were able to see that the locked box was stuffed with mail. Perhaps Ruby thought that if he could take some action, any action, he would feel more in control of a world he saw sinking rapidly out of control.

When Jack Ruby went to the Dallas police headquarters and shot alleged assassin Lee Harvey Oswald, the act was shocking to the nation but not within the city where it occurred. Most of the locals in the entertainment and law enforcement worlds understood the thinking behind the action.

Dallas nightclub owners always worked closely with law enforcement. They understood that their annually renewed licenses were examined in a number of ways. One of these had to do with the number of times someone other than a club owner or one of his employees called the police to report a problem. The club staff could call for help whenever they felt they needed help with a belligerent patron, drugs on the premises, or some other problem, and there would be no record of it reported when it came time for license renewal. However, calls from the public were logged and used against the club. The attitude was that no matter how much illegal activity was taking place, so long as it was not tolerated by the club owner and his staff, the club was not a detriment to the community.

Jack Ruby was always on the telephone, always reporting anything that looked suspicious. He was heading off both real trouble and any undercover police action that might otherwise work against him. In fact, the harassment and jailing of Candy Barr was often seen as a warning to everyone connected with the clubs. They also could be set up for noncooperation.

Ruby was proud of his friendship with local government officials, including Mayor Cabell. He loved the city, loved feeling himself to be one of the good guys. This was especially important in his mind because he was Jewish. He would later say that one of the reasons for his actions was that he needed to show that "Jews have balls." He thought he would be respected for getting rid of Oswald, a man who had made local law enforcement and the city itself look bad. He thought he might be released after his trial and that he certainly would not do hard time.

What shocked Ruby was the harsh reaction to his shooting. His "friend," the mayor, was upset because it looked as though the Dallas police were incompetent fools. It looked as though they could not protect a suspect. It was the most dramatic shooting the nation had witnessed in many years. Worse, Oswald was wearing handcuffs when he was shot.

The general attitude in Dallas was that it was all right to shoot Oswald if he was not wearing handcuffs or other restraints. He was restrained, though, so Ruby should have limited his actions to beating up the man. Friends were both surprised, and in some instances disappointed, that Jack had not confined himself to hurting the alleged assassin, especially since it was doubtful that the police would have stopped him until he was done. Instead, he was facing a first degree murder charge, the city was embarrassed, and anyone who might have been involved became immediately suspect. This included the woman Ruby had so recently called—Candy Barr.

A number of people were watching Juanita during this time. Her father, though still somewhat active, was terminally ill by then, and Gary was trying to take over some of his work. Gary, worried about Juanita's safety, insisted she own a handgun for self-protection. It was illegal for a convicted felon to own a gun, but Juanita was not worried about returning to prison. She felt as strongly about having access to weapons as she had before her arrest. There had been too many times in her life when her situation might have changed had she been better able to protect herself.

There was also the belief among some of the people in Edna that the Mafia was targeting Juanita for death. Certainly her life had been at risk on the trip to Mexico. Too little time had passed for anyone to have forgotten about her relationship with Mickey Cohen. Even her old friend Jack Ruby was reaching out to her by telephone to get in touch with one of the mobsters she knew. He was more than $30,000 in debt to the Internal Revenue Service, and even he thought Candy Barr had mob connections for loans. Thus the weapon was to keep her safe from any dangers that existed.

Juanita was sick one evening and had just taken a pill prior to lying down when she realized that someone in a car seemed to be checking the house. It came around and around, moving so quietly, had the house not been isolated, the car might have gone unnoticed.

Juanita listened as the sound of the car continued. Finally she got up from bed, certain she had to defend herself. "I got the gun and I said, 'Fuck it, fuck it, fuck it,' so I went out there and shot at the car. And the sons of bitches came back. Now that's bold!

"I shot again and they buzzed off. So I run into the house. I had my nightgown and slippers. I picked up my knife automatically. I had a switchblade. Always kept one. And I had a stiletto, and I just automatically picked it up when I went in the house."

Juanita called the sheriff's office before doing anything else. She was told the deputy on duty would respond right away, but he didn't. "The guy that was on patrol that night, he was out fucking somebody. I did call twice, so they vouched for the fact that I called for assistance and nobody came. They couldn't find him, their night patrol man."

Juanita, frustrated, went to the police station, still wearing her shorty nightgown and slippers. She told the dispatcher that she would find the deputy herself. Then she took off, catching up with the car holding the drivers who had been harassing her.

"I tracked that car down and I pulled them over, and I yanked those kids—it was a couple of kids." Only one boy was in the car, the other one across the street. She dragged the one boy out of the car. "I drew back my arm. I was getting ready to punch him. Just then the sheriff's deputy comes riding up and he stops me. So I tell him, 'You tell this kid where I've been and what I've been doing, and if he ever comes around my house again . . . ' I wasn't going to file charges on him because of the parole board and all.

"So I whipped across the street. I didn't care at that point. I was tired of this mess, scaring my family, and me never knowing who was coming for me. I was in their territory. I had to protect them. All my life I've been protecting others and it really pisses me off!

"So I ran across the street and I grabbed this kid. I flipped that switchblade knife. Now I've worked with my blades so much all my life that I could flip the blade and cut your belly."

There was a service station nearby, and people there were watching. Juanita knew that if she acted, she would be going back to prison because of all the witnesses, but she didn't care. "And I grabbed his throat, so he leaned back to hit me. And I said, 'Look here, you little cocksucker, you hit me and I will cut you in front of all these people. I don't really care anymore.' So after it all calmed down, he kept saying, 'I'm not going to hit you. I'm not going to hit you.'

"So I said, 'Fine, just don't come 'round my house anymore.' "

Juanita knew there would be a reaction to her pulling the knife, so she took steps to protect herself. "I broke down my damn knife and whittled me out a wooden blade that's bent back with masking tape around it. And I put it in my little knife frame. I had to tear up my good knife and everything, so when they wanted to see the weapon, they could see it was harmless.

"The next morning they hit me, of course, hard and long." But Juanita knew that one of the boys was the son of the banker. She went to the bank and explained that she was going to tell the judge about how the banker's son was a peeping tom.

"Now if you all want to file charges, you do it," she told them, "but I'm going before the court and I'm going to tell the judge that your boy was out in front of my house playing with his peter. Now if you want him to be known as a window peekin', peter playin' person, you do that. Now what do you want to do, because I am not messing with you people anymore?"

Her tactic worked. "Well, nobody ever did anything. The law stood up for me because I called them twice.

"Louis [the sheriff] was okay. He wasn't straight, but he ran the town and he was okay."

One person Juanita found she could not trust was one of the parole officers. Apparently influenced either by his imagination or a request from someone trying to get Juanita back in jail, he sent in a report that she was working again. She was allegedly dancing in some liquor joint and her costume consisted of two postage stamps and a playing card. Perhaps had the parole officer not gone to such an extreme there would have been no problem. However, even Juanita's enemies knew her act was not about sex. There was no way she would dance while covered in the manner described. The report did not result in her returning to jail.

What Juanita did not expect was to have to see the sheriff and the FBI shortly after President Kennedy was shot. It was no more than ten hours after Ruby's shooting of Oswald that the FBI came to interrogate Juanita concerning her part in an alleged plot to kill the president. The interrogation went on hour after hour.

Everyone was desperate to save face or avoid embarrassment after Oswald was shot while in police custody. The FBI was potentially in the most embarrassing position of all. Although it was not widely known at the time, Lucky Luciano, Meyer Lansky, and other mob leaders back before World War II had compromised the FBI director, J. Edgar Hoover. Hoover was a cross-dressing homosexual who maintained a long-term relationship with his bureau assistant Clyde Tolson. A deal had been reached in which Hoover would avoid investigating organized crime and the criminal leaders would not release their photographs. In addition, Hoover was periodically rewarded by being alerted to the assured outcome of certain horse races. The director was known to delight in going to the racetrack, but he always bet just $2 each time. What went unsaid was that other agents would bet in his place at the $100 windows, and those horses always won.

There were rumors of organized crime's involvement in the Kennedy assassination. Some criminals, including the New Orleans mob boss Carlos Marcello, actually claimed to have been involved, though ultimately it was found that far more people hinted at participation than had a role. It became a mark of honor among some of the more disreputable Kennedy haters to be rumored to have been involved. However, Hoover felt he dared not investigate any real mob involvement, so a theory developed about a conspiracy involving Oswald, who had once had a menial job in a Ruby club, Ruby himself, and the notorious Candy Barr.

Ruby's action was soon felt by Juanita in Edna, Texas. "They yanked me up the night he killed Oswald," Juanita recalled. "They bothered my family and me, way up into the seventies I lived in Brownwood.

"He'd been through Edna and they figured he was the bag man, and he'd come through here and I knew everything.

"My daddy came down there and he got me and my brother. They walked in there, and it was something. My brother said, 'Where is my sister?'"

Juanita had alerted her brother when the officials first came to her door. "I asked them if they had an arrest warrant, and they said no, so I said, I'll be down there. So I called my brother and I said, 'The FBI or whoever they are is down here and they want to take me down to the sheriff's office and question me about Jack.' And he said, 'I'll be right there.' There come my daddy with a .22 pistol. And my brother walk in, and Louis, he was the sheriff, said, 'You can't go back there, Gary.'

"And he said, 'The hell I can't.'

"My brother wasn't much bigger than I am. He was a little tiny fart. And my brother came through that door like he was ten feet tall. It was really kind of funny.

"Gary said, 'I don't know what all you're doing, but we've had enough of this. Let's go.'

"And Louis said, 'You can't take her.'

"And Gary said, 'The hell I can't.'

"And my daddy's standing out there. And they came out and Daddy took that little .22 pistol and said, 'Now Louis, you just go and tell these men to leave us alone until we get Nita home.'

"Louis said, 'Doc, you can't do that.'

"He said, 'Louis'—'cause Daddy knew all of Louis's secrets, see. My daddy knew everything everyone ever did in his life. And my daddy could shoot a string in two at a carnival with a pistol—'Louis, I can do any fuckin' thing I want to because I'm a dyin' man. Now tell those men to stay here until I get Nita home.' He said, 'Now I don't want any more of this mess. Leave her alone.'"

And they did. There would be conspiracy theorists, government researchers, and others who did not know the truth who would make the pilgrimage to Edna to learn firsthand from the notorious Candy Barr all that she knew about the Kennedy assassination. She would even come to believe that she was marked for death by those trying to hide facts she did not have. But with Doc's stance against the sheriff, the greatest pressure was over. Juanita would be able to live out the remainder of her parole in relative peace.

TWENTY-EIGHT

Still Feisty, Still Sexy

"I didn't do too good today, did I? And I may not do too good tomorrow either, but I'm aware of that. But it doesn't mean I've failed. It's just that I couldn't handle a few of your jokes today."

—Juanita, talking to the picture of her
"Chief"—Jesus—hanging in her bedroom

Candy Barr should have been dead, replaced by the chastened, disgraced, and ruined Juanita Sahakian. Her life had been brief. She was born on a Dallas, Texas, stage and rode to fame in Los Angeles and Las Vegas, and her enemies expected her to die when simple prison whites replaced the long gowns, the cowgirl outfit, and the other costumes that made Candy so appealing.

It had been all right to resurrect the stripper for the three prison rodeos where she performed during her time in Goree. However, these were muted, last-gasp appearances during which she was considered just one of the Goree Girls, albeit the most famous. And the clothing she wore during the rodeos stayed firmly, though fetchingly, on her body. The audience applauded the professionalism of the born entertainer, though they did not see the full genius of the woman whose dancing had electri-fied audiences and made her wealthy. Still, when Juanita was released and confined to Edna, Texas, more than 300 miles from Dallas, Candy Barr should have been but a memory—R.I.P.

The first hint of problems occurred when men started showing up in Edna, trying to destroy Juanita. People in Dallas sent them, though. They were not locals. If anything, the decent people of Edna had shown they would rally around one of their own whose life, they realized, had been a living hell. Their actions might have been illegal to those outside the area, but small-town Texans know how to take care of their own.

Not that there weren't fools. Edna, Texas, had gotten smaller over the years. Jobs became scarce, and many of the young people preferred places where there was more to do than get drunk, get pregnant, and ride around town. Those who stayed were not always the best and the brightest, and a handful of them became a nuisance for Juanita.

For example, there was the teenager who was fascinated by Candy Barr. He would use a few beers for courage, then get in his car and start following Juanita everywhere. He didn't approach her at first. He didn't even think he was calling attention to himself, not realizing that Juanita's training as a getaway driver for Billy Dabbs was not forgotten. She always knew exactly who was around her at all times. She knew when there was going to be trouble, and she was grateful to her brother, Gary, for making certain she had a gun. Possession of the weapon was illegal for a convicted felon out on parole, but Candy did not worry about such matters. She was not going to be hurt again.

After several days of stalking his fantasy conquest, the teenager drove his car alongside Juanita's vehicle after she had come to a stop. "What's on your mind, honey?" she asked, quietly taking hold of the handgun on her lap.

"I thought we'd get acquainted, maybe have a little party," he told her.

"I've noticed you driving behind me for three nights," Juanita told the youth. "I guess you like to play games."

Candy slowly eased up the barrel, making certain no one other than the youth could see it. As he stared in shock, she quietly explained, "I'm going to tell you, honey, if I catch you following me any more, I'm going to blow you away." She never saw him again.

The most serious problem, one that brought tears to Juanita's eyes, was with the people who should have known better, the members of the local church where Juanita expected to find a spiritual home. Religious theology had changed between the 1940s and when Juanita finally was able to return to the church. Groups ranging from Pentecostals to Catholics had individual churches experimenting with what today is called prosperity theology, the belief that God rewards the good and punishes the bad—that reward is immediate, on earth, and relates to financial success. Wealth is proof of one's goodness.

Prior to this time, and for most churches of the day, there was the belief that God loves the downtrodden. All humans were sinners in the Old Testament concept of the word "sin"—to fall short of the mark. The Bible preached forgiveness and redemption. The poor, the downtrodden, the afflicted, and those in jail were loved, forgiven, and in the case of those who had fallen short of the mark (including criminals and the physically disabled, once thought to be bearing the mark of family sin), given a new chance. The stories were numerous, such as the one of the adulterous woman about to be stoned. The men who would kill her were reminded of their own imperfect pasts, and the woman was told she was forgiven but to not sin again. This combination of sin, repentance, and forgiveness was a bulwark of most religious thinking. The various Protestant groups might argue the exact nature of the theology and issues concerning the factual nature of the Bible. But traditionally a woman such as Juanita would be embraced as much for what she had overcome as for where she was headed in life.

The variation of prosperity theology Juanita encountered when she returned to a church that had once nurtured her did not allow for anyone notorious to be in the midst of the "good" people. She entered the church seeking a spiritual home. She joined the choir, anxious to lend her voice to the musical praise worship of God. She entered with Jesus a real friend in her heart. She even had thoughts of studying to be a missionary, having survived abuse, oppression, discrimination, and wrongful imprisonment, all while feeling ever closer to Jesus. She was a woman who could have walked into many churches in the nation and had the congregations shout "Alleluia." Perhaps there was such a church in or near Edna. Tragically, the one in which she put her hopes and dreams was mired in hypocrisy, acting as if God sought only those people without spot or wrinkle. A "fallen woman" such as Candy Barr had a life that was visible proof of her failings and the failings of her family. White trash didn't belong in a house of God.

Perhaps had Juanita sought a different spiritual home, there would have been no problem. Perhaps had some of the good people of the community reached out to her, openly disagreeing with the pastor and those members of the congregation who scorned her, things would have been different. Instead she was thrown away, a stranger in a familiar land. It was one stress too many and Juanita gave up on people.

"I never had any heroes or idols except one. The only hero I have is Jesus. There's no one to compare with him. Why should I deny it?" Juanita told Gregg Barrios of the *Los Angeles Times*, her remarks appearing in the October 14, 1984, edition of the paper.

What should have been freedom from the past occurred late in 1967 when Texas Governor John Connally again involved himself in Juanita's life. After reviewing the case, he ordered a full pardon. Juanita was truly a free woman. Candy Barr could again dance in clubs.

Back in 1958, no one was certain just when Juanita would be in jail. She signed contracts that had to be fulfilled, even if her career was interrupted. As a result, as soon as Connally freed her, she was on her way to the Los Angeles Largo Club and making appearances in the Las Vegas Bonanza Hotel as well as returning to the Colony Club in Dallas where her career first took off. Tragically, the commitments, which Juanita was determined to fulfill, did not mean a return to the glory days of the past.

It had been eight years since Candy Barr's style of dance electrified the stage. It had been eight years since the public had seen a woman act as one with musicians, creating jazz improvisations with her body the likes of which had never been seen before. It had been eight years of Candy Barr impersonators, bumping and grinding in cowgirl outfits and ponytails, selling sexual sensation, not improvisational brilliance.

Perhaps had Juanita been allowed to develop her act again things might have been different. She had long had an athlete's body, but the height of her fame came when she was dancing for hours every day. She was stretched, practiced, as one with the music with which she worked on a regular basis. In 1968, without adequate time to stretch her body and develop the relationship with the musicians that had created the past genius, she was placed back on stage. Worse, in the case of the Largo, she was ordered to wear a prison-style uniform and pretend to be working a rock pile as part of her dance. It was the club owner's idea, not her own. It was a concept to which she could not relate, yet she had to try.

The reporters who covered Candy Barr's return to the stage were disappointed. The brilliance of the past was gone. They did not know the limitations that she struggled with. Forced into unnatural circumstances by contracts she had to honor and a need for money to help her extremely ill father, the brilliant dancer was forced to become a weak caricature of her former self.

Not that the fans were lacking. When Candy Barr could play a club where she still had control, her dancing still was better than anyone else's on the circuit. As she moved back into Las Vegas and Dallas for a few appearances, there was standing room only. She was like an aging athlete, the former superstar who has lost the luster for which she was known yet who is still superior to anyone foolish enough to challenge her skills.

The world was changing, though. The unions were dominating the entertainment industry. Strippers had to join the American Guild of Variety Artists if they wanted to work. Musicians had to join the Musicians Union. Minimum rates were being negotiated on the players' behalf. Minimum and maximum hours were being established. There would be rates for overtime, a demand for breaks, and other requests that did not fit the gypsy, counterculture lifestyle of burlesque. Many a musician worked a seven-day week, and the drummers might be in the theaters for twelve hours a day. Travel accommodations for the burlesque stars who worked the circuit were increasingly a part of negotiations. The club and theater owners began cutting back expenses.

First the musicians were let go. Recorded music replaced the men with whom Juanita related so well. It was impossible to improvise. It was impossible to do more than have a set act. To dance to a recording was to be forced into a mold she had never fit.

Next the quality of the performers degenerated. Sex became the focus of entertainment. Dancers were chosen for the size of their breasts and the way they worked the men. Doc Johnson sex aids became common in the clubs. These ranged from penis extenders to various lubricating creams meant to increase sexual desire and enhance performance. Some clubs were experimenting with bringing the dancers close enough to the audience so they could be touched. Men were allowed to put tips in the woman's G-string or a garter that was worn to hold the money.

The idea of a full stage show gradually went out of fashion. Dancing meant taking off your clothes to music, all the time playing to the fantasies of the men. Prostitution was not allowed in the clubs, but many of the club owners began ignoring the fact that the dancers were meeting customers just outside the building for "dates" that might last a few minutes in the back of a car.

Burlesque was dying. The clubs that did not make a complete switch to raunchy acts were making a gradual change, often adding what were then called XXX movies. They were often innocent by today's standards, such as *The Saucy Aussie*, the story about a man from Australia who developed a headache while visiting the United States and discovered that each time he took two aspirin tablets, he would see women naked. He looked at women doctors, waitresses, female police officers, and other women. Always they were beautiful. Always they were fully clothed at first. And always they appeared naked just to him (and the viewing audience) when he took the aspirin.

There was a hint of innocence in the naughtiness, yet the clubs' addition of such films was an omen. Burlesque was in its last gasps, and true burlesque clubs were almost impossible to find.

Perhaps Juanita could have made the transition from dancer to showgirl in Las Vegas. She had starred in elaborately staged musical numbers. She had made large sums of money. She had headlined in the manner of entertainers such as Jimmy Durante, Frank Sinatra, and others. But Candy Barr had become an outlaw legend. Candy Barr was notorious. She was "remembered" for her sex with animals in *Smart Aleck*. She was "remembered" for her use of drugs and sex in a lifestyle of hedonistic wildness that had been both voluntary and extreme. She was "remembered" for the fantasies of men and women who had never seen her perform or dared not admit they had once forced sex on a captive teenager. Candy Barr was morally reprehensible. Candy Barr was an ex-convict with no redeeming social value. Candy Barr was . . .

At the same time, the club owners had no interest in Juanita, trailer trash from Edna, Texas. Juanita Phillips or Juanita Sahakian wasn't a name that could fill a local bar much less draw people to the lounge or the main stage in a Las Vegas casino.

Juanita was aware of the changed nature of the clubs. "You don't take an entertainer that's danced to live music and make them perform to a tape," she said. "You just don't do it. So I don't care what they say about the performance, if you can't live on the stage, you can't live on the stage. But that's what was happening at that time, taped music everywhere. They had no more music, so I had no desire to dance and work. But I did go in and fulfill my obligations."

For less than a year, Juanita tried to settle in Edna with Jim Wilson, a man who strung wire for the railroad. It was the late 1960s and Juanita had thoughts of settling down. The trouble was that Juanita was very sensitive to families. She could not cause a rift between a man and his parents, a man and his siblings, a man and his relatives. This was the reason she was never a threat to the men who had abused her when she was in the Capture. She knew they were acting out their dirty little fantasies that would ruin their families' lives if made public. And this was why her marriage to Jim would be short lived.

"Jim was cute," Juanita said. "More than that, he was a nice person." The problem was that when they became close, "his whole family turned distant and I tried to tell him not to separate himself from his family to have a relationship with me."

Children at this time were frequently taught the importance of family. "Don't do anything that might embarrass the family," was a common comment. "Remember, the only people who will always love you, no matter what you do, are family." And in many communities, especially small towns like Edna, family did matter. Everyone lived close together, the ownership of homes sometimes passing through several generations. To be estranged from parents, siblings, aunts, uncles, or cousins was sadness almost beyond comprehension. Juanita knew that Jim would never be happy if he pursued their love, since he would lose his family. Still he persisted.

"And then when it all did finally happen," Jim being excluded from family gatherings and ridiculed by his relatives because of Juanita, "it wasn't that I didn't care about Jim, but I felt I had to marry him because of the fact that he was always so abused by his family because he cared about me.

I just couldn't walk off and say, 'That's tough luck, buddy.' I didn't dislike him. I liked him well enough, 'cause he was pleasant. That's how we married, actually. Nothing else could be done about it. I wasn't going to hurt that young man, 'cause he cared about me."

The failure of the marriage was inevitable, not only because of the circumstances but also because of Juanita's attitude. "I had nothing else to do with my time. I was free and single." The couple was married by a justice of the peace in El Capo, Texas, twenty-seven miles up the road from Edna. They moved in with her father and Etta after the ceremony. Eventually Jim lost his job, "and they persecuted the boy because he cared about me."

Jim and Juanita were trapped in Edna because of the social mores of the time. Today the couple would move to another town, starting over away from parents and other relatives. Back then, you stayed where you were, making the hostilities within the family much more difficult.

Juanita was torn as Jim became more devoted to her with each passing day, his emotions preventing reconciliation with his family. "You can't sit by and let somebody's life [be] destroy[ed] because they love you more and more. You can't do that. You release them so they can start trying. . . . You've got to let them go."

Juanita stressed the importance of family over marriage because she had seen how fragile supposedly committed relationships could be. She didn't expect Jim to cheat on her as other men had done to their wives when they paid to use Juanita sexually. But she felt that she was the one responsible for his pain. "You're the person they're blaming for why this is happening, too, and you know that this is happening because of your relationship, so you have to let them go."

Jim sadly accepted the idea that the relationship could not continue. He agreed to the divorce, eventually getting a desk job with a gas and oil company. "He got married and had babies, and we remained friends. I gave him my full support.

"I was friends with most of my ex-sweethearts 'cause I did leave with a clear conscience."

Juanita's father was dying, and because he was a veteran, he was able to get help in the VA hospital in Brownwood, Texas, and Juanita eventually moved there. At the hospital, she met a woman whose husband was also being cared for. The woman, Dorothy, was a dog groomer, a career that intrigued Juanita. She loved dogs, loved all animals. She also knew that dogs wouldn't make sexual passes at her, ridicule her past, or try to set her up to go to jail.

"I had these dogs," Juanita related, "and I decided that I would move over there and I would learn how to groom dogs and have a profession. So I had one room in the back [of Dorothy's house] and her husband was in the VA hospital where my daddy was."

Juanita left her trunks of possessions in the room, not bothering to unpack. She just wanted to be useful, to have a profession in which she could make a living. "I knew I wasn't going to be going back to dancing. When my daddy died, I didn't need the money. I knew I could live on grooming money. I had honored the [dancing] contracts that I had drawn [advance] money on. They were done regardless of what kind of job I did."

Brownwood, Texas, was not going to be the change Juanita had hoped. As she made friends with a number of the locals, she learned that one woman she befriended had a husband who was a professional gambler. Elaborate gambling equipment, illegal to own under Texas law, was kept in the house. Another friend was dating a man who supplemented his pay as a railroad worker by dealing in drugs.

Years later Juanita laughed about how naïve she was concerning her neighbors. "Why didn't someone offer me an upper, damn it? I can't believe, here I am one of the world's greatest drug offenders right next door to people who are dealing in drugs and they never offer to get me any. I said, 'Golly, that's cold!' They never offered to sell me a nickel's worth of nothing. I didn't know it was going on."

The drug problems in the area were worse than Juanita realized. One of the women she befriended had a husband who obtained barbiturates through the mail. The use of the post office to receive illegal substances turned the matter into a federal offense. The neighborhood in which Juanita was living was what was considered a federal arrest zone. Federal law enforcement officers were watching everyone. Anyone could be arrested if it appeared he or she was involved. And in the midst of all that was a woman who had already been railroaded into the state penitentiary.

There was more to Brownwood than problems, though. It was the type of community that seemed to be part of a past other cities had moved beyond. Brownwood had a touch of the small-town America that was idealized in Norman Rockwell cover paintings for the *Saturday Evening Post*. The men wore business suits for all but the dirtiest of laboring jobs. A trip to the Safeway supermarket required housewives to dress up as though going to a fancy coffee shop to meet friends. The Douglas MacArthur Academy and Howard Payne College were academic institutions in which the citizens took great pride. And there was a sense of history regarding the high schools that kept the name of Chili Rice alive almost three decades after he graduated from twelfth grade. Rice had been the physically small halfback on the Brownwood High School football team when, in 1940, the school beat Breckenridge High, its archrival. The defeat was only the second time in thirty-six years that Brownwood had triumphed, so Chili Rice's name remained a part of local lore, as big as Michael Jordan would become during his basketball playing days with the Chicago Bulls.

The town had its eccentricities as well. There was a reform school that had programs considered among the most innovative in the state. There was a pecan research station and several ranches. There was also a pig farm proud to have the cleanest pork available. All the pigs were potty trained, their feet wrapped in plastic booties. They were carefully penned so that they never touched the ground from the moment they were born until they were slaughtered for the market.

The people in the town knew about Candy Barr. They knew that Juanita had served time in Goree. They also recognized that she had paid the price for whatever was done, that it was time to forgive and forget. It was an attitude the town seemed to hold to everyone known to have gone to prison. There was an acceptance of people for who they were, not what they had been.

By March 1969, Juanita hoped that her past was behind her. She and her thirteen-year-old daughter were living together in a white-shingled cottage on the rim of a lake in Brownwood. There were questions about her source of income, questions that continue to this day, but whatever was happening, the nastier comments about her being a $100 prostitute, as some believed, were untrue. Juanita would herself joke that it was "$100 an *hour.*" But the truth was that the money was a combination of cash from friends and money that came from selling some of her possessions. Exactly who was paying her and why has never been revealed, including by Juanita. What is certain is that the payments came neither from bribery nor prostitution. There were always men who cared, including those wealthy enough to help someone who had been so horribly wronged from childhood.

On March 10, 1969, when her daughter was staying with friends, Juanita was driving with Dorothy on a road outside Brown County. It was late at night and Juanita was taking Dorothy home before returning to her cottage. As she came over the crest of a hill, there "was this black animal and it was running down the road, and I thought I hit it.

"Dorothy said, 'Don't go back there.'

"And I said, 'I have to see if I hit it.' And there was a dog on the side of the road, but it was cold and still."

The dog was also on the wrong side of the road from where she thought she might have hit it. Her car had not killed the animal. It had been dead far too long. Yet there was no question she had seen such a dog. Juanita was not sure what had happened, but she suspected the incident had greater meaning.

Juanita's mother had always talked about omens. The incident seemed a warning to not return home. Since she had to travel to Waco the next morning in order to take her dogs and those of Dorothy to a veterinarian whose skills they both trusted, she spent the night at Dorothy's place. Then she took the animals to Waco, calling Dorothy, who reported a break-in at Juanita's home. It appeared to Dorothy that there had been a burglary, and though she could not tell what was missing, she did spot a black dress that had been removed from the closet and was lying on the bedroom floor.

The burglary had not been a burglary in the traditional sense. At 2:30 a.m. on March 11, while Juanita was out of town, police officers entered her home. The police later said that they "found a music box that plays *Smoke Gets in Your Eyes*" and that inside was "a little cache of marijuana seeds." Other news stories from the day mention a shoebox, not a music box, and a "cache" consisting of marijuana seeds and stems.

The officers were allegedly investigating a break-in, though nothing was missing. "They smashed this little box," Juanita recalled, "so they knew what they went for and they knew what they were doing."

Dorothy agreed to help Juanita obtain a lawyer, an action that immediately brought police suspicion on herself. They went to her car and found the remains of a suspicious substance that they proceeded to vacuum and take to their crime lab. The suspicious substance proved to be dog-biscuit crumbs.

Once again Candy Barr was alive, well, and under arrest. The past that Juanita so long wished to put behind her was again part of the headlines. The *Dallas Times Herald* of August 24, 1969, headlined: "Candy Barr: Last 'Queen of Burlesque' in Trouble Again." She was released on $25,000 bond and was scheduled to go to trial in Brownwood on September 18. Outraged, Juanita told the press, "I'm not going back to Goree! This is a great error, and I will fight it and fight it and fight it until any and all things that need to be exploited are exploited—unless I am destroyed, and they will have to destroy me physically."

This time law enforcement authorities discovered how much sentiment turned against the railroading of a woman whose only crime had been trying to survive in life. On August 13, 1970, Brownwood District Attorney George Day was shocked to discover that Judge Joe Dibrell would allow Juanita's long-delayed trial to continue only if the marijuana was withheld from evidence. The marijuana had been illegally obtained. The search warrant was improper according to some sources, non-existent according to others. Either way, this was not to be a repeat of the improprieties she had suffered a decade earlier. The law did not act properly, the judge believed.

Four days later, when Judge Dibrell commenced proceedings, District Attorney George Day placed a motion that the trial should be ended and charges dropped since the marijuana seeds and stems could not be used for evidence. Juanita's final court trial was over thirty seconds after it began. Juanita then left Brownwood to go to Edna, where she had left Troylene.

TWENTY-NINE

Over the Hill? What Hill?

"Newsmen horrify me. I am afraid to even look at newsmen."

—Juanita, following the dismissal of charges
of marijuana possession in Brownwood, Texas

The greatest tragedy of Juanita's life was not the abuse of her childhood, nor did it involve her prison time. Instead, it was the way she was broken by day-to-day living.

Juanita was a brilliant woman. Her fiery temper was unleashed often, though always justifiably. Yet while most observers focused on her outlaw image, her anger, or her great beauty, few looked at her compassion for others. It is little wonder that the one person to whom she remained faithful was Jesus, a man ridiculed in his home town, denounced for being counterculture and associating with lowlifes, then murdered when he upset local politicians.

While Juanita survived because of her deep spirituality, she never used her full potential. She stopped trying to be part of a church when the one location in which she put her hopes failed her. She did not continue as a writer despite creating poetry that proved she was gifted. She even became an emotional recluse despite always desiring to help others.

The last time there seemed hope for a better future for Juanita was when she was still in Brownwood despite the troubles she had there. The friends she needed during her years immediately after her release from jail were often men having their own difficulties. Mickey Cohen was fighting the Internal Revenue Service. Sammy Davis Jr. was in a haze of drugs, booze, women, and racism, an entertainer who recognized that his brilliance would never be fully appreciated. Only Jack Ruby had genuinely tried to help her, seemingly without strings attached.

Abe Weinstein was in the midst of Juanita's life for a while during her last months of dancing and with her writing. He took her poetry in the form in which he first encountered it—scrawled on cheap paper and decorated by hand in ways that were heartfelt yet amateurish. Then he tried to promote it, going so far as to claim to the press that it was "in the hands of Doubleday right this minute." Abe wanted the listener to think he meant the publishing company, but he had actually given Juanita's poems to a friend, Bill Gilliland, who worked at the downtown Dallas Doubleday Bookstore and was storing the papers. As usual, Abe made local headlines with his flash and fancy talk, but the truth of what he was selling was lost in the hype.

Juanita eventually published the poetry herself, promoting the book wherever she could, usually without advance notice. For example, Terlingua, Texas, was known for its annual chili cook-off that attracted thousands of people a year. By 1975 she had taken to showing up unannounced, waiting for a crowd to gather, then making an appearance from a trailer on the grounds where she had been waiting. She always looked beautiful. She always encouraged fans to take photographs. And she always tried to sell her book of poetry that was published without photographs in order to be certain people would read her words, not just buy a sexy image of Candy Barr. Unfortunately there were usually more curiosity seekers than individuals who would take her work seriously.

There were also offers for her to sell her life story. Juanita was certain that her memoirs would be in demand, and she was equally sure she had found her writer when famed author Gay Talese journeyed to Brownwood in 1974. Talese had spent several years working on a book about American sexual practices that would eventually be published under the title *Thy Neighbor's Wife*. He had interviewed men such as Hugh Hefner, the founder of *Playboy* magazine and the Playboy Clubs. He had taken jobs in sex-related businesses in order to meet the men and women who were part of the sexual underground. And in 1974 he traveled to Brownwood to learn about Jack Ruby, Mickey Cohen, Joe De Carlo, and the other players who had an impact on both Dallas and Candy.

Juanita was outraged by that focus. She refused to talk on tape. She refused to detail the people she had always shielded. She wanted only to discuss her memoirs that she believed Talese wanted to write. For almost two days the writer and the former burlesque queen went round and round about both books, Talese constantly stressing his lack of time and interest in the memoir. His own book was late. The stress of the work, as well as the counterculture lifestyle he was leading while doing his research, would eventually contribute to the end of his marriage.

There would be rumors about his meeting with Candy Barr. There would be stories of Juanita stripping naked and sitting on the floor at the end of the time Talese was trying to interview her. There would be allegations that he grabbed the first flight out of town immediately after leaving her home. All that can be confirmed is that Talese managed to convince the editors at *Oui* magazine in Chicago that she should be photographed for the magazine. Talese would be given expenses for trying to set up the interview that he still hoped to handle himself. Juanita would be given $5,000 to pose.

Oui was a low-budget rival to the more familiar *Playboy* and *Penthouse* publications. Candy Barr appeared in the June 1976 issue, which stressed three stories on its cover: "Sex Tapes Take You Around the World," "Warning: College May Be Hazardous to Your Head," and "Candy Barr: Porn's First Star in a Wild Pictorial." The cover blurb told it all. Once again Juanita had not been able to be herself. There was the attitude conveyed by the cover, and then there was the sexually explicit inside art. Even the most sophisticated "men's" magazines of the day tended to have what they called a "beaver shot," an image that stressed the vaginal area. At the same time, the story and captions showed a respect for the forty-one-year-old ex-dancer. An opening image showing a naked Candy Barr, lying back on cushions and drapes, one of which strategically covers the area below her waist, is a signed photograph that has written on it: "For you Abe—With tender affection—Candy." The story also stresses that she was a "burlesque queen, ex-con, Jack Ruby's pal, porno's first (reluctant) star and a real lady."

Juanita and her friend Dorothy were flown to Chicago, where Talese and the editors of the magazine tried to conduct the interview during the time she was being photographed. It was not a good period for any of them.

First there was the constant reference to "Candy," long an accepted sore point. Candy Barr danced a little over four years. Juanita had a long life separate from her stage name. She understood why people used "Candy," but she also knew that anyone who understood her would call her Juanita.

Next there was the issue of the tape recorder. She didn't like talking to a machine and she resented the more intimate questions about her past. She seemed to be aware that many of her experiences, taken out of context, could cast her in a negative light. (The magazine story would include a series of still images from *Smart Aleck*, seemingly justifying some of her concerns.) At the same time, she explained that she was proud that, at the age of forty, she remained in great shape and did not mind people knowing it.

Perhaps the most telling aspect of the trip was an experience during her last night in Chicago. She went to her hotel bar and ordered a glass of ginger ale. Almost immediately a male customer almost twice her size began bothering her. She asked him to stop, and when he persisted, she struck him four times in the face. The security guards rushed over and dragged him out of the bar.

There should have been something more. The nude spread in *Oui* should have led to something, but it is hard to know what. A job in Hollywood? Television work? More magazine spreads?

There was a little attention. The *Oui* spread led to Gary Cartwright traveling to Brownwood to visit Candy Barr for the December 1976 issue of *Texas Monthly* magazine. They talked about her green 1974 Cadillac with custom upholstery, a CB radio, and a pawn ticket for the mink coat she had to let go for money. They talked about her past and about her latest mission in life, a seventy-six-year-old electrician named O. E. Cole, whom she had never met.

Juanita had read about Cole in the Brownwood paper. She had no idea what his race, religion, or personal bias might be. All she knew was that he was a hard-working man like her late father. He had worked and saved for fifty years when his wife, Nettie, suffered a stroke, not dying for eighteen months. He paid for her care with the couple's life savings, then spent another $500 on her headstone. He was left with $157, just enough money to cover the mortgages on his home and shop. Then a gunman shot him and the bank refused to look at the circumstances when he wanted credit while rebuilding his life. They were going to foreclose and take the last vestiges of his life.

Juanita took her mink to a pawnshop where she was given $250. She then used her CB radio to contact friends from the entertainment world who shared her outrage. In a matter of hours she raised $400, which she then took to Cole's home in Dallas, giving the astonished man the money and a copy of her poetry book. Then the two of them talked about Cole's problems, her daddy, and life in general throughout the night, something that surprised the electrician. It was not until the *Texas Monthly* writer told Cole who his benefactress had been that he learned Juanita Dale Phillips was the notorious Candy Barr.

Brownwood proved to be a relatively short-term home for Juanita. She became convinced that the sheriff was corrupt. She had no idea if he was benefiting from the local drug trade and other crimes that were common knowledge (or commonly rumored) in the 1970s. She did believe that he was aware of them, though, and that nothing took place without his knowledge. When she believed he was attempting to frame her brother, Gary, she began following the sheriff as much as she could. She also let her home be used by members of the Drug Enforcement Administration (DEA) who were working in Brownwood, pursuing some of the same rumors that Juanita had come to believe.

Eventually the corruption and violence became more than Juanita wanted to handle. She and a young local judge under indictment for crimes Juanita believed he had not committed began working together against the sheriff and other community leaders they thought were the dishonest ones. There were anonymous threats, and more than once she had to wait tensely, holding a gun, getting ready to shoot men who were menacing her house. The men never went that one step too far, trying to break into her home, but they did ambush the young judge. He died in a car wreck that was officially declared an accident, yet today, more than twenty years later, is still believed by locals to have been murder.

One of the DEA men who befriended Juanita and used her home as the base for their investigations brought in a load of marijuana that had been confiscated. While most of it was needed for evidence, the two of them removed a small portion for personal consumption. The agent chopped the marijuana into tiny pieces while Juanita assembled the ingredients for meat loaf and brownies. Then the two of them created a meal in which the marijuana was an integral though unnoticeable and essentially tasteless extra ingredient. The meal was served for the other agents who arrived a couple of hours later. None of them realized what had been added to the food, but Juanita thought the party that followed in her living room was one of the wilder events to take place in Brownwood.

Eventually Juanita decided to return to Edna. The sheriff in Brownwood cooperated with the DEA agents, eventually leaving the Brownwood area under a cloud of suspicion that a deal was made to avoid prosecution. Even today the Brownwood community is split, some people feeling he was a great, compassionate man unfairly maligned by rumor and innuendo, and others thinking he was guilty of crimes for which he escaped punishment by making deals. Either way, Juanita had grown less welcome in many ways.

Edna was in an area where Juanita still had close relatives, though she considered herself more available to them than they were to her. As with O. E. Cole, her many acts of loving compassion were done anonymously, a fact that also caused others to either ignore them or belittle her life in its declining years. Her lungs deteriorated and her health declined. She needed surgery to remove the lower lobes of her lungs, yet she was not certain she was strong enough to survive the operation. She had to rest frequently and nap between chores, though she still remained available to relatives who sought her help for their problems.

Personal memorabilia from the Candy Barr era was destroyed in flooding from one of the many hurricanes that struck the area. Duplicates of some items were available on the Internet, but she did not have the money to buy them.

By the time Juanita was in her sixties, life had become harsh. She desperately desired financial help from the wealthy men who said they cared about her. At the same time, she both resented any male who was a part of her life and quietly received assistance when she was short of money. Her car was in constant need of repairs. She had a roof over her head but had to haul in water for cooking.

Newspapers and magazines ran occasional stories mentioning Candy Barr, some of them accurate, others perpetuating the myth of the willing prostitute, porn star, and outlaw. A publication called *Black Book* mentioned her relationship with Mickey Cohen in a story that ran in its fall 1998 issue. The *Black Book* story was essentially accurate, but no one interviewed Juanita in order to learn that the love affair was one-sided, that she was not a willing participant in his world.

Juanita had hoped to one day be accepted for herself, but that did not happen. Candy Barr rose too far, too fast, gaining too much notoriety to ever go away. And so she endured, still beautiful in her sixties, at times bitter, refusing to suffer fools or those who would not listen and remember her words during conversations and interviews. Yet with the toughness, her failure to pursue the still attainable dreams she once held—of doing missionary work in some form, of writing, of truly helping others—shows how badly she had been shattered by others.

Interviewing Juanita for this book had its surprises. I worked with Juanita by telephone, talking for many hours, sometimes listening to her angry diatribes, sometimes laughing over some humorous incident in the past, sometimes shocked by the way she had been treated. Yet Juanita was never comfortable with me as a writer. She continued talking to me long after she dismissed others from her life because of my personal situation. She learned that my wife and I were the parents of three "throw-away" children, special-needs boys from two different biological families who had been through physical and emotional hell before we adopted them. It was our love for our oldest son, severely mentally ill and deteriorating during the time she knew me, that touched her most. She cared about those who cared for children she felt other adults would dismiss as a nuisance, and it was a side of Juanita I had not realized existed.

As for Candy Barr, I came to learn that in Las Vegas, Los Angeles, and Dallas, there remain old men, some of them musicians, who recall the real burlesque queen whose active career lasted little more than four years. They reminisced, though requesting anonymity, fearing the wrath of wives and children who might think they enjoyed more than her stage presence. Yet all of them talk of her dancing, her skills on the stage, the improvisations that created a new form of jazz in which her body was as capable of riffs as the musicians with whom she worked. They are the ones who remember the real Candy Barr. They are the ones who know the truth about that period in her life. And they are the ones who can still close their eyes and smile blissfully at the unfolding memory of the woman who once danced in the night music.

EPILOGUE

Trying to write a biography of a person whose life has been in turmoil can be an exercise in personal judgment. You listen to the subject for hours and hours, making careful notes, then cross-checking facts. You contact people who knew or know the subject and interview them. You find people who can help you re-create the times in which the subject became famous, the social conditions under which the person lived. You compile many hours of tapes, fill notebooks with information, then try to analyze all that you have heard to be as objective as possible. Such was the case with the woman who both briefly and forever has been known as Candy Barr.

One of the people I had hoped to interview was Jack Sahakian, the man who married Juanita Phillips shortly before she went to Goree. He was a man for whom Juanita always had great respect. And she never said he tried to take advantage of her. Yet he was another individual who seemingly abandoned her to her prison stay and was out of her life not long after her release. Given Juanita's intense distrust of men and her frequent attacks on the past men in her life, all of whom seem to have been controlling, manipulative, and denying her the freedom that could only come from being in charge of her own destiny, Jack Sahakian did not stand out.

Juanita long complained about the ways in which men used her. Having been victimized by pedophiles, forced into white slavery, and chased not only by mobster Mickey Cohen but also by the "good guys" and "bad guys" who were trying to stop Cohen's racketeering, her complaints seem justified. But then the full story of Jack Sahakian is revealed.

Jack Sahakian was more than an honest, caring man who became Juanita's husband during the most volatile time in her life, the weeks prior to her entering prison. He was a man deeply in love with her, who understood her abusive past, her sometimes counterculture lifestyle, and the way some men held her in disdain. He also loved the woman she was, ignoring the person she had been.

Sahakian was a rising businessman when he met Juanita, but like many up-and-coming entrepreneurs, his steadily increasing income was needed for his work. He was a hairdresser with a growing clientele and an actor when he could find work, but he was young, not yet established, and willing to do anything to help the woman he loved. That was why he put his own life on hold to rescue Juanita when she fled from Mexico after being sent away by Mickey Cohen. That was why he endured the break-ins, the endless questioning by law enforcement, and the implied threats of mobsters who claimed to not be happy that he was Juanita's new lover.

Adding to Jack's stress was the fact that Juanita went to prison. First there was the image of prison. Hollywood in the 1950s delighted in making low-budget movies about women behind bars. They created the image of a place were rape and violence were commonplace, where the women who were jailed were always guilty, and where any man who loved such a woman was a fool or worse.

It is easy to say that Juanita was railroaded into jail. It is easy to look at the facts and be outraged over the abuse Juanita endured. And based on interviews conducted, it seems to have been easy to be a resident of Dallas, Texas, and look on the jailing as little more than getting a foul piece of rubbish off the streets. Moreover, the press either vilified her or considered her just a woman of questionable morals with a great body who was always good for copy. But Jack Sahakian loved her. This meant that Jack was likely seen as a fool or a man who must somehow be mixed up in things that were against the law. Certainly neither his personal nor his professional lives were enhanced by his relationship.

Long after Sahakian's death, his son John, by then older than his father had been when he married Juanita, looked through his father's papers.

That was when several factors became clear. First, Jack Sahakian loved Juanita Phillips. He was not a user. He was not an abuser. He was a good and honest man whose eventual declaration that Juanita was leaving dancing was accurate. The couple planned a life together. In what Jack Sahakian wrote and in the stories he told his son when he talked about Juanita, they were going to start life as a family whenever Juanita was released from prison. Jack, Juanita, Troylene, and Jack's two children by a previous marriage would live together and work for a better future.

Jack called his mother to talk about Juanita, a woman whose reputation was obviously not one a mother might be pleased to encounter in a daughter-in-law. He explained that the past was over. It could not be changed. What mattered was who Juanita was today and what she chose to do with her future. He loved the woman she had become. He wanted the life they could have in the future. No matter who she was, no matter what she had done, no matter what had been done to her, it was all past.

Juanita felt she had always known Jesus, that God had blessed her by keeping her healthy and sane in the midst of the hell that had been her teenage years. In Jack, a man who would become a born-again Christian in a few years, she had found someone who reflected Jesus' values and compassion. If she was like the New Testament's adulterous woman about to be stoned by the men of Dallas, Texas, Jack Sahakian understood Jesus' sole admonition to her—sin no more.

Jack Sahakian married a professional dancer, not a prostitute. He married a woman who loved entertaining but was ready to rid herself of the image of Candy Barr, a woman who was willing to walk away from great wealth because it meant being owned by others, managed by others, controlled by others, in a world filled with sexual hypocrisy. He married someone he was proud to love, proud to have become the mother of his children, proud to say that he would be father to Troylene.

Jack remained faithful during the time Juanita was in jail. He worked whenever and wherever he could to raise the money to visit her, a struggle she later did not mention. He came to see her as often as he could, again something that went unspoken. He was constantly exhausted, both from dealing with the threats and the work he was doing to ensure there would be money for the new Sahakian family that would become his life's reality after Juanita was freed. He appeared in movies such as *Irma La Douce*, taking whatever roles he could obtain, then finding time to maintain his shop for clients such as Jack Lemmon and Shirley MacLaine.

Jack Sahakian used all his time and talent to prepare for the future, and then, when Juanita was soon to be released, he received a letter telling him the relationship was over. Juanita wanted a divorce.

Exhausted, in shock, and with all the plans for the future suddenly shattered, Jack Sahakian went into a deep depression. For three years he went from day to day, a shell of his former self. He lacked enthusiasm for anything, yet fought the depression, fought the desire to give up.

Eventually Sahakian recovered. He put Juanita in the past. He became deeply involved with the church and took formal study in Christianity. And he found a woman who looked upon the word "forever" as having meaning. He was able to love anew with the same sense of faith and commitment he had put into the relationship with Candy Barr. But unlike Juanita, this time his wife was as committed as he was. His son John was born of this new union.

What does all this mean? It is impossible to say. Perhaps one additional tragedy in the life of Juanita, or Candy Barr, is that in her pain and bitterness, she stopped being able to discern that which was the fulfillment of some of her prayers. Perhaps in her vehemence, she destroyed the one relationship that might have made the past thirty-five years a joyous time instead of one of increasing bitterness, isolation, and anger.

Death came on December 30, 2005. Juanita was still beautiful, but her lungs were ravaged from smoking, her body weakened by a less-than-healthy diet and the emotional stress of her adolescence. She was seventy years old and spent her last days suffering from pneumonia in a Victoria, Texas, hospital. There were no reporters staging a vigil outside the hospital, as would have occurred in her prime. The *National Enquirer* had no aggressive reporters trying to get her medical records. There were no interviews with family members or friends.

Burlesque was dying when Candy Barr was railroaded into jail. Candy Barr died faster in the few years immediately following her release from the Texas prison system. Only Juanita remained in the end, enduring a slow but desired spiral into near anonymity, interrupted only by an occasional magazine writer seeking to tell one aspect of her life or another. But for those who really cared, she sent her poetry, the one epitaph she would have desired had those who claimed to be her friends been listening.

> Hate the world that strikes you down,
> A warped lesson quickly learned.
> Rebellion, a universal sound,
> Nobody cares . . . No one's concerned.
> Fatigued by unyielding strife,
> Self-pity consoles the abused,
> And the bludgeoning of daily life
> Leaves a gentle mind . . . Confused.

BIBLIOGRAPHY

Allen, Robert C. *Horrible Prettiness: Burlesque and American Culture*. Chapel Hill: University of North Carolina Press, 1991.

Burger, Rowland. *The Night They Raided Minsky's*. New York: Simon & Schuster, 1960.

Cary, David. *A Bit of Burlesque: A Brief History of Its Times and Stars*. San Diego: Tecolote, 1997.

Cohen, Michael (Mickey), with John Peer Nugent. *Mickey Cohen: In My Own Words*. Englewood Cliffs, NJ: Prentice-Hall, 1975.

Corio, Ann, with Joseph DiMona. *This Was Burlesque*. New York: Madison Square Garden Press, 1968.

Davis, Sammy, Jr. *Hollywood in a Suitcase*. New York: William Morrow, 1980.

Davis, Sammy, Jr., Jane Boyar, and Burt Boyar. *Yes I Can: The Story of Sammy Davis Jr*. New York: Farrar, Straus and Giroux, 1965.

———. *Why Me?*. New York: Farrar, Straus and Giroux, 1989.

Levy, Shawn. *Rat Pack Confidential*. New York: Doubleday, 1998.

Minsky, Morton, and Milt Machlin. *Minsky's Burlesque*. New York: Arbor House, 1986.

Rella, Ettore. *A History of Burlesque*. San Francisco Theater Research, vol. 14. San Francisco: Works Progress Administration, 1940.

Rothe, Len. *The Queens of Burlesque: Vintage Photographs of the 1940s and 1950s*. Atglen, PA: Schiffer, 1997.

Scot, David Alexander. *Behind the G-String: An Exploration of the Stripper's Image, Her Person, and Her Meaning*. Jefferson, NC: McFarland, 1996.

Sobel, Bernard. *A Pictorial History of Burlesque*. New York: Putnam, 1956.

Storm, Tempest, with Bill Boyd. *Tempest Storm: The Lady Is a Vamp*. Atlanta, GA: Peachtree, 1987.

Sullivan, Steve. *Va-va Voom! Bombshells, Pin-Ups, Sexpots, and Glamour Girls*. Los Angeles: General, 1995.

Zeidman, Irving. *The American Burlesque Show*. New York: Hawthorn, 1967.

INDEX

National Organization for Decent
   Literature, 96
Newton, Jack, 161–62
Nichols, Red, 197–98
Nixon, Richard, 162
Novak, Kim, 190, 192

O'Connor, Donald, 4
oral sex, 43, 85, 95, 98–99
organized crime. *See* Mafia
Orwell, George, 96
Oscowski, Frank, 120
Oswald, Lee Harvey, 149, 175, 215,
   221, 258–59, 262
Otash, Fred, 184, 211
Oui (magazine), 279–80
outcall, 8, 39–40, 43–44, 78, 84, 86–89,
   91–92
Owens, George, 162, 169–70, 178, 181
Owens, Maureen, 162

Paris, Texas, 28–31
Pearson, Drew, 209
Pentacostal church, 23
Penthouse (magazine), 279
Perea Nina, 124
Phillips, Troy, 72–73, 75–79, 83–88, 91,
   98, 101–5, 109–10, 112, 114,
   147, 154–58, 166, 175, 222, 253
pimps, 40, 43–44, 47, 70, 79, 84–87,
   148
Pixie Lynn. *See* Smith, Helen
Playboy (magazine), 96, 279
Podell, Julie, 188
pornographic films, 93–98, 270
porters. *See* African American porters
Prabhupada, Swami, 247
Presley, Elvis, 147, 199, 245

Presser, Bill, 121
Prevost, Frank, 127
Price, Ray, 245
Prima, Louis, 184
Profaci, Giuseppe "Joe," 120
prosperity theology, 9–10, 267
prostitution, 7–8, 47, 70, 78–79, 101,
   148–53, 270. *See also* Capture,
   the; outcall

race:
   desegregation in Dallas and, 41–42
   and prejudice, 143–44, 181, 187–91
religion:
   Candy Barr and, 23, 154, 166, 223,
      244–45, 266–68, 277, 287
   prosperity theology, 9–10, 267
   Ruby, Kennedy, and, 256
   Sahakian and, 287–88
reservoirs, 45–46
Revill, Jack, 165, 168
Rice, Chili, 274
Richburg, W. E. "Bill," 169–70,
   177–79
Ritz Brothers, 202
rodeos, 240
Roosevelt, Franklin Delano, 256
Rose La Rose, 129–30
Rosenbloom, Slapsy Maxie, 185
Round-up Club, Dallas, 59, 77–78, 93
Ruby, Eva, 48–49, 59, 61
Ruby, Jack, 48–49, 59, 61, 66, 73, 80,
   149, 175–76, 214, 221, 252,
   254–60, 262, 278–79
runaways, 10–11

Sahakian, Jack, 215, 219–21, 223, 226,
   241, 253, 285–88